SAFETY

In the Classroom

- Read all of the directions. Make sure you understand them. When you see ▨, be sure to follow the safety rule.

- Listen to your teacher for special safety directions. If you don't understand something, ask for help.

- Wash your hands with soap and water before an activity.

- Wear safety goggles when your teacher tells you to wear them and whenever you see ▨. Wear them when working with anything that can fly into your eyes.

- Wear splash-proof goggles when working with liquids.

- Wear a safety apron if you work with anything messy or anything that might spill.

- If you spill something, wipe it up right away or ask your teacher for help.

- Tell your teacher if something breaks. If glass breaks do not clean it up yourself.

- Keep your hair and clothes away from open flames. Tie back long hair and roll up long sleeves.

- Be careful around a hot plate. Know when it is on and when it is off. Remember that the plate stays hot for a few minutes after you turn it off.

- Keep your hands dry around electrical equipment.

- Don't eat or drink anything during an experiment.

- Put equipment back the way your teacher tells you.

- Dispose of things the way your teacher tells you.

- Clean up your work area, and wash your hands with soap and water.

In the Field

- Always be accompanied by a trusted adult—like your teacher or a parent or guardian.

- Never touch animals or plants without the adult's approval. The animal might bite. The plant might be poison ivy or another dangerous plant.

Responsibility

- Treat living things, the environment, and each other with respect.

McGRAW-HILL
SCIENCE

MACMILLAN/McGRAW-HILL EDITION

RICHARD MOYER ■ **LUCY DANIEL** ■ **JAY HACKETT**
PRENTICE BAPTISTE ■ **PAMELA STRYKER** ■ **JOANNE VASQUEZ**

NATIONAL
GEOGRAPHIC
SOCIETY

McGraw-Hill
School Division

New York   Farmington

PROGRAM AUTHORS

Dr. Lucy H. Daniel
*Teacher, Consultant
Rutherford County Schools,
North Carolina*

Dr. Jay Hackett
*Emeritus Professor of Earth
Sciences
University of Northern
Colorado*

Dr. Richard H. Moyer
*Professor of Science
Education
University of Michigan-
Dearborn*

Dr. H. Prentice Baptiste
*Professor of Curriculum and
Instruction
New Mexico State
University*

Pamela Stryker, M.Ed.
*Elementary Educator and
Science Consultant
Eanes Independent School
District
Austin, Texas*

JoAnne Vasquez, M.Ed.
*Elementary Science
Education Specialist
Mesa Public Schools,
Arizona
NSTA President 1996–1997*

NATIONAL
GEOGRAPHIC
SOCIETY

Washington, D.C.

CONTRIBUTING AUTHORS

Dr. Thomas Custer
Dr. James Flood
Dr. Diane Lapp
Doug Llewellyn
Dorothy Reid
Dr. Donald M. Silver

CONSULTANTS

Dr. Danny J. Ballard
Dr. Carol Baskin
Dr. Bonnie Buratti
Dr. Suellen Cabe
Dr. Shawn Carlson
Dr. Thomas A. Davies
Dr. Marie DiBerardino
Dr. R. E. Duhrkopf
Dr. Ed Geary
Dr. Susan C. Giarratano-Russell
Dr. Karen Kwitter
Dr. Donna Lloyd-Kolkin
Ericka Lochner, RN
Donna Harrell Lubcker
Dr. Dennis L. Nelson
Dr. Fred S. Sack
Dr. Martin VanDyke
Dr. E. Peter Volpe
Dr. Josephine Davis Wallace
Dr. Joe Yelderman

The Book Cover, *Invitation to Science*, *World of Science*, and *FUNtastic Facts* features found in this textbook were designed and developed by the National Geographic Society's Education Division.
Copyright © 2000 National Geographic Society

The name "National Geographic Society" and the Yellow Border Rectangle are trademarks of the Society and their use, without prior written permission, is strictly prohibited
Cover photo: Stuart Westmorland/Tony Stone Images

McGraw-Hill School Division

A Division of The McGraw-Hill Companies

Copyright © 2000 McGraw-Hill School Division,
a Division of the Educational and Professional
Publishing Group of The McGraw-Hill Companies, Inc.

McGraw-Hill School Division
Two Penn Plaza
New York, New York 10121

Printed in the United States of America

ISBN 0-02-277435-1 / 3

8 9 058/046 05 04 03

CONTENTS

UNIT 1

LIVING THINGS
LIFE SCIENCES

UNIT 2

LIFT IT, PUSH IT, PULL IT
PHYSICAL SCIENCES

UNIT 3 MATTER AND ENERGY
PHYSICAL SCIENCES

EXPLORE ACTIVITIES

FACTS PROBLEMS PUZZLES

YOUR TEXTBOOK at a Glance

Begin each topic with an **Explore** question. Investigate further by doing an **Explore Activity.**

...HY IT MATTERS

...e Sun's energy
...ou every day.

A Closer Look

Could you tell time without a clock or calendar? Ancient people had to, because there were no clocks or calendars!

NATIONAL GEOGRAPHIC
World of SCIENCE

Science, Technology, and Society

SCIENCE MAGAZINE

EYES ON MARS

Look up at the sky on a clear night. Even without a telescope, you can spot Mars. It's a bright, red point of light. With powerful telescopes, scientists can see Mars's mountains, large plains, and polar ice caps.

For years people have wondered if there was life on Mars. Space exploration has let us see Mars up close and personal and look for signs of life.

In 1964, the U.S. launched the space probe *Mariner 4*. It was the first to fly by and send back to Earth images of Mars. Since then, space probes have sent back thousands of pictures of the red planet. None showed signs of life, but scientists were surprised to see giant volcanoes and dry canyons. Did the canyons mean that water had once flowed on Mars?

In 1976, the U. S. celebrated its 200th birthday and landed two spacecraft on Mars. Both *Viking 1* and 2 took pictures of the rocky plains around the landing sites. Again, there was no evidence of life on Mars.

On July 4, 1997, the U.S. spacecraft *Pathfinder* landed on Mars. Aboard was *Sojourner*, a robot on wheels that could travel to rocks and report what they were made of. Scientists on Earth could choose a rock and send *Sojourner*

to make a close-up examination. The *Pathfinder* mission showed that Mars once had the water that could have made life possible!

The U.S. plans a Mars mission every two years. Will they find life? Stay tuned!

DISCUSSION STARTER
1. Why would finding water on Mars prove that there is or was life on the planet?
2. How was *Pathfinder* different from other space missions?

To learn more about Mars, visit www.mhschool.com/science and enter the keyword ONMARS.

interNET CONNECTION

Discuss an exciting **Science Magazine** after each topic. **National Geographic World of Science** is the first magazine in each unit.

Here Comes the Sun

What difference would it make if the Sun were larger or smaller than it is? Every day you see how the Sun brightens the sky. Even though the Sun is far away, you can see and feel its energy. How does the energy from the Sun affect Earth?

EXPLORE

HYPOTHESIZE Each day Earth receives light and heat from the Sun. How does this affect Earth's temperature? Write a hypothesis in your *Science Journal*.

...WORDS

...e of gases that

...of the Sun

...ea on the

...layer of

...e Sun

...ned to pro-

DID YOU KNOW?

In a single tree in a rain forest in Peru, scientists found 43 different kinds of ants. That's more types of ants than are found in ...re United

...o you think ...rest supports ...ds of ants ...United

NATIONAL GEOGRAPHIC
FUNtastic Facts

The world's tallest tree is a coast redwood, a kind of conifer found in California. It is 111 meters (364 feet) high. It is also one of the world's oldest trees. How long do you think it took to grow this tall?

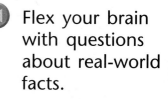

Flex your brain with questions about real-world facts.

Brain Power

Astronauts visiting the Moon left footprints. How long do you think these footprints will last? Explain.

EXPLORE ACTIVITY

Investigate How the Sun's Energy Affects Earth

Use a model to explore how the Sun's energy affects Earth's temperature.

MATERIALS
- lamp with light bulb, 60 watt
- aluminum can
- thermometer
- black paper
- meter stick
- tape
- *Science Journal*

PROCEDURES

1. MAKE A MODEL Cover the can with black paper. The can represents Earth. Place the thermometer in the can, and set the can on a table 20 cm from the lamp. The lamp represents the Sun.

2. COLLECT DATA Read the temperature inside the can. Record the number in your *Science Journal*.

3. COLLECT DATA Turn on the lamp. Record the temperature of the can every two minutes for 10 minutes.

CONCLUDE AND APPLY

1. IDENTIFY What was your first temperature measurement? What was the temperature after 10 minutes?

2. EXPLAIN Was the temperature of the can still increasing after 10 minutes? How do you know?

3. INFER Why did the temperature of the can stop increasing? Where do you think the energy from the lamp is going?

GOING FURTHER: Problem Solving

4. EXPERIMENT Suppose the can were twice as far from the lamp. How warm do you think it would get in 10 minutes? Write your prediction. Test it.

EXPLORE ACTIVITY

Design Your Own Experiment

WHAT IS THE VOLUME OF JUPITER?

PROCEDURES

1. If Earth had the volume of a bean, Jupiter would have the volume of the bowl.

2. MAKE A MODEL How can you estimate how much larger the volume of the bowl is than the volume of the bean?

3. COMMUNICATE Write your plan in your *Science Journal*. Share your plan with your teacher.

4. EXPERIMENT Try your plan.

MATERIALS
- 2 lb. bag of beans
- plastic bowl
- small cup
- *Science Journal*

CONCLUDE AND APPLY

1. USE NUMBERS How much greater is the volume of the bowl than the volume of the bean?

2. DRAW CONCLUSIONS How much

Use a Telescope

...makes faraway objects, like the Moon, look ...scope also lets you see stars that are too faint ...just your eyes.

HANDBOOK

UNIT REVIEW

USING IDEAS AND SKILLS

16. PREDICT Two seeds are planted in some soil. Only one of the seeds is watered. Which seed is more likely to grow into a plant?

17. List three things a kitten needs to live and grow.

18. Describe the pupa of a butterfly. What happens inside the pupa?

THINKING LIKE A SCIENTIST

19. CLASSIFY Many animals move by using their legs, fins, or wings. Think of two examples for each type of movement. Make a table like the one below. Write the names of the animals in the table.

LEGS	WINGS	FINS

20. Make a drawing of a cell. Label the cell membrane, the nucleus, and the cytoplasm.

WRITING IN YOUR JOURNAL

SCIENCE IN YOUR LIFE
Give some examples of the special needs of puppies, kittens, or babies. Tell how these needs are taken care of.

PRODUCT ADS
Some ads on TV try to make you hungry so that you respond by eating the foods shown. Describe an ad like this that you have seen and tell if it made you respond.

HOW SCIENTISTS WORK
Tell why scientists do experiments instead of just guessing or making up stories about how things work.

Design Your Own **Experiment**
How does an ant move? Write a hypothesis. Design an experiment that lets you see the parts of an ant and how it moves. Think safety first. Review your experiment with your teacher before you try it.

interNET CONNECTION
For help in reviewing this unit, visit www.mhschool.com/science

...How do the acorns move to... ...mals help. Squirrels find the acorns. They bury ...acorns in the ground to store them for winter. Most of the acorns get eaten by the squirrels, but a few of them are forgotten. They stay buried in the ground, far from the tree. They will grow into new trees.

...bury
...to store
...winter.

QUICK LAB

Traveling Seeds

HYPOTHESIZE Animals with fur often help plants spread their seeds. How might they do this? Write a hypothesis in your *Science Journal*.

PROCEDURES

1. PREDICT What will happen when you toss the seeds onto the fur? Record your prediction in your *Science Journal*.

2. EXPERIMENT Test your prediction. Have your partner hold up the fur. Toss different seeds at it. Record the results.

MATERIALS
- seeds
- fake fur
- *Science Journal*

CONCLUDE AND APPLY

1. IDENTIFY Which of the seeds stuck to the fur?

2. INFER How might animals with fur help plants spread their seeds?

Design Your Own Experiments, do **Quick Labs,** use **Internet Connections,** and try **Writing in Your Journal.** Use the **Handbook** for help.

Reading Graphs, Diagrams, Maps, and **Charts** help you learn by using what you see.

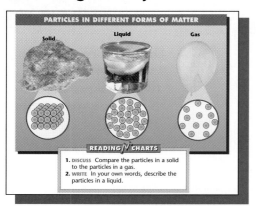

PARTICLES IN DIFFERENT FORMS OF MATTER

Solid — Liquid — Gas

READING CHARTS

1. DISCUSS Compare the particles in a solid to the particles in a gas.

2. WRITE In your own words, describe the particles in a liquid.

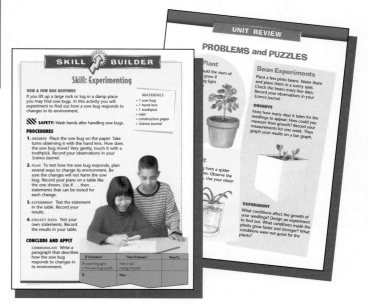

SKILL BUILDER

Skill: Experimenting

HOW A SOW BUG RESPONDS
If you lift up a large rock or log in a damp place you may find sow bugs. In this activity you will experiment to find out how a sow bug responds to changes in its environment.

SAFETY: Wash hands after handling sow bugs.

MATERIALS
- 1 sow bug
- 1 hand lens
- 1 toothpick
- ruler
- construction paper
- *Science Journal*

PROCEDURES

1. OBSERVE Place the sow bug on the paper. Take turns observing it with the hand lens. How does the sow bug move? Very gently, touch it with a toothpick. Record your observations in your *Science Journal*.

2. PLAN To test how the sow bug responds, plan several ways to change its environment. Be sure the changes will not harm the sow bug. Record your plans on a table like the one shown. Use if . . . then . . . statements that can be tested for each change.

3. EXPERIMENT Test the statement in the table. Record your results.

4. COLLECT DATA Test your own statements. Record the results in your table.

CONCLUDE AND APPLY

COMMUNICATE Write a paragraph that describes how the sow bug responds to changes in its environment.

If Statement	Then Statement	Results
If something gets the sow bug tooth	then it will change its path	
2.	then. . .	

UNIT REVIEW

PROBLEMS and PUZZLES

...Plant
...uild the stem of ...grow if ...ng light

Bean Experiments
Plant a few pinto beans. Water them and place them in a sunny spot. Check the beans every few days. Record your observations in your *Science Journal*.

OBSERVE
Note how many days it takes for the seedlings to appear. How could you measure their growth? Record your measurements for one week. Then graph your results on a bar graph.

...t:
...from a spider ...ter. Observe the ...Use your obser-

EXPERIMENT
What conditions affect the growth of your seedlings? Design an experiment to find out. What conditions made the plants grow faster and stronger? What conditions were not good for the plants?

Build your skills with Skill Builders and **Problems and Puzzles.**

NATIONAL GEOGRAPHIC

READ ALOUD

INVITATION TO SCIENCE

Even as a young boy, Ballard loved the sea!

Aboard a research ship, Ballard and his crew study images taken by an underwater camera.

Robert Ballard

Robert Ballard's love for the sea began when he was a boy in southern California. Other Californians liked to surf the waves, but Ballard was more interested in what lay beneath the ocean's surface.

To explore that world safely, he knew he had to learn as much as possible. He says, "I needed to learn a lot about geography, navigation, meteorology, geology, biology, and many other things."

His hard work has paid off! Now Ballard leads expeditions to explore the bottom of the sea. He and his crew travel in underwater vehicles called submersibles.

He is most proud of discovering unusual volcanoes on the sea floor. Hot water and minerals flow from the volcanoes, supporting many strange kinds of animals. "Most of the creatures my colleagues and I found," he says, "were completely new to science."

To help other people enjoy the thrill of discovery, Ballard started the JASON project. It uses satellite broadcasts and Internet connections to let students take part in real scientific expeditions!

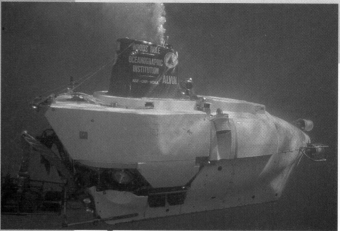

The submersible *Alvin* can carry scientists deep underwater.

Ballard discovered strange forms of life on the ocean floor.

BE A SCIENTIST

Have you ever looked at the Moon through a telescope? The light places you see are mountains and hills. The dark places are flat lands. Can you see parts that look like rings or holes? These are called **craters** (krā′tərz). A crater is a hollow area in the ground. A crater has a flat floor with walls rising around it. Craters are found in different sizes. Some can be smaller than a dime. Others can be miles across. How did they get there?

EXPLORE

Why are craters different sizes? Write a possible explanation in your *Science Journal*. How might you test your explanation?

S4

Investigate Why Craters Are Different Sizes

How does the size of a falling marble affect the size of the crater it forms? How does the height of a falling marble affect its crater size? Think of a sentence about craters that you can test. Example: A large marble will make a larger crater than a small marble.

MATERIALS

- flour
- aluminum pie tin
- marbles of different sizes
- newspaper
- meterstick
- ruler
- safety goggles
- *Science Journal*

PROCEDURES

 SAFETY: Wear goggles.

1. **MAKE A MODEL** Place newspaper on a flat surface. Fill a pie tin with flour. Smooth the flour's surface.

2. **OBSERVE** Compare the sizes of the marbles. Discuss with a partner which marble will make the biggest crater. What do you mean by big? Deep or wide, or both? Write your ideas in your *Science Journal*.

3. **MEASURE** Drop the smallest marble into the flour from a height of 25 cm. Measure the size of the crater it creates. Record your results.

4. **MEASURE** Repeat step 3 from heights of 50 cm, 75 cm, and 100 cm.

5. **REPEAT** Try the activity again with a large marble.

CONCLUDE AND APPLY

1. **INTERPRET DATA** What happened to the size of the crater as the marble was dropped from greater heights? Why?

2. **INTERPRET DATA** What happened to the size of the crater as the size of the marble increased? Why?

3. **INFER** Why are craters on the Moon different sizes?

Why Are Craters Different Sizes?

The Explore Activity shows that craters form when an object hits a surface. Scientists call this event an impact. That is why they often call craters *impact craters*.

The Explore Activity also shows that the width of the crater depends on the size of the object hitting the surface. How deep the crater is changes depending on how fast the object is traveling when it hits. The greater the height the marble was dropped from, the greater its speed. Greater speed results in deeper craters.

Did the craters you made in the tin of flour remind you of any other craters you have seen? Could the craters on the Moon be caused by impacts from objects traveling in space?

A large crater on the Moon

How Do Scientists Work?

One scientist who asked these same questions was **geologist** (jē ol′ə jist) Eugene Shoemaker. A geologist is a scientist who studies the characteristics of rocks to tell how the rocks may have formed. He investigated craters on Earth, and it made him wonder about the craters on the Moon.

Dr. Eugene Shoemaker was a geologist.

Dr. Shoemaker's interest in craters started when he was in school. He saw a crater in Arizona called Meteor Crater and wondered how it formed. He wanted to learn everything he could about it. He studied the crater's shape, and he chipped away at the rock inside it to see what he could learn from it.

The more Dr. Shoemaker studied Meteor Crater, the more he became interested in the craters on the Moon. He was so interested he decided to become an astronaut. He wanted to "bang on the Moon" with his own hammer!

Meteor Crater in Arizona is over one kilometer wide!

Unfortunately, Dr. Shoemaker's health was not good enough for him to be an astronaut. He didn't get a chance to go to the Moon, but he did train astronauts who went into outer space.

He also traveled to craters on every part of Earth. Thanks to his work, scientists now think Meteor Crater was made by a chunk of rock from outer space that hit Earth. The rock was as big as a house! Rocks from outer space enter Earth's **atmosphere** (at′məs fîr′). The atmosphere is the layer of gases that surround the planet. The rocks that enter Earth's atmosphere are called **meteors** (mē′tē ərz). When they hit an object like Earth or the Moon, they are called **meteorites** (mē′tē ə rīts′).

Dr. Shoemaker investigated more questions he had about craters. Were all craters the "footprints" of meteorites? Were craters on the Moon formed the same way as craters on Earth? Dr. Shoemaker and other scientists studied many other craters. They found **evidence** (ev′i dəns) of more than 100 large craters on Earth. Evidence is a word for clues used to solve a problem.

Meteorites are made up of mostly stone and iron.

How Do Scientists Use the Work of Other Scientists?

Dr. Shoemaker compared his ideas with what other scientists had discovered. He learned that meteorite craters had several features in common:

- They are all shaped like circles.

- The floor of the crater is lower than the land around it.

- The rim of the crater is higher than the land around it.

- The rim is made of rock material thrown out of the crater.

- The rocks thrown out of the crater are like those just below Earth's surface around the crater.

- Rock layers under the crater floor have many cracks.

- Pieces of the rock from space may be found buried in the floor of the crater. They also may be found in the ground around the crater. These rocks are different from rocks on Earth.

Henbury Crater is a meteorite crater found in Australia.

How Can a Computer Help Scientists?

Dr. Shoemaker collected evidence about his ideas. He compared craters on Earth to craters on the Moon. He concluded that they were alike. When you **draw conclusions**, you put together in a statement all the facts you have learned.

Scientific conclusions are different from opinions. An opinion is a statement about something that has not been measured or cannot be measured. It may be what someone believes—a hunch or an idea. Here's an opinion: "The Moon is a more interesting place than Earth." You may agree or not, but this is not something you can back up by collecting evidence.

You may have opinions, too. Most people do! In science, however, it is important to back up statements with supporting evidence—as you do when you record observations and make measurements.

Dr. Shoemaker used a computer to help answer some of his questions. He made a computer **model** (mod'əl) that showed what it's like when a meteorite hits Earth. A model is something that represents an object or event. In the computer model, the rocks at the center of the spot where the meteorite hit were thrown the farthest away. Rocks around the edges of where the meteorite hit moved only slightly. The rocks now formed the rim of the crater.

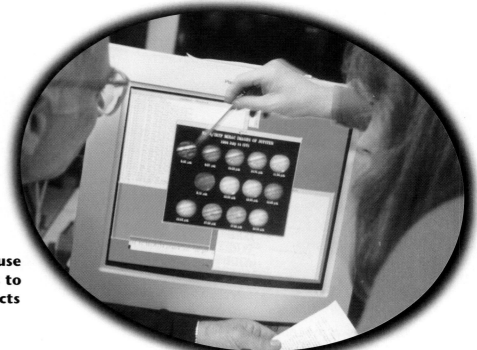

Scientists use computers to study objects in space.

Dr. Shoemaker repeated his **experiment** on the computer using **variables** (vâr′ē ə bəlz). Variables are things in an experiment that can be changed or controlled. Each time he repeated the experiment, Dr. Shoemaker changed the size of the meteorite. The larger the meteorite he used, the larger the crater formed. All of the information he gathered supported his explanation. Earth's craters were formed by meteorites that hit its surface.

Studying Things That Are Far Away

Dr. Shoemaker wanted to learn more about the craters on the Moon. Most scientists agreed that most of the Moon's craters were also formed by meteorites. How could Dr. Shoemaker find out more about how these craters formed? How could he study the Moon's craters without going to the Moon?

Craters cover most of the Moon's surface.

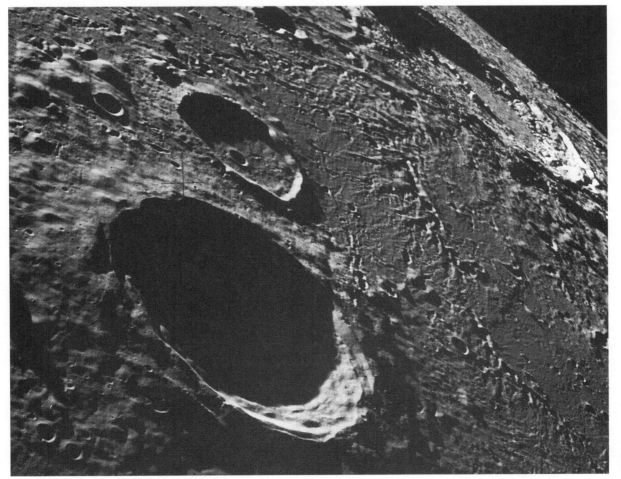

How Can a Scientist Prove His or Her Ideas?

Dr. Shoemaker and other scientists studied photographs of the craters. The pictures were taken through large telescopes. The pictures could be enlarged, making the images much bigger and easier to see. Guess what they found out?

- The Moon's craters are shaped like circles.
- The floors of the Moon's craters are lower than the land around them.
- The rims of the Moon's craters are higher than the land around them.
- The rim around the Moon's Copernicus Crater is much like Meteor Crater's rim in Arizona.

Telescopes are tools used to make faraway objects appear closer.

Based on the evidence, the scientists concluded that Copernicus Crater was made when a large meteorite hit the Moon.

What would it take to make this explanation more certain? Astronauts would have to visit Copernicus Crater and bring back rock samples from it.

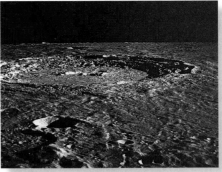

Copernicus Crater on the Moon

The explanation seems correct. Most scientists agree with it. It can be defended using the evidence from photos. The photos can be compared with the evidence collected at Meteor Crater in Arizona.

In the future you may be able to find new evidence as an astronaut or scientist. Maybe you will think of new questions about the Moon's craters. Maybe you will investigate to find the answers.

Astronauts have brought rocks from the Moon back to Earth.

How Can I Be Like a Scientist?

How do flower petals open? How are rainbows made? Why are Moon craters round? You may have asked yourself questions like these. Being curious and wondering about things is the first step in learning. Finding answers to questions based upon evidence is how science works.

Let's go back and look at how you found answers in the Explore Activity to your questions about craters and the objects that made them.

You Asked Yourself Questions

To be a scientist, you start by **observing**! Before the Explore Activity, you knew that craters came in different sizes. You **asked questions**. Which marble will make the biggest crater in the flour? Does it make any difference how fast the marble falls? What shape will the crater have? How can I test these questions and find answers?

This photograph of a rainbow over Scotland was taken from space.

You Set Up an Experiment

Your sentence at the start of your Explore Activity is called a **hypothesis** (hī poth ə sis). A hypothesis is a statement in answer to a question; you must be able to test the statement. You made a plan to test your hypothesis with marbles of different sizes.

You compared the size of the marble to the size of the crater it made. You also compared the height of the drop and the speed of the marble to how deep a crater was formed. You observed the results and measured with a ruler. Next you recorded and organized the measurements. That made them easier to compare.

You Used the Results of Your Investigation to Answer Questions

You thought about the measurements and what they meant. From this evidence you formed answers to your questions. You decided that large marbles make bigger craters than small marbles. You also decided that the faster a marble falls, the deeper the crater it makes. Marbles falling into flour are like meteorites hitting Earth or the Moon. You used a model to help test your ideas and find answers to your questions. You also wrote the results in your *Science Journal* to **communicate** your findings.

Now repeat the Explore Activity. See if the results are the same. Think of how a scientist works each time you do a step.

In this book you will be doing many Explore Activities. Complete all the steps you just learned each time. It's called using scientific methods. It's how you work like a real scientist! Answers are important. In science, *how* you find the answers is also important.

SCIENTIFIC METHODS

The work of geologists like Dr. Shoemaker is very important. Geologists find useful materials inside Earth. They help decide if places are safe to build homes on. They also study volcanoes and earthquakes. They help save lives because they can predict when a volcano is going to erupt. They're trying hard to be able to predict earthquakes, too.

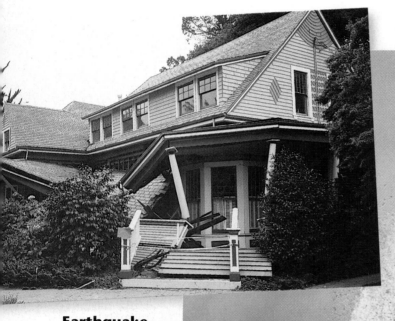

Earthquake damage

A volcano

Luckily, Earth's atmosphere protects us from most meteors. The Moon is constantly bombarded with meteorites because it has no atmosphere. That makes it a good place to study meteorites but a bad place to live! Now we know that meteorites have hit Earth and the effect they have had. Dr. Shoemaker's work has helped us understand our planet a little better.

REVIEW

1. What is the difference between a meteor and a meteorite?

2. How do scientists like Dr. Eugene Shoemaker learn about craters?

3. What did Dr. Shoemaker learn about craters?

4. What do geologists study?

BE A SCIENTIST Glossary

These are skill words that you will see printed in red in the Explore Activities, Skill Builders, and Quick Labs throughout this book.

analyze to separate anything into its parts to find out what it is made of and how it is put together

ask questions to ask about what you don't know based on what you see around you

cause and effect something (cause) that brings about a change in something else (effect)

classify to group objects according to characteristics

collect data to put together all useful information

communicate to share information

compare and contrast to find out how things are the same (compare) and how they are different (contrast)

define to make up a description that is based on observations and experience

draw conclusions to put together in a statement all the facts you have learned

evidence clues used to solve a problem

experiment a test that is used to discover or prove something

explain to tell the meaning of or tell how to do something

hypothesis a statement in answer to a question; you must be able to test the statement

identify name or recognize

infer to form an idea from facts or observations

interpret data to use the information that has been gathered to answer questions or solve a problem

make decisions to make up your mind from many choices

measure to find the size, volume, area, mass, weight, or temperature of an object or how long an event occurs

model something that represents an object or event

observe to use one or more of the senses to identify or learn about an object or event

plan to think out ahead of time how something is to be done or made, including methods and materials

predict to state possible results of an event or experiment

repeat to do something again the same way to see if the results are the same

sequence a series of things that are related in some way

test the examination of a substance or event to see what it is or why it happens

theory an explanation based on observation and reasoning

use numbers to explain data by ordering, counting, adding, subtracting, multiplying, and dividing

variables things in an experiment that can be changed or controlled

These are new Science Words that you learned in Be a Scientist. You will see and learn more Science Words printed in blue as you read this book.

atmosphere the layer of gases surrounding a planet

crater a hollow area in the ground

geologist a scientist who studies the characteristics of rocks to tell how the rocks may have formed

meteor a piece of rock from outer space that enters Earth's atmosphere

meteorite a meteor that has fallen to Earth

METHODS OF SCIENCE

Here is a chart that shows the steps to follow when solving a problem in science.

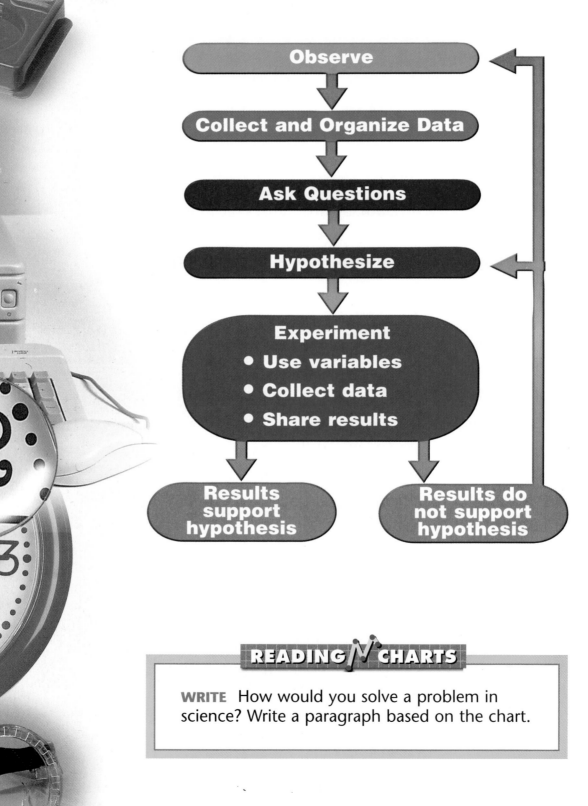

READING CHARTS

WRITE How would you solve a problem in science? Write a paragraph based on the chart.

CHAPTER 1

THE WORLD OF LIVING THINGS

Everything in the world is either living or nonliving. Sometimes it can be hard to tell a living thing from something that is nonliving. To be able to tell the difference, you need to know what it means to be living.

In Chapter 1 you will compare and contrast things. When you compare and contrast things you state how they are alike and how they are not alike.

WHY IT MATTERS

Being able to tell if something is a living thing or a nonliving thing is a valuable skill.

SCIENCE WORDS

organism a living thing

development the way a living thing changes during its life

reproduction the way organisms make new living things just like themselves

environment the things that make up an area, such as land, water, and air

respond the way a living thing reacts to changes in its environment

communicate to share information

An Inside Look at Living Things

What types of things do you see in this picture? Make a list. Some things in the photograph are living. Some are nonliving. How can you tell a living thing from a nonliving thing? What are the differences between them?

EXPLORE

HYPOTHESIZE What features do you think living things have? Write a hypothesis in your *Science Journal.* How could you test your ideas?

2

Investigate the Features of Living Things

Observe pea seeds and gravel to find out the features of living things.

PROCEDURES

1. MEASURE Mark a piece of white paper A. Place the pea seeds on it. Mark another piece of paper B. Place the gravel on it.

2. OBSERVE Look at the seeds and gravel with the hand lens. Describe what you see in your *Science Journal.*

3. Mark a plastic cup A. Place the seeds in it. Mark the other plastic cup B. Place the gravel in it. Pour the same amount of water into each cup. Make sure the seeds and gravel are completely covered with water.

4. PREDICT What do you think will happen after two days?

5. OBSERVE Look at the soaked seeds and gravel every few hours for two days. Record your observations.

CONCLUDE AND APPLY

1. EXPLAIN What happened to the seeds? What happened to the gravel? Which do you think is living? Why?

2. INFER What are some features of living things?

GOING FURTHER: Apply

3. COMPARE AND CONTRAST From what you have observed, what are some differences between living and nonliving things?

MATERIALS

- 25 pea seeds
- 25 pieces of gravel
- 1 hand lens
- 2 $3\frac{1}{2}$ oz. plastic cups
- 2 pieces of white paper
- marker
- water
- *Science Journal*

Acorn

Green sapling

Young tree

What Are the Features of Living Things?

The Explore Activity demonstrates some of the features of **organisms** (ôr′gə niz′əmz). An organism is a living thing. How can you tell an organism from a nonliving thing? Sometimes it is easy. You can probably tell a living frog from a non-living toy frog. Sometimes it is not easy. There are three ways to tell a living thing from a nonliving thing.

Living Things Grow and Change

A living thing grows. It starts out small. Then it gets bigger. An oak tree begins as an acorn. Then it grows to become a green sapling (sap′ling). This is a very young tree.

Organisms also change as they grow. The way a living thing changes during its life is called **development** (di vel′əp mənt). As an oak sapling grows into a tree, its branches and trunk become thicker and stronger. The oak tree also changes shape and color as it develops.

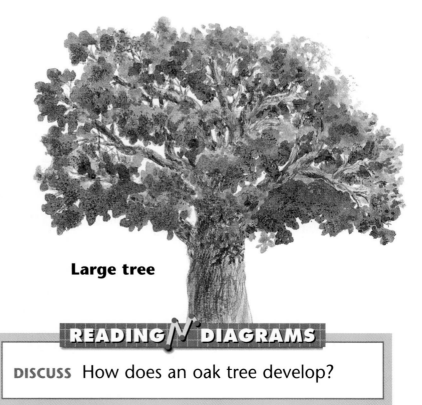

Large tree

READING DIAGRAMS

DISCUSS How does an oak tree develop?

4

Living Things Make More of Their Own Kind

The Explore Activity showed one feature of living things—they grow and change. When water was added to the pea seeds, new plants began to grow.

Another feature of living things is that they make more of their own kind. Plants grow from seeds. Chicks hatch from eggs. Some animals, like puppies, are born live. All these are examples of **reproduction** (rē′prə duk′shən). Reproduction is the way organisms make more of their own kind.

How is a puppy similar and different from its parents? Some new living things, or offspring, are not exact copies of their parents. Most animal offspring, including you, are not exact copies of their parents. A puppy is a mixture of both parents. It is not exactly like either parent.

Some offspring are not exact copies of their parents. They have a mixture of features from both parents.

Brain Power

A photocopy machine makes perfect copies of an original. Is the machine a living thing? Explain.

What Is the Third Way to Tell a Living Thing?

Living Things React

You and all organisms live in an **environment** (en vī rən mənt). An environment is made up of everything that surrounds an organism. It can include the air, the water, the soil, and even other organisms.

An organism **responds** (ri spondz´) to changes in its environment. When an organism responds to a change, it reacts in certain ways. All living things respond in some way.

Have you ever noticed how plants and insects respond to light? Plants bend toward light. Insects fly toward light.

These plants respond by bending toward the sunlight.

Living things also respond in other ways. The leaves on some trees respond to a change in season. In autumn, they turn colors, then fall off the branches. Animals also respond to a change in season. Squirrels save nuts for the winter. Bears sleep through the winter in a cave.

You respond to your environment in many ways, too. You may shiver if you are cold. What other ways do you respond to changes in your environment?

SKILL BUILDER

Skill: Experimenting

HOW A SOW BUG RESPONDS

If you lift up a large rock or log in a damp place you may find sow bugs. In this activity you will experiment to find out how a sow bug responds to changes in its environment.

SAFETY: Wash hands after handling sow bugs.

PROCEDURES

1. OBSERVE Place the sow bug on the paper. Take turns observing it with the hand lens. How does the sow bug move? Very gently, touch it with a toothpick. Record your observations in your *Science Journal.*

2. PLAN To test how the sow bug responds, plan several ways to change its environment. Be sure the changes will not harm the sow bug. Record your plans on a table like the one shown. Use if. . . then. . . statements that can be tested for each change.

3. EXPERIMENT Test the statement in the table. Record your results.

4. COLLECT DATA Test your own statements. Record the results in your table.

CONCLUDE AND APPLY

COMMUNICATE Write a paragraph that describes how the sow bug responds to changes in its environment.

MATERIALS

- 1 sow bug
- 1 hand lens
- 1 toothpick
- ruler
- construction paper
- *Science Journal*

If Statement	Then Statement	Results
If something gets in the sow bug's path	then it will change its path	
If...	then...	

How Do Living Things Use Their Senses to Respond to the Environment?

Living things use their senses to gather information about their environment. As the Skill Builder activity showed, a sow bug uses its senses to collect information about its environment. Then it responds.

Living things especially use their senses when they **communicate** (kə mū′ni kāt′), or share information. To communicate, organisms send, collect, and respond to signals. They use their senses of sight, smell, hearing, or touch to collect information.

How do living things communicate? They communicate in many ways. For example, fireflies flash lights to attract mates. Some birds sing to mark their territory, or area. When a male red-wing blackbird sings it is saying to other males, "Stay out of my territory!" Skunks sometimes spray a strong-smelling liquid to communicate. If you have ever smelled a skunk, you know it is warning you to stay FAR AWAY!

When a red-wing blackbird sings, other male red-wing blackbirds know to keep their distance.

Your sense of smell tells you a skunk is warning you to stay away.

Living things can be identified from nonliving things in three ways. Living things grow and develop, reproduce, and respond to their environment. It is important to be able to identify living things. For example, some living things like this poisonous stonefish look like nonliving things. You would treat a nonliving thing very differently than a living thing.

Just stepping on this poisonous stonefish can cause a lot of pain and even death.

REVIEW

1. What is an organism?
2. How is a living thing different from a nonliving thing?
3. How do living things gather information about their environment?
4. 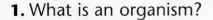 **EXPERIMENT** How would you test the way a plant may respond to changes in its environment?
5. **CRITICAL THINKING** *Evaluate* Suppose your pet dog lost its sense of smell. How would this change the way it responds to its environment?

WHY IT MATTERS THINK ABOUT IT
Suppose you were an explorer in a rain forest. You find something that looks interesting. You are not sure if it is a living thing. How could you find out?

WHY IT MATTERS WRITE ABOUT IT
Describe your discovery. What features did it have that helped you tell whether it was a living thing?

Hand Talk

After Koko used a hand sign to ask for a cat, her keeper gave her a kitten of her own!

A Closer Look

Can animals talk to people? Some gorillas and chimpanzees can. Two gorillas, Koko and Michael, use sign language. They talk with their hands!

Koko began learning to sign in 1972. She was just one year old then. Now she understands more than 1000 signs! She uses the signs to talk with her keepers. Michael began signing in 1976, when he was three. Now he uses 500 different signs.

Five chimpanzees have also learned sign language. They sign with their keepers and each other. Washoe, the oldest, was born in 1965. She uses 240 signs.

The animals often combine signs and make "sentences" of up to seven signs. They also put signs together in new ways. For example, the chimps named watermelon "drink fruit." They call a radish "cry hurt food."

How did the animals learn to sign? It's a case of "monkey see, monkey do." They watched their keepers sign, then copied the movements. After Washoe learned to sign, she taught her adopted son, Loulis!

"Talking" with the animals helps us learn more about how they—and people—think and learn.

A chimp learns the sign for "eye."

Discussion Starter

1 Why would gorillas and chimps want to talk with people?

2 Why would the chimps call watermelon "drink fruit"? What do you think they'd call broccoli?

*inter*NET CONNECTION To learn more about sign language, visit www.mhschool.com/science and enter the keyword **SIGN**.

Topic 2
LIFE SCIENCE

WHY IT MATTERS

All organisms need certain things to live and grow.

SCIENCE WORDS

energy the ability to do work

oxygen a gas that is in air and water

migrate to move to another place

hibernate to rest or sleep through the cold winter

What All Organisms Need

What would you pack for a trip to the bottom of the ocean? These divers are getting ready for such a trip. They can pack only what they need. Their needs include food and fresh water. They also have some other needs. Can you tell what these other needs are? How would the divers take care of these same needs on dry land?

EXPLORE

HYPOTHESIZE What do you think organisms need to live and grow? Write a hypothesis in your *Science Journal.* How could you test your ideas?

FOOD

FOOD

WATER

H₂O TANK

BATTERIES & LIGHT BULBS

O₂ O₂ O₂

SUPPLIES

WASTE TANK

EXPLORE ACTIVITY

Investigate What Organisms Need

Observe caterpillars and pea plants to find out what organisms need to live and grow.

PROCEDURES

1. Plant 6 of the soaked pea seeds in each milk carton. Cover the seeds with $\frac{3}{4}$ cup of soil. Place one carton in a sunny area. Water it as needed. Place the other container in a dark place. Do not water it.

2. Place the container with the caterpillars in a cool place out of the sun.

3. **OBSERVE** Look at the caterpillars and seeds two or three times each week. Record what you see in your *Science Journal*.

CONCLUDE AND APPLY

1. **EXPLAIN** What happened to the caterpillars?

2. **DRAW CONCLUSIONS** What do caterpillars need to live and grow? What do pea plants need to grow?

3. **INFER** What do pea plants get from the soil?

GOING FURTHER: Apply

4. **DRAW CONCLUSIONS** How are the needs of caterpillars different from those of pea plants?

MATERIALS

- container with 3 caterpillars and food
- hand lens
- 2 half-pint milk cartons
- $1\frac{1}{2}$ cups soil
- soaked pea seeds from Topic 1
- water
- *Science Journal*

13

What Do Organisms Need?

What do you need every day to live and grow? The Explore Activity shows that organisms have certain needs like food, water, air, and a place to live.

Food gives an organism **energy** (en′ər jē). Energy is the ability to do work. An organism is like a machine. Both need energy to run. Fuel, such as gasoline, runs a machine. Food is an organism's fuel.

Different kinds of organisms get food in different ways. Plants make their own food. Leaves make food using sunlight for energy, water, and air. Some animals eat only plants. Some eat only other animals. Some animals eat both plants and animals. Other organisms, like mushrooms, get food from dead organisms.

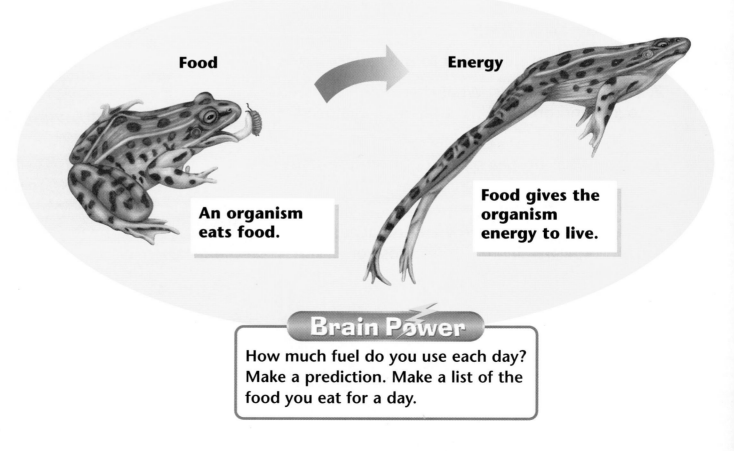

Food

Energy

An organism eats food.

Food gives the organism energy to live.

Brain Power

How much fuel do you use each day? Make a prediction. Make a list of the food you eat for a day.

Why Do Organisms Need Water?

Most organisms are made up mostly of water. For example, a large part of the human body is made up of water. Water is taken into the body and lost from the body. It leaves the body as sweat and liquid waste. Organisms must take in water to replace lost water.

Water also has several important jobs.

- It helps the body use food as fuel.
- It helps some animals stay cool.
- It helps get rid of body wastes.
- Plants take in water, sun, and air to make their own food. Water also helps a plant keep its shape.

A jellyfish is more than $\frac{9}{10}$ water! MATH LINK

Watch Water Travel Through a Plant!

HYPOTHESIZE How does water travel through a plant? Write a hypothesis in your *Science Journal.*

PROCEDURES

SAFETY: Wear goggles.

1. MEASURE Put about 2 inches (5 cm) of water in the plastic glass. Add 10 drops of food coloring.

2. PREDICT Put a celery stalk in the glass for 2 hours. What do you think will happen?

CONCLUDE AND APPLY

1. EXPLAIN What did you observe after 2 hours?

2. INFER How does water travel through a plant?

MATERIALS

- 1 clear plastic container
- 1 celery stalk with leaves
- food coloring
- water
- safety goggles
- *Science Journal*

Why Do Organisms Need Air?

Most organisms need air because it contains **oxygen** (ok′ sə jən). Oxygen is an important gas. Like many organisms, you can live for a few days without food or water. However, you would die in just a few minutes without oxygen.

Why is oxygen important? All your body parts need oxygen to live and grow. Plants and animals also need oxygen to get the energy they need from food.

How do organisms get oxygen? Some absorb it through their body coverings. Others get it by taking air into their bodies. Some land organisms take in air with their lungs. Lungs are body parts inside the chest. Most water animals breathe through gills. Gills are body parts that take oxygen out of water.

How Do Organisms Get Rid of Wastes?

Using the energy in food creates three forms of waste—solid, liquid, and gas. Organisms must get rid of wastes. Wastes can be poisonous if they stay inside the body. The body parts that break down food also help get rid of solid waste. Body parts called kidneys (kid′nēz) help get rid of liquid waste. Organisms with lungs breathe out waste gas.

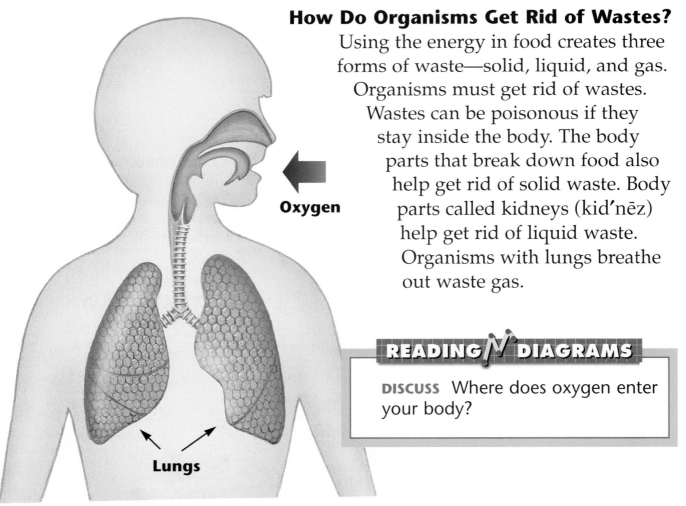

Oxygen

Lungs

READING *N* DIAGRAMS

DISCUSS Where does oxygen enter your body?

How Do Living Things Respond to Inner Needs?

How do you know you are hungry? Does your stomach make noises? Some needs, like the need for food, are inner needs. Signals inside an organism's body tell it what to do to respond to an inner need. When you are hungry your brain gets the message: Eat!

A whale swimming underwater begins to run out of oxygen. Waste gas also builds up in its body. These events give the whale's brain a message: Go up for air! A horse running on a hot day sweats and loses body water. The horse's brain gets a message: Drink! What happens when you play games or run? Do you lose water? How does your body tell you that it is time to drink?

How do you think you would feel after running in a race?

After running, the horse will probably be very thirsty.

How Do Organisms Respond to Changes in Their Environment?

How do you respond if you step outside and find that it is very warm? You may take off your jacket. How might you respond if it is cold? You might put on a hat and gloves. When you do these things, you are responding to a change in your environment.

All organisms need a place to live—their environment. Living things respond to changes in their environment in different ways. For example, daylight signals some flowers to open to welcome insects. Bats return to their caves to sleep.

What happens when the weather gets colder and the days get shorter? Some animals gather food for the winter. Geese and butterflies **migrate** (mī'grāt). Animals that migrate move to another place to live. Other animals find places to **hibernate** (hī'bər nāt'). Animals that hibernate rest or sleep through the cold winter.

Changes in the weather and the seasons signal plants and animals to do different things. How do you plan for a changing season?

WHY IT MATTERS

All living things have needs. These needs include food, water, air, and a place to live. It's important to know about your needs. It's also important to be careful about how you meet your needs. Keeping the water and air clean is one way to be careful. Keeping the land clean so healthy foods can grow is another way. Taking care of your environment now will help take care of everyone's needs in the future.

Help take good care of your environment!

REVIEW

1. What are the needs of plants?

2. How do organisms use food and water?

3. How do organisms take in oxygen?

4. **PREDICT** Suppose you were going on a trip to the North Pole. What might your outer needs be?

5. **CRITICAL THINKING** *Evaluate* How can people help make sure that their needs are met in the future?

WHY IT MATTERS THINK ABOUT IT
What if you had to do without one basic need for one day? Which basic need might you be able to go without?

WHY IT MATTERS WRITE ABOUT IT
Write a paragraph about how you meet your basic needs at home.

Chasing

Students at the Blake School in Minnesota read about monarchs. They learned that monarchs east of the Rocky Mountains fly to Mexico in the fall. Monarchs west of the Rocky Mountains fly to the coast of California. Some fly up to 4,500 kilometers (2,500 miles)! They fly by day and rest at night. The trip takes up to three months.

The students went to the eastern monarchs' winter home. It's in the mountains west of Mexico City. There they saw millions of monarchs. The butterflies stay in Mexico until spring. Then they fly north. The females lay eggs along the way.

Monarch Fall Migration

As temperatures drop in the fall, monarchs migrate south.

Kids Did It!

Butterflies

Now the Blake students want to help protect the places where monarchs rest during the winter. Without these places, monarchs would disappear!

DISCUSSION STARTER

1. Why do monarchs migrate?
2. How could people protect the places where the monarchs rest during winter?

To learn more about butterflies, visit *www.mhschool.com/science* and enter the keyword FLUTTER.

*inter*NET
CONNECTION

21

WHY IT MATTERS

Some organisms go through amazing changes as they live and grow.

SCIENCE WORDS

life cycle all the stages in an organism's life

metamorphosis a change in the body form of an organism

inherited trait a characteristic that comes from your parents

learned trait something that you are taught or learn from experience

The Life of an Animal

How do animals change over a lifetime? Compare a dog and a caterpillar. Both change as they grow, but in very different ways. Which one seems to grow more? Which one seems to change more?

EXPLORE

HYPOTHESIZE How does a caterpillar change over its lifetime? Write a hypothesis in your *Science Journal.* How could you find out?

Investigate How an Organism Changes as It Grows

Observe and record how a caterpillar grows and develops over a period of time.

MATERIALS

- caterpillars and container from Topic 2
- 1 hand lens
- *Science Journal*

PROCEDURES

1. OBSERVE Look at the caterpillars with the hand lens. Make a drawing of them in your *Science Journal.*

2. OBSERVE Look at the caterpillars twice each week. Record your findings and make a drawing of what they look like. Answer these questions: How have the animals changed? How do the animals act?

CONCLUDE AND APPLY

1. EXPLAIN What happened to the caterpillars?

2. EXPLAIN What does the caterpillar become when it is an adult?

3. COMPARE In what ways are the young and adult forms different?

GOING FURTHER: Apply

4. CLASSIFY How many different forms of development do the caterpillars go through?

How Does an Organism Change as It Grows?

The Explore Activity showed some of the **life cycle** (līf sī′kəl) of a butterfly. A life cycle is all of the stages in an organism's life. Organisms go through these stages:

• **Birth** The organism's life begins.

• **Growth and Change** The organism gets larger. It may take on a new form.

• **Reproduction** The organism creates new organisms like itself.

• **Death** The organism's life ends.

LIFE CYCLE OF A MONARCH BUTTERFLY

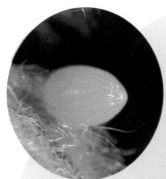  

STAGE 1: EGG
The female lays eggs on a leaf. Each egg grows until it is ready to hatch.

STAGE 2: CATERPILLAR
After about 1 week, a caterpillar hatches from the egg. The caterpillar eats often. It is storing food energy for the next stage in its life cycle.

STAGE 3: PUPA
The caterpillar stops eating. It forms a hard case around itself called a pupa (pū′pə). Inside, the caterpillar goes through many changes.

STAGE 4: ADULT
After about a week, the adult butterfly comes out. Its body is now completely different. A female butterfly will lay eggs to start a new life cycle.

How have you changed since you were five years old? Some organisms, like people, get larger as they grow older. Unlike people, some organisms go through life cycle changes called **metamorphosis** (met′ə môr′fə sis). Metamorphosis means a change in body form. It causes big changes in insects like the butterfly.

Other animals, such as frogs and toads, also go through metamorphosis. For example, young frogs live only in the water. Adult frogs live both in and out of water. Their bodies must change to live in different places.

LIFE CYCLE OF A FROG

STAGE 1: EGG A female lays eggs in water. Each egg grows for about 12 days until it is ready to hatch.

STAGE 2: TADPOLE A fish-like tadpole hatches from each egg. Tadpoles spend all their time in the water. They get oxygen from the water through their gills.

STAGE 3: ADULT A tadpole's tail finally disappears. Lungs replace its gills. A tadpole can now breathe air. It is a frog. A female frog lays eggs to start a new life cycle.

LATER IN STAGE 2 Over time, a tadpole grows legs and its tail shortens.

What Are the Life Cycles of Other Animals?

Have you ever seen a kitten or puppy grow into an adult? What changes did it go through?

Almost all animals come from eggs. Some offspring, like frogs, birds, and turtles, hatch from eggs outside the female's body. Some go through **metamorphosis**, like frogs. Others, like birds and turtles, do not.

Other offspring, like cats and bears, grow and **develop** inside the female's body. They look a lot like the adults. As they grow and change, they do not go through metamorphosis. Use these charts to compare the life cycles of a bird, a bear, and a turtle.

BEAR

Bear
A bear egg develops inside a female's body. The developing bear goes through many changes before it is born.

Young Cub
The young bear is called a cub. Its mother teaches it to hunt, fish, and find plants and berries to eat.

Adult
Adult bears begin to reproduce between $2\frac{1}{2}$ and 6 years of age. One to four cubs are born at a time.

BIRD

Bird
Bird eggs develop outside of the female's body. Bird egg shells are hard. Each egg contains a developing bird and yolk. Yolk is food for the developing bird.

Young Bird
Young birds, or nestlings, have few feathers. Parents take care of them. Most young birds will not leave the nest until they know how to fly.

Adult
To show they are ready to reproduce, some birds have bright feathers.

TURTLE

Turtle
Turtle eggs develop outside of the female's body. They are usually soft and leathery.

Young Turtle
Once hatched, the young turtle is on its own. It immediately begins to walk toward the water.

Adult
Turtles begin to reproduce when they are between 3 and 8 years old.

READING CHARTS

1. **DISCUSS** How is a young turtle different from a bear cub or a young bird?
2. **WRITE** How is the egg of a bear different from the egg of a bird or a turtle?

What Makes You YOU?

Have you ever been told, "You have your mother's eyes"? This is an example of an **inherited trait** (in her′itəd trāt). Inherited traits are characteristics that come from your parents. How do you inherit traits? People start out life as an egg. That egg contains special material from both parents. This material determines your traits.

Not all traits are inherited. Some are **learned traits** (lûr′nid trāts). Learned traits are ones you are taught or that you learn from experience. You learn to ride a bicycle or speak a language. Even if your parents speak Spanish, you will not speak Spanish unless you learn it from someone.

QUICK LAB

Name that Trait Game!

HYPOTHESIZE What traits do you think you inherited from your parents? What things did you learn? Make a list for each in your *Science Journal.*

PROCEDURES

1. Write a trait that can be inherited on each of two cards. Write a trait that can be learned on each of the other two cards. Do not show your partner what you write.

2. Take turns holding up a card. Ask your partner to identify the trait as inherited or learned.

MATERIALS
- 8 index cards
- *Science Journal*

brown eyes

speak Spanish

CONCLUDE AND APPLY

1. **CLASSIFY** Arrange the cards into two groups.

2. **COMMMUNICATE** Make an illustrated chart of the traits in your *Science Journal.* Evaluate your results.

Brain Power

How have you changed from the time you were born? Draw pictures to show these changes.

WHY IT MATTERS

As you get older, you will go through many changes in your life. Knowing the stages of the life cycle helps you better understand some of these changes.

Studying the life cycles of animals helps you to appreciate nature. If you ever see a pupa hanging from a branch you will know what it is. You will be able to identify tadpoles in a pond.

REVIEW

1. How many stages does a butterfly go through in its life cycle?

2. How does a butterfly go through metamorphosis?

3. Which kinds of animals are born live? Which hatch from an egg?

4. INFER Suppose you have a dog that likes catching balls. Is this an inherited trait or a learned trait? Explain.

5. CRITICAL THINKING *Apply* You are asked to study the adult stage of a moth. In what form would the moth be right before it becomes an adult?

WHY IT MATTERS THINK ABOUT IT
You are still growing and changing. How do you think you will change by the end of the year?

WHY IT MATTERS WRITE ABOUT IT
Write a paragraph about something you want to learn to do by the end of the year. How will you learn it?

READING SKILL How are the life cycles of birds and frogs alike? How are they different?

WHY SO MANY EGGS?

A female frog can lay thousands of eggs at a time. Lots of frogs live in the same pond, so imagine all the frog eggs there could be! Will the pond soon overflow with twisting and turning tadpoles?

Probably not. Many fish eat frog eggs. Some kinds of frogs eat other frogs' eggs, too. Sudden cold weather can chill and kill the eggs. If insecticides or other chemicals get into the pond, the eggs will absorb them and die. If a pond dries up, so do the eggs!

Some eggs will survive and become tadpoles. However, fish and ducks eat tadpoles. Cold or dry weather or water pollution can kill tadpoles. Some might not find enough food. All in all, few tadpoles live to become adult frogs.

Although they lay lots of eggs, the number of frogs worldwide goes down every year. Water and air pollution are two causes. People have also filled in many ponds where frogs once laid their eggs. Without places to live, the number of frogs may continue to decrease.

Frog eggs

Math Link

DISCUSSION STARTER

1. Are all those frog eggs necessary? Why or why not?

2. Most birds lay just a few eggs. Why do they survive?

To learn more about animal survival, visit **www.mhschool.com/science** and enter the keyword SURVIVE!

*inter*NET CONNECTION

WHY IT MATTERS

Plants grow and reproduce in different ways.

SCIENCE WORDS

embryo a young organism that is just beginning to grow

germinate to begin growing

flowering plant a plant that produces seeds inside of flowers

conifer a tree that produces seeds inside of cones

The Life of a Plant

Do you think that plants, like animals, have different kinds of life cycles? Why or why not?

Look at the trees in the photograph. How do you think a tree changes in each stage of its life cycle?

EXPLORE

HYPOTHESIZE How does a plant's life begin? Write a hypothesis in your *Science Journal.* How could you test your ideas?

Investigate How a Plant Life Cycle Begins

Grow a pea plant to observe the beginning of its life cycle.

MATERIALS

- 5 pea seeds
- 1 hand lens
- 1 plastic cup
- $\frac{1}{4}$ cup of water
- paper towel
- 1 self-sealing plastic bag, pint-sized
- *Science Journal*

PROCEDURES

1. OBSERVE Look at the seeds with a hand lens. Record your observations in your *Science Journal.*

2. Soak the seeds in water in the cup overnight. Make sure the seeds are totally covered with water.

3. OBSERVE Look at the seeds the next day. How are they different? Peel away the outside of one seed. Look at the seed with a hand lens. Record your observations. Separate the two halves of the seed. Use a hand lens to observe each half. Draw what you see.

4. Moisten a paper towel. Fold it and place it inside the plastic bag. Place the other four seeds at the bottom of the plastic bag on top of the paper towel. Seal the bag.

5. PREDICT How do you think the peas will change? Observe the peas each day. Make drawings to show how the peas change.

CONCLUDE AND APPLY

1. EXPLAIN How did the seeds change after they were soaked? What did you find between the two halves of the seed?

2. INFER Which part of a plant's life cycle is the seed?

GOING FURTHER: Apply

3. EXPLAIN What changes did you observe as the tiny plants grew from the seeds?

How Does a Plant Life Cycle Begin?

The Explore Activity shows how seeds begin a pea plant's life cycle. The stages in a plant's life cycle are similar to an animal's life cycle. A plant begins life, grows and develops, reproduces, and dies.

A seed is a tiny capsule that contains a plant **embryo** (em'brē ō'). A plant embryo is a young plant that is just beginning to grow. Each seed also contains food for the embryo to use as it grows. The food contains *nutrients* (nü'trē ənts). A nutrient is a substance in food that an organism needs to live. The food helps the embryo survive during the time it cannot make its own food. A tough outer case protects the embryo.

Seeds do not always **germinate** (jûr'mə nāt') right away. A seed that germinates begins to grow. Seeds can wait for months, or even years, until the conditions for growth are just right. A seed needs light, water, nutrients, oxygen, and the right temperature to germinate.

What kinds of seeds have you seen? You can see seeds in many different kinds of plants. Pumpkins, peanuts, corn, and watermelons all contain seeds. Each of these seeds can grow into a new plant.

The life cycle of plants can be very short or very long. A tomato plant lives for a few months. A redwood tree can live for hundreds, or even thousands, of years.

GERMINATION OF A BEAN SEED

Bean seed

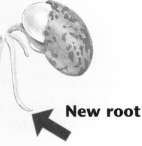

New plant

New root

How Are Seeds Made?

Most plants, like the pea plant, make seeds. There are two main groups of plants that reproduce by making seeds. **Flowering plants** (flou'əring plantz) are plants that produce seeds in flowers. Most plants in the world are flowering plants. **Conifers** (kon'ə fərz) are trees that produce seeds in cones.

Flowering Plants

What are the parts of a flower? Flowers can have male parts and female parts. The female parts make eggs that become seeds. The male part makes *pollen* (pol'ən). Pollen is a powdery material that is needed by the egg to make seeds.

To make seeds, pollen and eggs must come together. The wind, insects, and birds bring pollen to eggs. Many animals love flowers' bright colors. They also like a sugary liquid in flowers. This is called nectar (nek'tər). While they drink nectar, pollen rubs off on their bodies. As they move, some of this pollen gets delivered to the female flower parts.

Over time, the female parts turn into fruits that contain seeds. Animals often eat the fruits. The seeds pass through their bodies as waste. The animals don't know it, but they are planting seeds as they travel!

LIFE CYCLE OF A FLOWERING PLANT

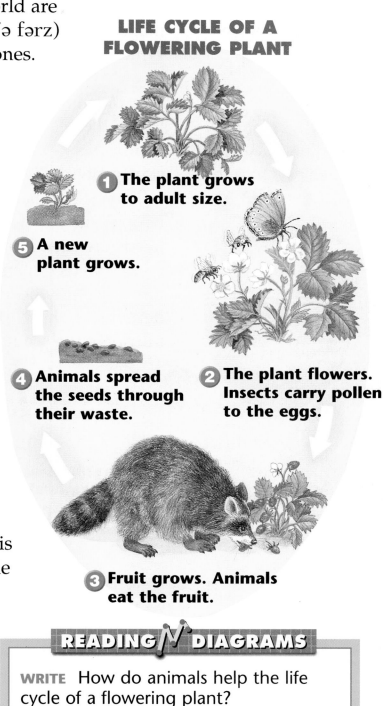

1. The plant grows to adult size.
2. The plant flowers. Insects carry pollen to the eggs.
3. Fruit grows. Animals eat the fruit.
4. Animals spread the seeds through their waste.
5. A new plant grows.

READING DIAGRAMS

WRITE How do animals help the life cycle of a flowering plant?

35

Conifers

Have you ever seen a pine cone? Pine cones come from conifers. Conifers include pine trees, spruce, and hemlock. Their leaves look like needles or brushes.

A pine tree makes two kinds of cones. They make small pollen cones and large seed cones. Wind blows pollen from the small cones to the large cones. When pollen attaches to the large cone, a seed is made. Seeds grow inside the large cones. When the seeds are ripe, they fall to the ground. If conditions are right, each seed can germinate and start growing. Over time, the seed becomes a tree.

Each seed made by a plant is able to produce a new plant. This will happen if all of the seed's needs are met. However, the number of seeds that a plant makes depends on several things. It depends on how many flowers are pollinated. It also depends on how much light, water, oxygen, and nutrients the plant gets.

MATH LINK

LIFE CYCLE OF A CONIFER

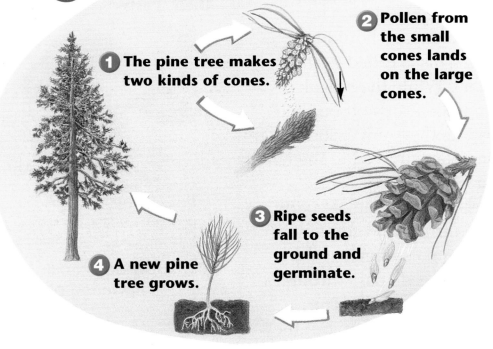

1 The pine tree makes two kinds of cones.

2 Pollen from the small cones lands on the large cones.

3 Ripe seeds fall to the ground and germinate.

4 A new pine tree grows.

When Do Flowers Bloom?

Seeds need the right conditions to germinate and grow. Flowers also need the right conditions to bloom. Most flowers use sunlight as their cue. Long-day plants bloom in the spring when days get longer. Short-day plants bloom in the fall when days get shorter.

Light or Shade

HYPOTHESIZE **Do seedlings need light to grow? Write a hypothesis in your *Science Journal.***

PROCEDURES

1. Cover the outside of one glass with black paper.

2. Wet the paper towels. Place one in each plastic glass. Put a seedling on the paper towel in each glass.

3. Place both glasses on a sunny window sill. Place a piece of the black paper over the top of the glass. Make sure the towels are kept wet.

4. **OBSERVE** Compare the seedlings after two days.

CONCLUDE AND APPLY

1. **OBSERVE** What happened to the seedling in the glass covered with black paper? What happened to the other seedling?

2. **INFER** What does this tell you about a seedling's needs?

MATERIALS

- 2 pea seedlings from the Explore Activity
- 2 10-ounce clear plastic glasses
- water
- 2 paper towels
- 1 sheet of black construction paper
- tape
- scissors
- *Science Journal*

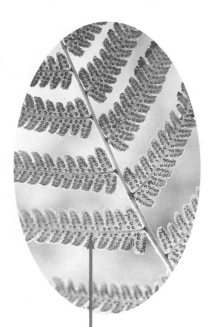

Each spot on this fern contains hundreds of spores.

What Other Ways Do Plants Reproduce?

Not all plants have seeds and pollen. For example, a fern uses *spores* (spôrz) to reproduce. Spores are not as tough as seeds. They do not have a food supply. When a spore has light, water, and nutrients, it can grow into a new plant.

Did you know that some types of plants can grow new plants from parts of themselves? These pieces are called *cuttings* because a piece of the plant is cut off. If a leaf or piece of a stem from certain plants is placed in water, new roots will grow. A new plant develops.

A *bulb* is an underground stem. A bulb is covered with leaves. One type of bulb is the onion. Each bulb can grow into a new onion plant just like the parent plant.

Do you know what a *tuber* (tü'bər) is? You may have eaten a mashed one for dinner last night! A potato is a tuber. A tuber is an underground stem. New plants that grow from a tuber are just like the parent plants.

This bulb will grow into an iris plant.

New roots grow from this cutting.

This potato is a tuber. Each white spot, called an eye, can grow a new plant.

38

WHY IT MATTERS

Plants need nutrients in soil to survive. Some of these nutrients can come from *compost* (kom′pōst). Compost is a mixture of plant materials, such as grass clippings, dead plants, leaves, and the unused parts of vegetables and fruits. Tiny organisms break the materials down into smaller pieces and nutrients. When it is all broken down, this mixture can be added to soil. This makes the soil rich in nutrients. New plants grow strong and healthy. Knowing about the life cycle of plants can help you prepare your own garden!

Brain Power

The leaves of a plant in your room suddenly start turning brown. What could be wrong? How could you find out?

REVIEW

1. Which part of a plant's life cycle is a seed?

2. What is a seed?

3. What are the ways plants can reproduce, other than seeds?

4. **COMPARE** Where do conifers and flowering plants produce seeds?

5. **CRITICAL THINKING** *Analyze* How can insects be helpful in your garden?

WHY IT MATTERS THINK ABOUT IT
Compost makes soil rich. It is also good for the environment in another way. What do you think it is?

WHY IT MATTERS WRITE ABOUT IT
Research how to make a compost bin. Check for local rules. Make a plan for how you would build one at home or at school. What materials would you need?

39

STAYING ALIVE

Water, sunlight, and nutrients keep plants alive and growing. Plant leaves absorb sunlight and use it to make food. Trees grow tall and use their leaves to get as much sunlight as possible. However, some plants are equipped to live in places with very little water, sunlight, or nutrients.

The cactus lives in the desert, where there's not much rain. The plant's roots absorb and store rainfall. Some roots grow way out to absorb as much water as possible. The cactus also stores water in its thick stem.

Cactus

Ferns grow on the ground, far from sunlight. These plants prefer the shade. They don't use as much of the Sun's light to make their food.

Fern

40

A Closer Look

Mosses grow close to the ground. They don't need much sunlight. Some grow even where it's shady. Their leaves are like tiny magnifying glasses. They focus any available sunlight into the plant.

Moss

The creosote bush, which grows in the desert, releases poisons into the soil. Then other plants don't grow too close and take nutrients from the soil. Soil doesn't supply all the nutrients a Venus flytrap needs. To get them, the plant catches and eats insects!

Venus flytrap

DISCUSSION STARTER

1. Where could a cactus get water if it hasn't rained for a long time?

2. How does a Venus flytrap get the nutrients it needs?

To learn more about adaptation to environment, visit *www.mhschool.com/science* and enter the keyword ADAPT.

*inter*NET
CONNECTION

SCIENCE WORDS

communicate p.8

conifer p.35

embryo p.34

energy p.14

flowering
plant p.35

germinate p.34

inherited
trait p.28

learned trait p.28

metamorphosis p.25

migrate p.18

reproduction p.5

respond p.6

USING SCIENCE WORDS

Number a paper from 1 to 10. Fill in 1 to 5 with words from the list above.

1. Organisms use food to get ___?___.

2. Changes in their environment may cause living things to ___?___.

3. Organisms make others of the same kind through ___?___.

4. Under the right conditions seeds ___?___.

5. A characteristic that comes from your parents is called a(n) ___?___.

6–10. **Pick five words from the list above that were not used in 1 to 5 and use each in a sentence.**

UNDERSTANDING SCIENCE IDEAS

11. How can you tell if something is a living thing?

12. What do seeds need to grow?

USING IDEAS AND SKILLS

13. **READING SKILL: COMPARE AND CONTRAST** How are plant and animal life cycles alike? How are they different?

14. **EXPERIMENT** Plan a flowering plant experiment. You need to find out if the temperature or the amount of daylight is more important for this plant to grow. Describe your experiment.

MATH LINK

15. **THINKING LIKE A SCIENTIST** You are studying the inherited traits and the learned traits of cats. Make a list of what might be inherited and what might be learned.

PROBLEMS and PUZZLES

Leaves Live Pull two leaves off the same plant. Make sure the stem of one leaf is always in water. Keep the other leaf dry. Give both leaves plenty of sunlight. What happens to each leaf after one day? After two or three days? Why?

CHAPTER 2
PARTS OF LIVING THINGS

All living things are made up of small and large parts. You may not think about it, but each part of your body helps you. All these parts work together and make you a living thing. In this chapter you will learn what jobs these parts have.

In Chapter 2 you will identify lists of parts. Identifying lists of parts will help you understand how the parts work together.

WHY IT MATTERS

Different body parts help an organism to survive.

SCIENCE WORDS

system a group of parts that work together

mineral a substance found in nature that is not a plant or an animal

Different Jobs for Different Body Parts

What types of body parts do you have? How do you protect your body? All organisms have body parts that do special jobs. What are those jobs?

Body coverings have a special job to do. Look at the body coverings of the organisms on this page. Welcome to nature's fashion show!

EXPLORE

HYPOTHESIZE What is the job of an organism's outer covering? Write a hypothesis in your *Science Journal.* How could you test this idea?

Design Your Own Experiment

WHAT ARE THE PARTS OF AN INSECT AND A PLANT?

PROCEDURES

1. OBSERVE Look at the caterpillars with a hand lens. What parts do you see? Draw a caterpillar in your *Science Journal.*

2. EXPERIMENT Use the materials to observe how a caterpillar uses certain parts of its body. How does it move?

3. OBSERVE Think of ways to closely examine the pea plant. In your *Science Journal,* draw the parts of the plant.

MATERIALS

- caterpillars in a 5-inch clear plastic petri dish
- 1 hand lens
- 1 pea plant from Topic 2 Explore Activity
- 1 sheet of white paper
- 1 toothpick
- paper towels
- *Science Journal*

CONCLUDE AND APPLY

1. EXPLAIN What are the parts of a caterpillar? How does a caterpillar use its parts?

2. EXPLAIN What are the parts of a pea plant?

GOING FURTHER: Apply

3. INFER How do you think the pea plant uses its parts?

What Are the Parts of an Insect and a Plant?

The Explore Activity shows the different parts of a caterpillar and a pea plant. Organisms can have four main kinds of parts. Each part helps the organism survive in some way.

What other body parts work together to do a job?

1. **Parts that Protect and Support** These include stems, skin, bark, shells, feathers, scales, and bones.

2. **Parts that Move** These include arms, legs, wings, fins, and other moving parts. Plants can't move from place to place. However, you may have seen plants grow toward light. The Venus flytrap has sensitive parts that close when touched by an insect.

3. **Parts that Get Information** These include eyes, ears, skin, noses, tongues, leaves, and roots.

4. **Parts that Take in Materials** These include roots, leaves, mouths, noses, skin, and other openings.

What parts do you have? How do they help you?

What Are Parts of Parts?

Look at any one body part. Is it made of smaller parts? These are parts of parts. Almost all body parts have smaller parts.

Together, parts work in **systems** (sis'təmz). A system is a group of parts that work together. Bones and muscles form a system that supports your body and helps you move. Can you think of any other parts that work together?

How Do Parts Protect and Support?

What outer covering protects your own body? How do you think outer coverings help organisms survive? Here are some important ways in which parts protect and support organisms:

Tiny duck feathers are called down. They are one of the warmest materials known.

- Some outer coverings keep organisms warm. Fur, feathers, and wool keep animals warm.

- Some outer coverings are waterproof, like skin and scales. For example, a fish's scales, a lizard's skin, and your skin keep water that is inside the body from escaping. The waxy coating on many leaves keeps water in plants. Skin also keeps outside water out.

- Outer coverings keep certain things in and out. Outer coverings work like a wall. The outer covering keeps important materials inside the organism. It also keeps out harmful materials, such as germs.

- Some outer coverings both protect and support. The shell of a crab supports the crab while it protects it. The trunk and bark of a tree perform a similar job. The trunk supports while the bark protects.

- Other parts support from the inside. Some animals have strong bones that help keep body parts in place.

A lizard has tough, waterproof skin.

47

An owl has very good hearing. This lets it find a meal in the dark. An owl can even hear a mouse walking by!

How Do Moving Parts Help Organisms Survive?

Being able to move helps organisms survive in different ways. Moving parts help organisms get food. Moving parts help some organisms escape from danger. Moving parts help organisms build or find homes. Moving parts also perform other jobs. Birds sing songs to communicate. Cats lick their kittens to keep them clean. Elephants use their trunks to spray water on themselves for a bath.

What Parts Collect Information?

How do you get information about what is going on around you? Which body parts do you use?

Different body parts collect different kinds of information. Eyes sense light information. Ears receive sounds. The nose smells information. The skin senses touch information. The tongue senses different tastes. Information about the environment helps organisms respond to changes, avoid danger, and find food.

This snowshoe hare has to move quickly to survive!

Brain Power

List all your moving parts. How does each help you survive? Make a chart. In one column, list your moving parts. In the second column, tell how each helps you survive. Illustrate your chart.

How Do Body Parts Take in and Get Rid Of Materials?

To survive, organisms use particular body parts to take in and get rid of certain materials. Here are some ways they do this.

- Parts of organisms take in materials to get energy. Most animals take in food and oxygen. They use this food inside their bodies to get energy. Most animals take in food with their mouths. Other kinds of organisms absorb food from their surroundings.

- Plants take in water and **minerals** (min'ər əlz) through their roots. A mineral is a substance found in nature that is not a plant or an animal. Plants also take in special gases through tiny leaf openings. Leaves also absorb sunlight. Plants use the food they make for energy.

- Parts that get rid of wastes also help organisms stay healthy. Many organisms get rid of materials the same way they came in. Gases both enter and leave plants through leaves. Animals also breathe gases in and out through lungs or gills. Most large organisms have solid and liquid body wastes. Special systems in their bodies help get rid of these wastes.

Some animals, like sharks, have very sharp teeth. These teeth easily tear food into pieces they can swallow.

Mushrooms absorb food from the substances they grow on.

Skill: Classifying

COMPARING DIFFERENT BODY PARTS

Classifying information helps you make sense out of the world. How could you classify the parts of different organisms?

PROCEDURES

1. List at least ten different plants and animals.

2. COMMUNICATE Make a table in your *Science Journal*. It should include headings for the types of parts you learned about in this topic. You can copy the table shown or design your own.

3. CLASSIFY In the table, group together the organisms from your list that have similar parts.

CONCLUDE AND APPLY

1. IDENTIFY Which organisms have similar parts that protect and support? Which organisms have similar moving parts?

2. IDENTIFY Which organisms have similar parts that take in materials? Which organisms have similar parts that get information?

3. CLASSIFY Look at your list of plants and animals. How else might you group these organisms? Make a new table that shows another way to classify them.

Parts That Protect and Support	
Moving Parts	
Parts That Take in Materials	
Parts That Get Information	

Next time you look at a plant or an animal, think about its different body parts. Each part has a job. Each helps the organism survive. Your own body is also made of parts that help you survive. Right now you are using some parts to gather information. Which parts are you using? How do these parts help you survive?

Which parts might you use to get information at a science center?

REVIEW

1. How are the parts of a pea plant different from those of a caterpillar?

2. What are the parts of organisms that help them to survive?

3. What kinds of homes can organisms build with body parts that move?

4. **CLASSIFY** How might you classify the following body parts: ears, skin, brain, hands, leaves, roots?

5. **CRITICAL THINKING** *Evaluate* Explorers find something that they think is an organism. The object has no way for materials to enter or leave its body. Could it be a living thing? Explain.

WHY IT MATTERS THINK ABOUT IT
How would your life be different if you were not able to use one of your parts that gets information?

WHY IT MATTERS WRITE ABOUT IT
If you could add a part to your body, what would it be? Think of a part that some other organism has. Draw what it would look like. How would it help you?

PLANT
HARM AND CHARM

How do plants protect themselves from animals or people? The plants don't have to pull up their roots and run away—nature gave them special ways to protect themselves.

In a dry desert, the cactus stores water in its stem. To protect the water from animals, the cactus has needles on its waxy skin. If an animal gets too close, the needles may stick in its nose, paws, or mouth!

A rose has thorns. They may stick a person trying to pick the plant or an animal trying to eat it. Some other bushes have thorns or brambles that stick anyone who gets too close.

The pine cones of lodgepole pine trees release their seeds when exposed to heat or strong winds. When a forest fire wipes out all the plants in an area, lodgepole pines are often the first trees to grow back!

Although some plants "scare away" animals, others try to get animals to come closer. Why? Many flowers depend on animals to spread their pollen. These plants have pleasant smells and beautiful colors to attract animals.

52

A Closer Look

Lodgepole Pine

Cactus

Some plants produce harmful substances to protect themselves. The oil on poison ivy leaves can give anyone who touches it an itchy rash. The poison hemlock has such a strong poison, it can kill anyone who eats it!

DISCUSSION STARTER

1. What would happen to an animal that tried to get water out of a cactus?

2. Why does poison ivy have a harmful oil on its leaves?

To learn more about nature's protection, visit **www.mhschool.com/science** and enter the keyword PROTECTION.

*inter***NET**
CONNECTION

53

WHY IT MATTERS

The large parts of living things are made up of smaller parts. Small parts are made up of even smaller parts!

SCIENCE WORDS

cell tiny box-like part that is the basic building block of living things

cytoplasm a clear, jelly-like material that fills plant and animal cells

cell membrane a thin outer covering of plant and animal cells

nucleus a main control center found in plant and animal cells

tissue a group of cells that are alike

organ a group of tissues that work together

A Look at Smaller Body Parts

What do you see when you look closely at the back of your hand? Is what you see the same on your other hand? Your skin is made up of smaller parts— little hairs, lines, and wrinkles. These are things you can see when you look closely. Are there even smaller parts of your hand that you cannot see? What might they be?

EXPLORE

HYPOTHESIZE How could you get a better look at some of the smaller parts of living things? Write a hypothesis in your *Science Journal.*

Investigate the Smaller Parts of Living Things

Observe the smaller body parts of a pea plant and caterpillar.

MATERIALS

- 1 pea plant from Topic 5
- 1 caterpillar in a petri dish
- 1 hand lens
- *Science Journal*

PROCEDURES

1. OBSERVE Look at the leaf of the pea plant very closely with the hand lens. Look at the caterpillar very closely with the hand lens. Describe what you see in your *Science Journal.*

2. OBSERVE Now look at the pictures. They show the smaller parts of a caterpillar and a pea plant very close up.

3. INFER Which picture belongs to the caterpillar? Pea plant? Why do you think so?

CONCLUDE AND APPLY

1. EXPLAIN What clues helped you identify which organism the pictures belonged to?

GOING FURTHER: Apply

2. INFER What would you need to see the smaller parts of an organism?

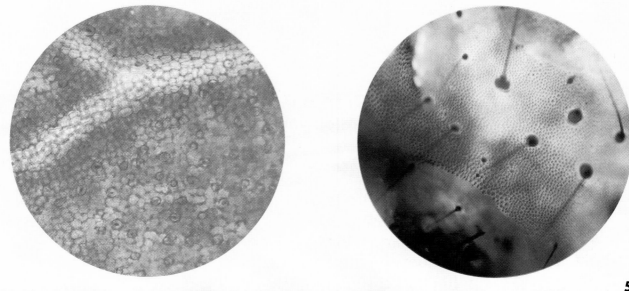

What Are the Smaller Parts of Living Things?

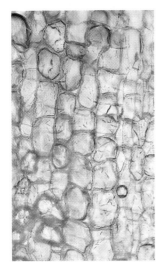

These cork cells are similar to the ones Hooke saw in 1665.

More than 300 years ago, scientist Robert Hooke looked at a thin piece of cork through a *microscope* (mī′krə skōp′). A microscope is a device made of glass lenses, similar to those in eyeglasses. A microscope allows people to see very small things. Hooke saw that the cork was made of tiny boxes. He called these tiny box-like shapes **cells** (selz).

Cells are the basic building blocks of life. Each picture in the Explore Activity showed an example of plant or animal cells. Since Hooke's time, scientists have learned that all living things are made of cells—even people. Your own body is made of billions of cells.

QUICK LAB

MATH LINK

Get to Know the Back of Your Hand

HYPOTHESIZE How small is a cell? Write a hypothesis in your *Science Journal*.

PROCEDURES

1. PREDICT With the pen, make the smallest dot you can on the back of your hand. How many cells do you think it covers? Write your prediction in your *Science Journal*.

MATERIALS
- pen
- beans
- *Science Journal*

2. USE NUMBERS Place all the beans in a solid circle. How many beans do you have?

CONCLUDE AND APPLY

DRAW CONCLUSIONS Each bean represents a skin cell under the dot on your hand. How many skin cells are under the ink dot? How does your prediction compare to this number?

How Are Plant and Animal Cells Alike and Different?

Plants are very different from animals. Yet plant and animal cells have many of the same parts.

Both plant and animal cells are filled with **cytoplasm** (sī′tə plaz′əm). Cytoplasm is a clear, jelly-like material. Both types of cells also have a **cell membrane** (sel mem′brān). A cell membrane is the thin outer covering of the cell. Plant and animal cells also have a **nucleus** (nü′klē əs). The nucleus is the main control center of the cell.

How can you tell a plant cell from an animal cell? Plant cells are usually larger than animal cells. Plant cells often have a box-like shape. Animal cells come in a wide variety of shapes. Plant cells have a stiff *cell wall* and a thin cell membrane. Animal cells only have a cell membrane. Many plant cells have green *chloroplasts* (klôr′ə plast′). Chloroplasts make food. Animal cells do not have chloroplasts.

DID YOU KNOW?

How small do you think a typical animal cell is? Look at the red dash. You could line up more than 300 cells along it! How many cells do you think you could line up along the blue dash?

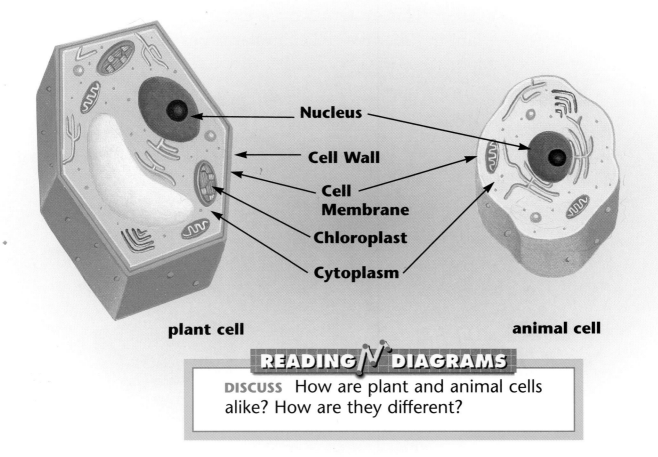

Nucleus

Cell Wall

Cell Membrane

Chloroplast

Cytoplasm

plant cell   **animal cell**

READING N DIAGRAMS

DISCUSS How are plant and animal cells alike? How are they different?

How Are Organisms Organized?

To understand how organisms are organized, think of your body as a house. Different parts of the house are made of different smaller parts. In a similar way, your body is made up of different cells.

A **tissue** (tish′ü) is like a wall of a house. Tissue is made up of a group of cells that are all alike. Muscle tissue is made of muscle cells. Nerve tissue is made of nerve cells. Muscle tissue is different from nerve tissue.

An **organ** (ôr′gən) is like a room of a house. It is a group of tissues that work together to perform a job. The heart, liver, brain, and stomach are organs.

Some organs work together in body systems. Body systems include the digestive system, nervous system, and muscular system. Each body system performs a special job.

A plant's organs include leaves, stems, and roots. Its organ systems include the water transport system. This system moves water up and down the plant in tube-like cells. Similar tubes also move food.

Organism

Cell

House

Brick

You have something in common with all other organisms: You are made of cells. Only living things are made of cells. Each cell in your body is also a living thing, but it cannot live by itself. Each of your cells must live as part of a larger living thing—you.

Knowing about the smallest parts of living things will help you to understand the natural world. You will probably look at plants in a different way. After all, they are made of cells, just like you.

One day, you might want to study cells more closely.

Brain Power

A house has telephone and cable lines to communicate with the outside world. What organs and body systems perform the same jobs for a human being?

REVIEW

1. What are the small parts on the back of your hand?

2. How big are cells?

3. What features do all animal and plant cells have in common?

4. **COMMUNICATE** Draw a picture to show how an organ is like the room of a house.

5. **CRITICAL THINKING** *Analyze* Why is Robert Hooke's discovery of cells important? How do you think people might have reacted to his discovery?

WHY IT MATTERS THINK ABOUT IT
Suppose you could shrink down to the size of a cell. What would it be like to take a tour of the human body?

WHY IT MATTERS WRITE ABOUT IT
Write a story. Describe some of the things you would see on a tour of the human body.

READING SKILL Read page 57. List the parts of a plant cell.

CHEERS FOR CELLULOSE

What do plant cells have that animal cells don't? Walls! The walls of plant cells have cellulose (sel' yoo lōs'), a substance humans have used for years.

For centuries, people took hairlike threads, or cellulose fibers (fi' barz), from cotton and linen plants. The fibers were twisted into rope, tied into nets, and woven into cloth. People made paper by pressing cellulose fibers into sheets.

In the 1800s, scientists discovered that cellulose is also in wood and straw. It is cheaper to produce wood and straw than to grow fiber plants, so people began making paper from wood cellulose.

Today many things are made from cellulose, including photographic film and a fabric called rayon. So give a cheer for cellulose!

All plant cells have walls made mostly of cellulose.

DISCUSSION STARTER

1. Where does cellulose come from?

2. Why is it less expensive to produce wood for cellulose than cotton or other fiber plants?

To learn more about cellulose, visit **www.mhschool.com/science** and enter the keyword CELLULOSE.

*inter*NET CONNECTION

SCIENCE WORDS

cell p.56   nucleus p.57

cell membrane p.57   organ p.58

cytoplasm p.57   system p.46

mineral p.49   tissue p.58

USING SCIENCE WORDS

Number a paper from 1 to 10. Fill in 1 to 5 with words from the list above.

1. A substance found in nature that is not a plant or an animal is a ___?___.

2. A tiny box-like shape that is a basic building block of life is a ___?___.

3. The clear, jelly-like material that fills plant and animal cells is ___?___.

4. The thin outer covering of plant and animal cells is the ___?___.

5. The control center of a cell is the ___?___.

6–10. Pick five words from the list above. Include all words that were not used in 1 to 5. Write each in a sentence.

UNDERSTANDING SCIENCE IDEAS

11. What jobs do your skin and bones have?

12. What parts of your body help you get food?

USING IDEAS AND SKILLS

13. **READING SKILL: RECOGNIZE A LIST** Read page 47. How do outer coverings protect and support organisms?

14. **CLASSIFY** Identify the following as an animal cell or a plant cell:

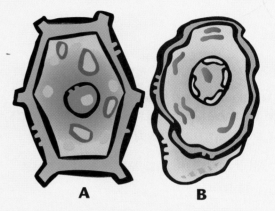

A   **B**

15. **THINKING LIKE A SCIENTIST** What are some movements an insect makes to help itself survive? Write a plan that describes how you could find out.

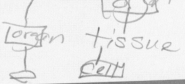

PROBLEMS and PUZZLES

Bug Boy Different living things have different body parts to help them survive. Pretend you are a superhero with the body part or ability of an animal, insect, or plant. What would your name be? Draw a picture of your super hero self. Write what your powers are.

SCIENCE WORDS

cell p.56

conifer p.35

embryo p.34

hibernate p.18

inherited

   trait p.28

life cycle p. 24

migrate p.18

organ p.58

organism p.4

oxygen p.16

respond p.6

system p. 46

tissue p.58

USING SCIENCE WORDS

Number a paper from 1 to 10. Beside each number write the word or words that best completes the sentence.

1. All living things, such as carrots and frogs, are ___?___.

2. Shivering when you are cold is one way that you ___?___ to the environment.

3. A gas that is in water and air is ___?___.

4. When the weather gets cold, bears find places to ___?___.

5. The stages of egg, caterpillar, pupa, and adult make up the ___?___ of a butterfly.

6. A dog cannot learn to have stripes because stripes are a(n) ___?___.

7. A young plant inside a seed is called a(n) ___?___.

8. Pine trees are examples of cone-producing plants called ___?___.

9. A group of parts that work together is a(n) ___?___.

10. Your heart is an example of a(n) ___?___.

UNDERSTANDING SCIENCE IDEAS

Write 11 to 15. For each number write the letter for the best answer. You may wish to use the hints provided.

11. Birds communicate with other birds by
    a. eating
    b. singing
    c. smelling
    d. nesting
    (Hint: Read page 8.)

12. Before winter begins, geese
    a. gather food
    b. hibernate
    c. migrate
    d. stay in caves
    (Hint: Read page 18.)

13. Which of the following is an inherited trait?
    a. eye color
    b. playing the piano
    c. reading
    d. counting
    (Hint: Read page 28.)

14. Which of the following is a source of nutrients for plants?
    a. bulbs
    b. conifers
    c. compost
    d. tubers
    (Hint: Read page 39.)

15. Which of the following did Robert Hooke discover with a microscope?
    a. cells
    b. corks
    c. organs
    d. organisms
    (Hint: Read page 56.)

USING IDEAS AND SKILLS

16. **PREDICT** Two seeds are planted in some soil. Only one of the seeds is watered. Which seed is more likely to grow into a plant?

17. List three things a kitten needs to live and grow.

18. Describe the pupa of a butterfly. What happens inside the pupa?

THINKING LIKE A SCIENTIST

19. **CLASSIFY** Many animals move by using their legs, fins, or wings. Think of two examples for each type of movement. Make a table like the one below. Write the names of the animals in the table.

LEGS	WINGS	FINS

20. Make a drawing of a cell. Label the cell membrane, the nucleus, and the cytoplasm.

inter**NET** CONNECTION

For help in reviewing this unit, visit **www.mhschool.com/science**

WRITING IN YOUR JOURNAL

SCIENCE IN YOUR LIFE
Give some examples of the special needs of puppies, kittens, or babies. Tell how these needs are taken care of.

PRODUCT ADS
Some ads on TV try to make you hungry so that you respond by eating the foods shown. Describe an ad like this that you have seen and tell if it made you respond.

HOW SCIENTISTS WORK
Tell why scientists do experiments instead of just guessing or making up stories about how things work.

Design your own Experiment

How does an ant move? Write a hypothesis. Design an experiment that lets you see the parts of an ant and how it moves. Think safety first. Review your experiment with your teacher before you try it.

PROBLEMS and PUZZLES

Potted Plant

Which way would the stem of a potted plant grow if you put a strong light underneath the plant? Write a hypothesis. Experiment to find out. You can use a camera to show how the plant changes. Make a table to organize and evaluate your data.

Bean Experiments

Plant a few pinto beans. Water them and place them in a sunny spot. Check the beans every few days. Record your observations in your *Science Journal.*

OBSERVE

Note how many days it takes for the seedlings to appear. How could you measure their growth? Record your measurements for one week. Then graph your results on a bar graph.

A New Plant

Place a small cutting from a spider plant in a cup of water. Observe the cutting for one week. Use your observations to make a drawing of the cutting each day. What changes take place? Use a camera to examine and evaluate your results. Make a table to record your observations.

EXPERIMENT

What conditions affect the growth of your seedlings? Design an experiment to find out. What conditions made the plants grow faster and stronger? What conditions were not good for the plants?

LIFT IT, PUSH IT, PULL IT

CHAPTER 3
HOW THINGS MOVE

What makes something move? Why do some things move faster than others? What makes an object stop moving?

In Chapter 3, you will read several diagrams. A diagram uses pictures and words to show how something works.

WHY IT MATTERS

All around you, things are always moving.

SCIENCE WORDS

position the location of an object

motion a change of position

speed how fast an object moves

On the Move!

The Circus Is in Town

The circus is in town!	Jugglers, dancers,
The circus is in town!	Twirling acrobats
Here come the tigers.	Dangerous animals,
Here comes the clown.	Balancing acts.
Here come the fliers	Up on the tight rope,
On the trapeze	Far from the ground
Soaring through the air,	Don't look now—
Hanging by their knees	The circus is in town!

• • • • • •

Who do you think moves faster—the tightrope walker or the acrobats? How do you know?

EXPLORE

HYPOTHESIZE **How much faster do you run than walk? Write a hypothesis in your *Science Journal*. How might you test your ideas?**

Investigate How Things Move

Compare the time it takes you to run a certain distance with the time it takes you to walk that same distance.

MATERIALS
- stopwatch
- 1 red crayon
- 1 blue crayon
- graph paper
- meter tape
- *Science Journal*

PROCEDURES

1. PREDICT Look at a distance of 10 meters. How long will it take you to run 10 meters? How long will it take you to walk 10 meters? Record your predictions in your *Science Journal*.

2. MEASURE Use the stopwatch to time how long it takes each person in your group to run 10 meters. Record each person's time.

3. MEASURE Time how long it takes each person in your group to walk 10 meters. Record each person's time.

CONCLUDE AND APPLY

1. COMPARE Look at your predictions of how long it would take you to walk and run 10 meters. How do they compare to the times you measured?

2. COMMUNICATE Print each person's name on a line at the bottom of the graph paper. Use a red crayon to mark an X above your name to show how many seconds it took to walk 10 meters. Use a blue crayon to mark an X that shows how many seconds it took to run 10 meters.

3. INTERPRET DATA What is the difference, in seconds, between your times for walking and running?

GOING FURTHER: Problem Solving

4. PREDICT Use your graph to predict how long it would take you to walk 20 meters.

How Do Things Move?

You've just seen many different types of movement. In the circus on page 66, tigers roared while acrobats soared. The Explore Activity shows that you can move in different ways, too. What are some different ways that you move?

How do you know an object is moving? Take a look at the toy cars in picture A. Do either of them seem to be moving? How can you tell?

A The Start

Start   **Finish**

Now look at picture B. Ten seconds have passed. The blue car seems to have moved because it changed **position** (pə zish' ən). What is position? To find out, keep reading.

B 10 Seconds later

Start   **Finish**

Position is the location of an object. Everything has a position. Your nose has a position in the middle of your face. The red car has a position at the starting line.

Some positions change. The blue car moves from the starting line to the finish line. Other positions don't change. Your nose stays in the middle of your face. The red car stays at the starting line.

How do you describe an object's position? You can compare it to the positions of other objects. Special words like *above* and *below, left* and *right, ahead* and *behind* give you clues about position. The pink fish is above the green fish. The yellow fish is behind the pink fish. The green fish is ahead of the yellow fish.

Which fish are above? Which are below?

Picture the Position

HYPOTHESIZE Do position words help you give directions? Write a hypothesis in your *Science Journal.*

PROCEDURES

1. Sit opposite your partner at a table. Prop up the notebook between you. Create a building with your blocks.

2. COMMUNICATE By describing the position of each of your blocks, instruct your partner to create the same building.

3. COMPARE Remove the notebook. Are the buildings the same? Switch roles and try it again.

CONCLUDE AND APPLY

DRAW CONCLUSIONS What would happen if your partner gave you directions without using position words? Could you still build the building?

MATERIALS

- 2 sets of 5–7 blocks
- a notebook
- *Science Journal*

What Happens When an Object Changes Position?

Think back to the toy cars on page 68. You knew the blue car moved because it changed position. When an object changes position, the object is in **motion** (mō'shən). Motion is a change of position.

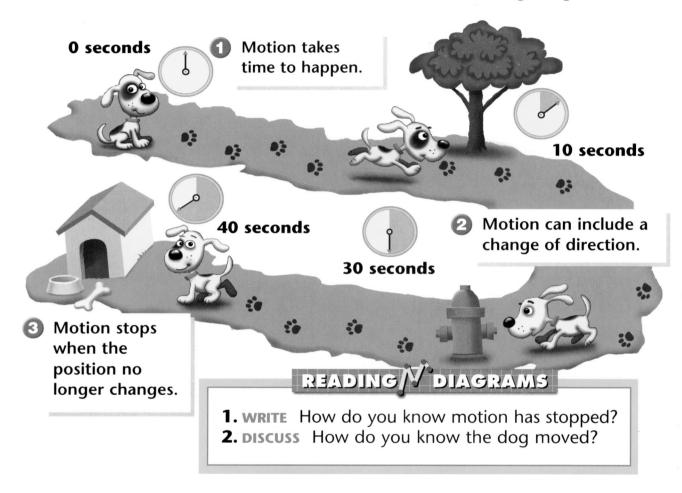

0 seconds

① Motion takes time to happen.

10 seconds

40 seconds

30 seconds

② Motion can include a change of direction.

③ Motion stops when the position no longer changes.

READING DIAGRAMS

1. **WRITE** How do you know motion has stopped?
2. **DISCUSS** How do you know the dog moved?

Some motions are hard to see. The ball is kicked so hard that it looks like a blur. The snail moves so slowly that it doesn't seem to be moving. What is the difference between these two motions? One happens very fast. One happens very slowly.

The snail moves slowly.

The ball is moving quickly.

How Fast Do You Go?

Some things move faster than others. Things that move faster have a greater **speed**. Speed is how fast an object moves. You can judge an object's speed by how quickly it changes position. A fast-moving object changes position quickly. A slow-moving object takes longer to change position.

How do you measure speed? You need to measure two things: time and distance. The distance an object travels in a period of time tells you its speed. Fast-moving objects go long distances in a short period of time. Slow-moving objects take longer to travel the same distance.

The Explore Activity demonstrates how to measure walking speed and running speed. Your running speed is faster than your walking speed. This means you can run a distance in a shorter amount of time than you can walk it. This chart shows what different speeds mean.

	SPEED	DISTANCE	TIME	WHAT IT MEANS
Bicycle	24 kilometers per hour	24 kilometers	1 hour	The bicycle travels 24 kilometers in 1 hour.
Swimmer	20 meters per minute	20 meters	1 minute	The swimmer swims 20 meters in 1 minute.
Insect	140 centimeters per second	140 centimeters	1 second	The insect flies 140 centimeters in 1 second.

READING CHARTS

WRITE What is the speed of the swimmer?

What Do Maps Tell You?

GEOGRAPHY LINK

A map is a flat drawing that tells you where objects are located. Maps tell you the positions of things.

You could draw a map like the one shown here. Maps tell you how to find things. To read a map, you need to use directions. Maps tell you which direction—north, south, east, or west, to find places or things. These directions help you find your way around.

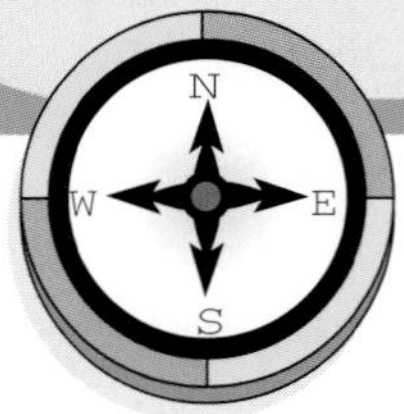

READING N' MAPS

1. **WRITE** In which direction would you walk to go from the basketball court to the playground?

2. In which direction is the track from the school?

3. **DISCUSS** How would you go from the front door of the school to the playground without going off the sidewalk?

4. Start at the front door of the school. Walk all the way around the school. Which directions will you go?

Motion is everywhere in your world. Your body moves when you run fast and even when you are sitting quietly. You know that you are moving because you change position. Sometimes you change position quickly, like when you throw a ball. Sometimes you change position slowly, like when you turn the pages of a book. Wherever you go and whatever you do, you move!

REVIEW

1. What is motion?

2. Two toy cars are rolling on the floor. The red car is moving faster than the green car. Both cars move for three seconds. Which car will move farther?

3. Use position words and distances to tell how to get from your class to the cafeteria.

4. **COMMUNICATE** Three children all live on the same street. Ann lives west of Peter. Peter lives east of Meg. Meg lives west of Ann. Draw a map of their street.

5. **CRITICAL THINKING** *Apply* A train is traveling at a speed of 60 miles per hour. How far will it travel after three hours?

WHY IT MATTERS THINK ABOUT IT Explain how you play your favorite game. Why is it your favorite?

WHY IT MATTERS WRITE ABOUT IT How are position, motion, and speed important in your favorite game?

Are we THERE Yet?

Each GPS satellite broadcasts its position with a radio signal. Ships and other vehicles use receivers to pick up the signals.

What if you're on a hike in the woods? How can you tell which direction you're going so that you don't get lost?

By day, look for the Sun. It's in the east in the morning and the west in the afternoon. At night, use the Big Dipper to help you find the North Star. Better yet, bring a compass. Its needle always points north.

How do you know how far you've gone? You could count every step. Each step is about two feet. Better yet, wear a pedometer. It's a tool that counts steps. If you know where you started, which direction you're heading, and how far you've gone, you can use a good map to figure out exactly where you are.

Long ago, sailors used stars or a compass to check direction. To check their speed, they tossed a piece of wood into the water. Then they timed how long it took for the ship to move past the wood.

Today there's a new way for travelers to figure out where they are. It's the Global Positioning System (GPS). It has 24 satellites that orbit Earth and constantly broadcast their positions. People who have special receivers can pick up the signals to figure out their own latitude and longitude. Then they can check a map to see exactly where that point is. Someday you may carry a small receiver as you hike and use GPS to find out if you're there yet!

If you know where north is, you can find east, south, and west, too!

Discussion
Starter

1 How can knowing which way is north tell you the other directions?

2 Suggest some uses for the GPS besides finding your way on a vacation trip.

*inter*NET
CONNECTION   To learn more about finding directions, visit
www.mhschool.com/science and enter the keyword **LOST.**

WHY IT MATTERS

You use pushes and pulls in many ways each day.

SCIENCE WORDS

force a push or pull

gravity the pulling force between two objects

weight the pull of gravity on an object

Pushes and Pulls

Why are some things harder to push or pull than others? Every day you use pushes and pulls to get things done. Sometimes you use a big push, like when you push your bike up a hill. Other times you use a small pull, like when you pull open a book.

Which push or pull pictured do you think was easiest? How do you know?

EXPLORE

HYPOTHESIZE Why are some objects harder to push or pull than others? Write a hypothesis in your *Science Journal.* How might you test your ideas?

EXPLORE ACTIVITY

Investigate Why Some Objects Are Harder to Pull

Measure the strength of different pulls.

PROCEDURES

 SAFETY: Wear goggles.

1. OBSERVE Look at your spring scale. What is the highest your scale can read?

2. PREDICT Which one of the objects will require the greatest pull to move? Record your prediction in your *Science Journal*. Then predict which object will require the next strongest pull to move. Record this prediction. Make a prediction for each of your objects.

3. MEASURE Hook the scale on an object. Place the scale and the object on a smooth, flat surface and pull at a steady speed. Record what the spring scale reads. Repeat with other classroom objects. Were your predictions correct?

CONCLUDE AND APPLY

1. IDENTIFY What did you feel when you pulled an object on the spring scale?

2. IDENTIFY Which objects made the scale read the highest when you pulled them?

3. EXPLAIN Why did it take a bigger pull to move some objects?

GOING FURTHER: Apply

4. EXPERIMENT How could you measure the strength of the pull needed to move your lunch box? If you took your lunch out of your lunch box, how would that affect your measurement?

MATERIALS

- spring scale
- safety goggles
- 5 objects from your classroom
- *Science Journal*

77

Why Are Some Objects Harder to Pull?

The Explore Activity shows that a spring scale can be used to measure different pulls. Spring scales measure in *newtons*. A newton is the unit used to measure pushes and pulls. The heavier an object is, the harder you must pull it to get it to move. The harder you pull, the greater the number of newtons the spring scale shows. When you pull an object, you feel a pull, too.

All pulls are **forces** (fôrs′ əz). A force can change the motion of an object. Pushes are forces, too. You see examples of forces in everyday life. You use a pulling force when you put on your backpack. You use a pushing force when you open a door. Do you think you could measure these forces in newtons? Which force would be greater?

FACTS ABOUT FORCES

1 *All pushes and pulls are forces.* Pushes move away from you. Pulls move toward you.

2 *Forces may change the motion of an object.* The heavier an object is, the more force you need to move it.

3 *Forces work in pairs.* Whenever you push or pull on something, you feel a push or pull, too. The push or pull that you feel is a force working in the opposite direction.

4 *Even though all forces push or pull, there are different kinds of forces.* Some forces push and pull on objects without even touching them. One of those forces is acting on you right now. Do you know what it is?

READING /V/ DIAGRAMS

1. WRITE In which direction do pushes move?

2. DISCUSS Do you need more or less force to move a heavier object?

What Force Is Always Pulling on You?

There is one force that is everywhere. The force of **gravity** (grav'i tē) is pulling on you right now. Gravity is the pulling force between two objects. It attracts, or pulls, objects together. It pulls everything on Earth.

The force of gravity between two objects depends on two things. It depends on how much *matter* is in the objects and how close they are to each other. Matter is what makes up an object. The more matter there is in the objects, and the closer the objects are to each other, the stronger the force of gravity between them will be.

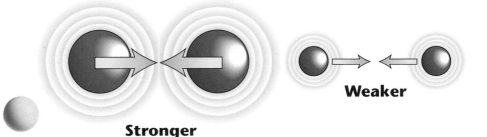

Stronger　　　　　**Weaker**

When things go up, the force of gravity pulls them down. Things fall to Earth because they are pulled by Earth's gravity. Most objects don't have enough matter in them to pull on each other enough to notice. Earth has a lot of matter. The pull between it and other objects is strong.

Brain Power

How would a basketball game change if there were no gravity? Draw a picture or write a story that shows what the game would be like.

Why Are Some Things Heavier than Others?

Some objects are heavy. Other objects are light. You can measure how heavy or light something is by measuring its **weight** (wāt). Weight is the pull of gravity on an object. Why do some things weigh more than others? Objects that weigh more have more matter in them. The more matter there is in an object, the greater the pull of gravity is on that object.

Scientists measure weight in newtons. In everyday life, people in the United States measure weight in *pounds*. A pound is the unit used to measure forces (such as weight) in the English system of measurement. Newtons are the unit of force in the metric system. All scientists use the metric system.

The pull of gravity is just about the same all over Earth. So the weight of an object will be about the same anywhere on Earth. However, the pull of gravity is different on other planets. So objects might weigh more or less on different planets.

These apples weigh two pounds or nine newtons.

Skill: Interpreting Data

READING A BAR GRAPH

The bar graph below shows how much the dog weighs on each planet and on the Moon. Each bar gives us information, or *data*. For example, look at the bar labeled Earth. It lines up with 40 on the Pounds scale on the left. Now look at the bar labeled Jupiter. What number on the Pounds scale does it line up with? By answering this question, you are interpreting data.

Interpret the data in this graph to answer the questions below.

MATERIALS
- *Science Journal*

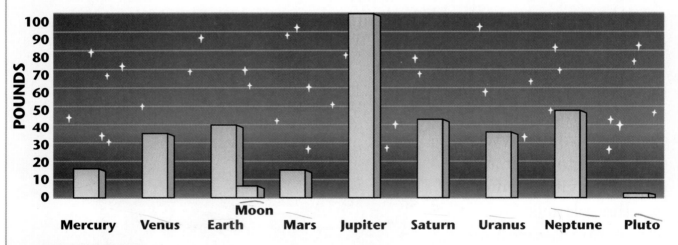

PROCEDURES

1. INTERPRET DATA How much does the dog weigh on Mars?

2. INTERPRET DATA On which planets would the dog weigh more than on Earth? On which planets would the dog weigh less?

3. COMPARE How much heavier is the dog on Jupiter than on Venus?

CONCLUDE AND APPLY

COMMUNICATE Make a chart showing how you interpreted the data from the graph in question 2.

This dog weighs 40 pounds on Earth. How much does it weigh on other planets?

Why Does a Dog Weigh Less on Mars?

Remember that the more matter an object has, the greater the pull of gravity. Jupiter has more matter than Earth, so the force of gravity is greater there. The stronger pull of gravity makes things weigh more on Jupiter.

On the other hand, Mars has less matter than Earth. The pull of gravity is weaker there. The weaker pull of gravity makes things weigh less on Mars.

Jupiter

Earth

Mars

WHY IT MATTERS

Almost everything you do requires a force of some type. When you brush your hair, you push your hair back. When you write your name, you push and pull the pencil across the paper. As you push and pull on things around you, one force is always pulling on you. Gravity is pulling on you and everything else on Earth all the time.

REVIEW

1. What is a force?

2. How do you use pushes and pulls in your everyday life?

3. If you took your books out of your backpack, how would that change the amount of force needed to lift the backpack?

4.  **INTERPRET DATA** Look back at the graph on page 82. How much does the dog weigh on Uranus?

5. **CRITICAL THINKING** *Apply* A planet has six times as much matter as Earth. Do you think an object would weigh more on this planet or less? Explain.

WHY IT MATTERS THINK ABOUT IT
A hairbrush is a tool that you use to make your hair smoother. A pencil is a tool you use for writing. Describe three other tools you use each day.

WHY IT MATTERS WRITE ABOUT IT
Knives, forks, and spoons are tools you use for eating. How do pushes and pulls help you use these tools?

SHOW YOUR MUSCLES

   Let's hear it for your muscles! They're what help you move and stay on the go. They help you run to score that touchdown, climb trees, swim and dive, and so much more!

   When you push or pull, you use muscles. Some of them come in pairs. Your upper arm has biceps and triceps. Both muscles stretch between a bone in your upper arm and one in your lower arm.

How are these children using their muscles?

84

Health Link

Muscles contract, or get shorter. When your biceps contracts, it pulls on the lower bone. Your lower arm moves up so you can lift objects. How would you carry all your books without biceps?

You use your triceps to push things. When your triceps contracts, your biceps relaxes. Your arm becomes straighter and you can push down.

Want to run a little faster? Hit a ball a little harder? The more you push and pull, the stronger your muscles get.

Walking, jogging, and swimming build up muscles in your whole body. They make many muscles pull against gravity.

Here's how to use gravity to strengthen your muscles:

 Increase the amount of weight you pull or push.

 Increase the amount of time you push or pull that weight.

☑ Increase how often you push or pull that weight.

Remember that muscles need time to rest between exercise sessions!

DISCUSSION STARTER

1. What kinds of things do you do that use your biceps and triceps?

2. What activities do you enjoy that use your whole body?

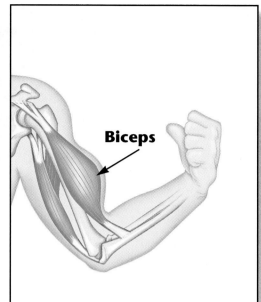

Biceps

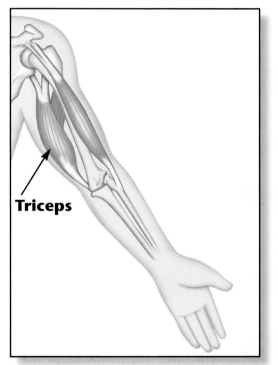

Triceps

To learn more about your muscles, visit **www.mhschool.com/science** and enter the keyword MUSCLES.

*inter*NET CONNECTION

WHY IT MATTERS

Forces can change an object's motion.

SCIENCE WORDS

friction a force that occurs when one object rubs against another

Forces in Motion

What must these children do in order to make their seesaw move? Just a few minutes ago, the seesaw was bobbing up and down. Then it stopped. What do you think caused it to stop? Why did it stop in the position it's in?

EXPLORE

HYPOTHESIZE Sometimes objects change position, and sometimes they stay still. What must you do to make a resting object move? Write a hypothesis in your *Science Journal*. How might you test your ideas?

Investigate What Causes a Change in Motion

Experiment to find out what makes a resting object move.

PROCEDURES

SAFETY: Wear goggles.

1. Cut two pieces of string that are slightly shorter than the width of your desk. Knot the strings together. Lay the knot in the middle of your desk and let the strings hang off opposite sides of the desk. Bend the paper clips to make hooks, and tie one to the free end of each string.

2. PREDICT Hold the knot in place and hang two washers on one paper-clip hook. What will happen if you let go of the knot? Write your prediction in your *Science Journal*. Test your prediction.

3. PREDICT Take the two washers off. Holding the knot in place, add one washer to each of the paper-clip hooks. Predict what will happen if you let go of the knot now. Test your prediction.

4. EXPERIMENT What could you do with the washers to move the knot toward one side of the desk? Test your idea.

MATERIALS

- washers
- 2 paper clips
- scissors
- string
- safety goggles
- *Science Journal*

CONCLUDE AND APPLY

1. COMPARE What did you observe in steps 2 and 3?

2. EXPLAIN In step 3, why didn't the knot move? In step 4, what did you do to make the knot move?

GOING FURTHER: Problem Solving

3. EXPERIMENT How could you move the knot back to the middle of your desk?

What Is a Change in Motion?

The Explore Activity shows that when there is one washer at each end of a piece of string, the knot in the center of the string does not move. However, when different amounts of weights are placed on the string, the knot moves.

When an object that is resting starts to move, there is a change in motion. A change in motion also occurs when a moving object speeds up, slows down, changes direction, or stops.

Here are the different types of changes in motion.

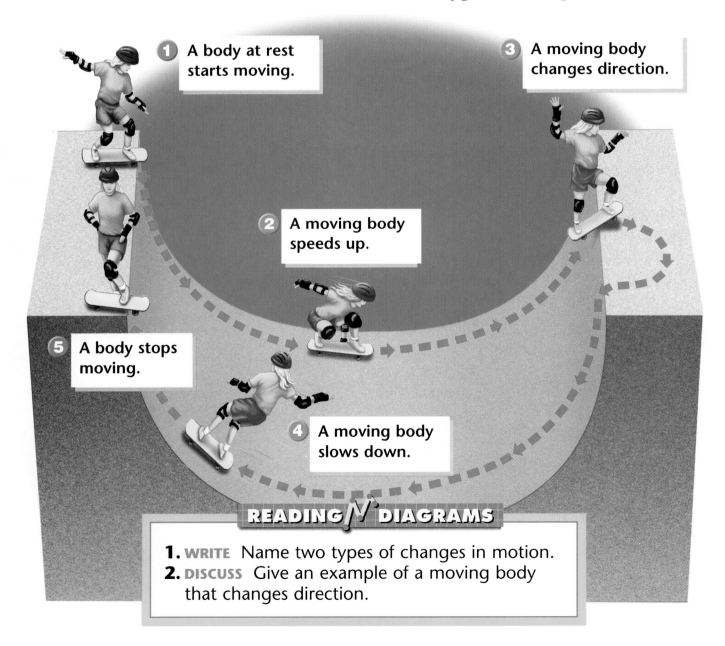

1 A body at rest starts moving.

2 A moving body speeds up.

3 A moving body changes direction.

4 A moving body slows down.

5 A body stops moving.

READING ✓ DIAGRAMS

1. **WRITE** Name two types of changes in motion.
2. **DISCUSS** Give an example of a moving body that changes direction.

What Causes a Change in Motion?

In the Explore Activity, one washer was put on each string. Two forces were acting on the knot at one time. The forces were balanced, so there was no change in motion. The knot stayed at rest. When different amounts of weights were put on the strings, the forces didn't balance anymore. There was a change in motion—the knot moved.

A change in an object's motion is the result of all the forces that are acting on the object. The same thing happens on a seesaw. You see a change in motion only when forces are unbalanced. Think of what happens when you get off a seesaw. The forces suddenly become unbalanced. Then the seesaw moves.

You can see how unbalanced forces create a change in motion in a tug-of-war. When both sides pull equally, forces balance. Nothing moves.

If one side begins to pull harder, the forces become unbalanced. Now there is a change in the position of the rope.

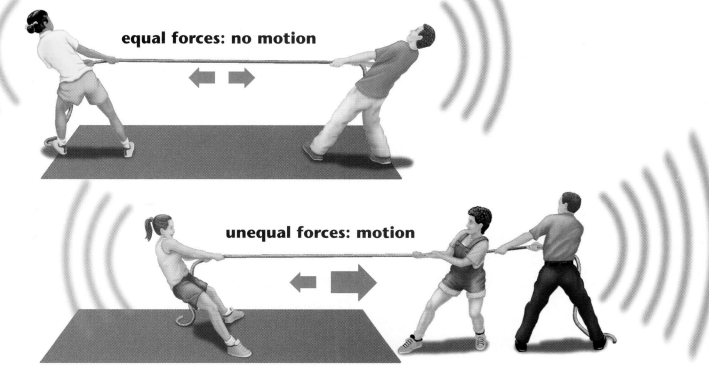

equal forces: no motion

unequal forces: motion

What happens if the rope breaks?

Robert Shurney, with glasses, is an inventor. He designed the tires that were used on the buggy driven by astronauts on the Moon.

Why Do Things Stop Moving?

A ball is rolling on the floor. Over time, it slows down. A force must be acting on the ball.

The force that slows the ball down is called **friction** (frik′ shən). Friction is a force that occurs when one object rubs against another. The ball rubbing on the floor creates friction.

Different materials produce different amounts of friction. Rough materials rub best. They produce a lot of friction. Most smooth materials don't rub well. They produce less friction. Other materials, like rubber, are smooth but still produce a lot of friction.

Friction keeps the car's rubber tires on the road, but ice on the road changes the amount of friction. The car slides!

Brain Power

Sand is sometimes put on icy roads. How does sand change the amount of friction on an icy road?

What objects rub together when you ride a bike? Friction slows the bike down even if you are riding on a very smooth sidewalk. You have to keep pedaling in order to keep the bike in motion.

How do brakes stop a bike's motion? When you squeeze the brake lever, the brake pad presses against the wheel. There is friction between the brake pad and the rim of the wheel. The wheel slows down. The bike stops.

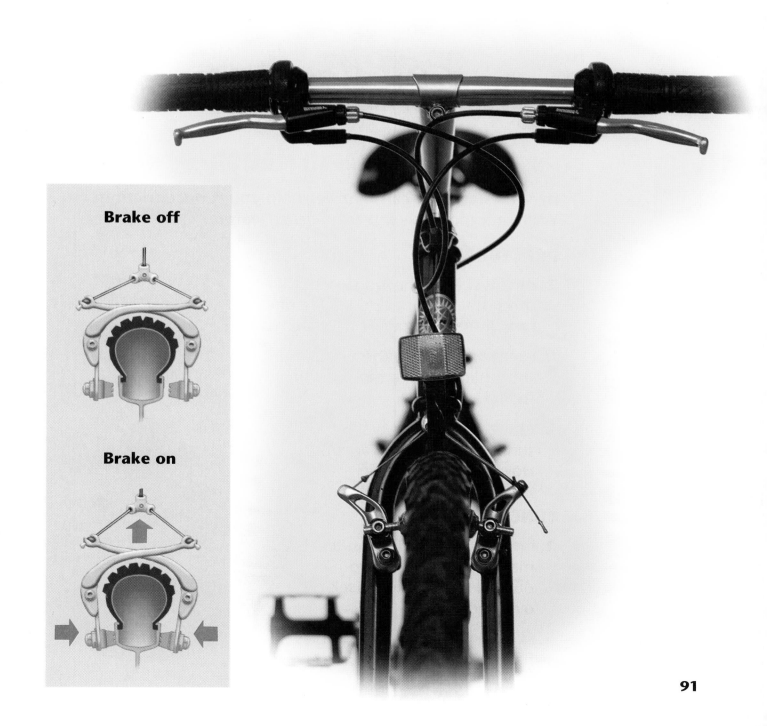

Brake off

Brake on

How Can You Control Friction?

Friction is a force that slows things down. You can't get rid of friction, but you can change the amount of friction you have. People use slippery things to decrease friction. For example, oil is often put on the moving parts of machines. To increase friction, people use rough or sticky things. In-line skates have a rubber pad that skaters use to slow down and stop.

Marbles in Motion

HYPOTHESIZE How can marbles help you reduce friction? Write a hypothesis in your *Science Journal.*

PROCEDURES

1. OBSERVE Push the wooden block over the surface of your desk. Describe how it feels in your *Science Journal.*

2. EXPERIMENT Place the marbles under the jar lid. Lay the block on top of the lid.

3. OBSERVE Push the block over the surface of your desk again. How does it feel now?

MATERIALS
- 10–20 marbles
- jar lid
- wooden block
- *Science Journal*

CONCLUDE AND APPLY

1. IDENTIFY When did you feel more friction: When you pushed the block by itself or over the jar lid?

2. EXPLAIN How did the marbles help to reduce friction?

Every time you move an object, you are unbalancing the forces acting on it. One force that affects you every day is friction. Without friction, you couldn't grip a door knob, or pick up a ball. You'd slip when you tried to walk. Once you were moving, you wouldn't be able to stop!

How do you make sure you don't slip on the basketball court? Put on some rubber-soled sneakers to increase friction.

REVIEW

1. What is a change in motion?

2. You see a ball resting on the ground. What can you do to make it move?

3. What is friction?

4. PREDICT Would it be easier to roller skate on gravel or concrete? How do you know?

5. CRITICAL THINKING *Apply* You are swinging on a swing. What must you do to swing higher? What must you do to stop?

WHY IT MATTERS THINK ABOUT IT Describe some of the sports you like to watch or play. What type of equipment do the players use? What sort of clothing do they wear?

WHY IT MATTERS WRITE ABOUT IT How does the clothing or equipment used in your favorite sport help the players to control friction?

READING SKILL Look at the diagram of the tug-of-war on page 89. Write a paragraph that explains what the diagram shows.

DANCING ON ROCKS

SPECIAL TOOLS

All this equipment is needed for safe climbing.

What's dancing got to do with rocks? Ask someone whose favorite sport is rock climbing. A climber will tell you it's like dancing on the side of a cliff. Like a dancer, a rock climber has to understand the use of friction and balance.

Climbers need friction as they climb. Their shoes have sticky rubber soles to keep their feet from slipping on the rocks. Climbers carry bags of chalk on their belts. As they climb, they rub chalk on their hands. That helps with the friction between their hands and the rocks.

Rock climbers use ropes as they climb, but not to pull themselves up. The ropes are for safety. They hang on the special harness climbers wear.

As climbers move, they put special metal bolts into cracks in the rock. Then they clip their ropes to each bolt. If a climber slips, the last bolt will grip the rope tightly. Friction will stop the rope from slipping. Climbers may fall a short way, but their ropes will stop them from falling too far. Then they can start climbing again.

Rock climbers learn to balance gracefully, like dancers. They know it's important to keep their weight evenly on both feet. If they lean, they lose their balance. Then they could really fall!

DISCUSSION STARTERS

1. What equipment helps rock climbers use friction?

2. How do rock climbers keep their balance while climbing?

To learn more about rock climbing, visit *www.mhschool.com/science* and enter the keyword CLIMBERS.

interNET CONNECTION

SCIENCE WORDS

force p.78

friction p.90

gravity p.80

motion p.70

position p.68

speed p.71

weight p.81

USING SCIENCE WORDS

Number a paper from 1 to 10. Fill in 1 to 5 with words from the list above

1. An object's location is its ___?___.

2. How fast an object moves is its ___?___.

3. When you throw a ball in the air, it falls down because of ___?___.

4. Snow and ice make the ground have less ___?___.

5. Unbalanced forces cause ___?___.

6–10. **Pick five words from the list above. Include all words that were not used in 1 to 5. Write each word in a sentence.**

UNDERSTANDING SCIENCE IDEAS

11. How can you measure your speed on a long car trip?

12. Two objects are pushed with the same force. The first object moves twice as far as the second object. Which object is heavier?

USING IDEAS AND SKILLS

13. **READING SKILL: READ A DIAGRAM** How do brakes stop a bike's motion? Hint: Use the diagram on page 91 to help you.

14. **INTERPRET DATA** Who is the fastest runner? What is the speed of the slowest runner?

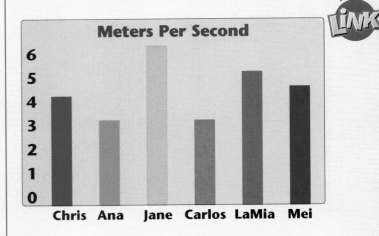

Meters Per Second

Chris Ana Jane Carlos LaMia Mei

15. **THINKING LIKE A SCIENTIST** Do dogs or cats run faster? How can you test your ideas?

PROBLEMS and PUZZLES

Long Distance You want to race your friend, who lives in a different country. How could you find out who is faster?

CHAPTER 4
WORK AND MACHINES

People do different kinds of work. Machines do work too. How do we define what work is? When is play really work? Read on to find out!

In Chapter 4 you will find some lists. A list gives you facts about something.

SCIENCE WORDS

work when a force changes the motion of an object

energy the ability to do work

Doing Work

Are you working right now? All day long you do different kinds of work. You do schoolwork at school and homework at home. You may have chores that you do to help your family, too.

Who is doing work in these pictures? How do you know?

EXPLORE

HYPOTHESIZE **What do you think work is? In your own words, write a definition of work in your** *Science Journal.* **How might you apply your definition of work to different kinds of actions?**

Investigate What Work Is

Use your definition of work to classify the actions below. Does your definition of work make sense?

MATERIALS
- 4 books
- pencil
- *Science Journal*

PROCEDURES

1. EXPERIMENT Complete each of the actions described below.

- Put four books on the floor. Lift one book up.

- Put four books on the floor. Lift all four up.

- Put a book on your desk. Push down very hard on top of the book.

- Pick up a pencil from your desk.

- Push against a wall with all of your strength.

2. CLASSIFY After each action, ask yourself: "Did I do work?" Review the definition of work that you wrote in your *Science Journal*. Does the action you did fit your definition? Tell your partner what you think. Together, decide whether the action was work or not.

CONCLUDE AND APPLY

1. EVALUATE Look at your responses to the question "Did I do work?" Think about your responses. Is there a pattern? What is it?

2. COMMUNICATE Write a sentence for each action explaining why you classified it the way you did.

GOING FURTHER: Apply

3. EVALUATE How might different people classify the actions? For example, would picking up one book be work for a baby? Would picking up four books be work for a very strong adult?

Is It Work?

The Explore Activity shows several actions. Some of the actions were **work**. Others were not work. You wrote your own definition of work. Is your definition correct? Scientists say that work is done when a force changes the motion of an object.

Take another look at some of the actions shown on pages 98 and 99. Did they involve work or not?

Who's Doing Work?

1. Picking up books
Force: Pulling force of hands
Object: Books
Movement: Books move up.
Conclusion: Work was done because a force changed the motion of the books.

☑ **Work**

☐ **Not Work**

2. Pushing against wall
Force: Pushing force of body
Object: Wall
Movement: None
Conclusion: No work was done because there was no change in motion.

☐ **Work**

☑ **Not Work**

3. Shaking rattle
Force: Shaking force of arm
Object: Rattle
Movement: Rattle moves back and forth.
Conclusion: Work was done because a force changed the motion of the rattle.

☑ **Work**

☐ **Not Work**

Brain Power

A ball is rolling on a flat surface. Is any work being done? You can ignore the effects of friction on the ball. Hint: Is there any change in motion for a ball traveling at a steady speed?

What Do You Need to Get Work Done?

To do work, you need **energy** (en′ ər jē). Energy is the ability to do work.

Energy exists in different forms. Moving things, like a rock rolling down a hill, have energy of motion. Sometimes objects have the ability to move because of their position. A rock that is on top of a hill is in a position to move. Energy that can cause an object to move is called stored energy. Sources of stored energy include food, fuel, and batteries.

Other forms of energy include heat, light, sound, and electricity.

A rock rolling down a hill has energy. How might a falling rock do work?

QUICK LAB

Changing Energy

HYPOTHESIZE What will happen when you rub a wooden block with sandpaper? Write a hypothesis in your *Science Journal.*

MATERIALS
- wooden block
- sandpaper
- safety goggles
- *Science Journal*

PROCEDURES

 SAFETY: Wear goggles.

1. **OBSERVE** Feel the temperature of the block.

2. **OBSERVE** Rub the block with sandpaper about 20 times. What do you feel through your fingertips?

CONCLUDE AND APPLY

EXPLAIN What happened to the temperature of the block?

How Does Energy Change?

Energy moves from place to place, and changes from one form to another. The Quick Lab shows how friction can change to heat. The steps below show how energy of motion can move from one object to another.

READING 〽 DIAGRAMS

1. **WRITE** How many changes of motion did you see in the diagram? Make a list.
2. **DISCUSS** Why did the green ball stop moving after hitting the yellow ball?

1 The green ball has energy of motion.

2 The green ball hits the yellow ball. Now the yellow ball has energy of motion. The force of the green ball has caused the yellow ball's motion to change.

3 Work has been done on the yellow ball. It has gained energy from the green ball.

4 The green ball has stopped moving. Its energy of motion went to the yellow ball.

When people talk about work, they usually mean a job that adults do. Whether you have a job or not, you work every day. You work when you pedal a bike. You work when you jump rope. You even work a little bit when you do your homework! Where do you get the energy to do all this work? From the energy stored in food! Food is the fuel your body uses to do the work you do each day.

REVIEW

1. You push against a brick wall as hard as you can. Your friend picks up a pencil. Who did more work?

2. What is energy?

3. How does energy change?

4. **INFER** Rub your hands together quickly. What energy change takes place?

5. **CRITICAL THINKING** *Apply* Write a definition of work. How did your definition change after finishing this lesson?

WHY IT MATTERS THINK ABOUT IT
Describe a job you would like to have when you grow up. Why do you think you would like it?

WHY IT MATTERS WRITE ABOUT IT
What kinds of actions would you do in the job you would like to have? Would you be doing a lot of work the way a scientist would define it?

Earth at Work

What kind of work does Earth do? It's not the same kind of work you do when you clean your room. Oh, no. Earth works a lot harder than that! Earth uses lots more energy to put rocks and soil in motion.

Deep within Earth there are layers of rock. These rock layers push against each other without moving. Energy builds up or is stored up between the layers.

Earth Science Link

Earthquakes can cause great damage.

An earthquake can release stored energy in rocks and cause a landslide.

To learn more about Earth's forces, visit *www.mhschool.com/science* and enter the keyword QUAKES.

*inter***NET** CONNECTION

Sometimes the rubbing and pushing breaks the rocks. Or the rubbing and pushing can make rock layers slide or pop out of place. The energy that builds up in the rocks is suddenly released. It's an earthquake!

Deep down beneath the surface of Earth, there are melted rocks. They are very, very hot. Sometimes an earthquake cracks a hard rock layer around the melted rock. It pushes up through the cracks to Earth's surface. The melted rock blasts or flows from the ground as lava.

Some of the lava's heat energy becomes mechanical, or moving, energy. Rivers of lava push everything out of their way. When the lava cools, it forms a volcano.

Rocks and soil on hills can become loose during an earthquake. This makes the solid rock under the surface of the hill weaker. The loose rocks and soil on the hill begin to fall. It's a landslide!

DISCUSSION STARTER

1. How can an earthquake help to form a volcano?

2. Do you think we'll ever be able to use the energy from volcanoes, earthquakes, or landslides? Why or why not?

WHY IT MATTERS

Tools can help you get work done faster and easier.

SCIENCE WORDS

machine a tool that makes work easier to do

simple machine a machine with few or no moving parts

lever a straight bar that moves on a fixed point

wheel and axle a wheel that turns on a post

pulley a simple machine that uses a wheel and a rope

Getting Work Done

Can you help these children with their gardening? They want to start planting, but there is a big rock right in the middle of the garden! They try pushing. They try pulling. No matter what they do, the rock is too heavy to move. What would you do? Can you think of a plan that would help you move the heavy rock?

HYPOTHESIZE Sometimes you want to move an object that takes a lot of force to move. How can you do it? Write a hypothesis in your *Science Journal.* How might you test your ideas?

Design Your Own Experiment

HOW CAN YOU MAKE WORK EASIER?

PROCEDURES

SAFETY: Wear goggles.

1. **ASK QUESTIONS** How can you invent a way to get the roll of tape from the floor to your desk? Your hands can help provide the lift, but you can't just pick up the tape and put it on the desk.

2. **COMMUNICATE** With your group members, think of as many different ways as you can to lift the tape. Write or draw two of your plans in your *Science Journal*.

3. **EXPERIMENT** After your teacher approves your plans, try one of them. Write down what happens. Does the plan work well? If not, what can you do to fix it? Try your other plan for lifting the tape.

CONCLUDE AND APPLY

1. **COMPARE AND CONTRAST** Which of your two plans worked better?

2. **IDENTIFY** What materials did you use in your most successful invention?

3. **EXPLAIN** What forces did you use? What force did you work against?

GOING FURTHER: Apply

4. **EVALUATE** Why did you think some plans for lifting the tape worked better than others?

MATERIALS

- a roll of masking tape
- safety goggles
- building materials
- *Science Journal*

107

How Can You Make Work Easier?

You need to move something. Normally, you move things with your hands. The Explore Activity demonstrates that sometimes you might need to find another way to get a job done. You may need a **machine** (mə shēn').

What is a machine? A machine is a tool that makes work easier to do. From Lesson 4, you remember that work is done when a force changes the motion of an object. How do machines make it easier for forces to move objects?

WHAT MACHINES DO

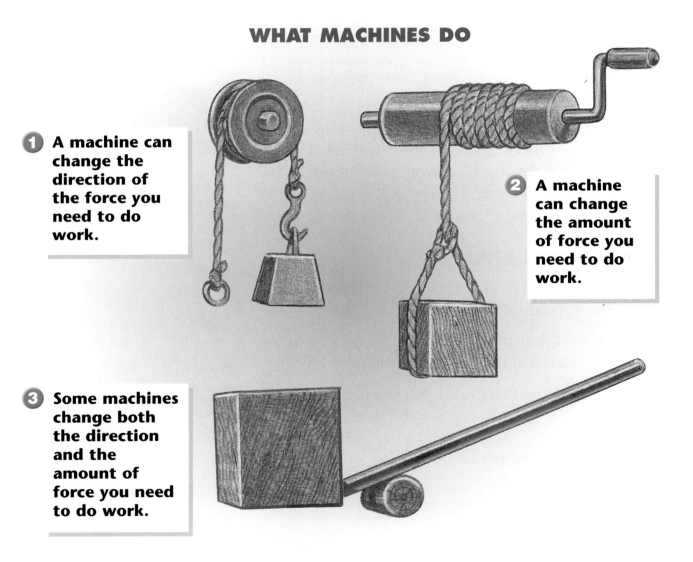

1 A machine can change the direction of the force you need to do work.

2 A machine can change the amount of force you need to do work.

3 Some machines change both the direction and the amount of force you need to do work.

What Is a Simple Machine?

A **simple machine** (sim′ pəl mə shēn′) is often used to make work easier. Machines with few or no moving parts are called simple machines. A **lever** (lev′ ər) is an example of a simple machine. A lever is a straight bar that moves on a fixed point. All levers have three important parts: the load, the fulcrum, and the force.

HOW LEVERS MAKE WORK EASIER

A lever makes moving a load easier in two ways. A lever lets you change the direction of a force. Sometimes it is easier to push one way than another. A lever lets you change the amount of force needed to move something.

The force is the push or pull that moves the lever.

The load is the object being lifted or moved.

The fulcrum is the point where the lever turns.

READING ⩕ DIAGRAMS

1. **DISCUSS** How do levers make work easier?
2. **REPRESENT** Draw a lever. Label the force, load, and fulcrum.

force

load

fulcrum

The load is in the middle on a wheelbarrow.

Are There Different Kinds of Levers?

The world is full of levers. Each one is set up differently. The force, fulcrum, and load can change places. Sometimes the fulcrum is in the middle. Sometimes it is on the outside. Take a look at how this lever works.

Make a Lever

HYPOTHESIZE What happens when you change the position of the fulcrum on a lever? Write a hypothesis in your *Science Journal.*

PROCEDURES

1. Use some clay to hold a pencil in place on your desk. Place the ruler over the center of the pencil.

2. **EXPERIMENT** Put 2 blocks on one end of your ruler. Add pieces of clay to the other end of the ruler. How much clay does it take to lift the blocks? What happens if you take a block away?

3. **EXPERIMENT** Change the position of the ruler on the pencil. Then repeat step 2. How does the new position change your results?

MATERIALS
- clay
- ruler
- pencil
- 2 small blocks
- *Science Journal*

CONCLUDE AND APPLY

1. **COMMUNICATE** Draw your lever. Label the force, load, and fulcrum. Describe how your lever works.

2. **DRAW CONCLUSIONS** How does the position of the pencil affect the amount of force you need to lift the load?

110

What Are Some Other Simple Machines?

Another kind of simple machine is the **wheel and axle** (hwēl and ak'sel). This simple machine has a wheel that turns on a post. The post is called an axle.

A wheel and axle makes work easier by changing the strength of a turning force. The wheel turns a long distance. The axle turns a short distance.

This windlass is used to raise water from a well. The bucket is tied to a rope. The other end of the rope is tied to the axle. At the end of the axle is the handle. When you turn the handle in a large circle, the axle turns in a small circle. The bucket moves up.

axle makes smaller movement

wheel makes larger movement

handle

axle

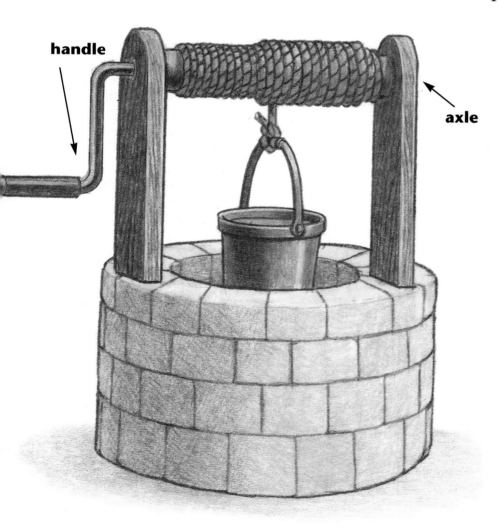

111

What Goes Down to Go Up?

Another simple machine is the **pulley** (pul′ē). A pulley is a simple machine that uses a wheel and a rope to lift a load. Some pulleys make work easier simply by changing the direction of a force. In a one-wheel pulley, the force and the load are equal. The pulley lets you pull down to lift the load up.

Some pulleys make work easier by changing the amount of force needed to do the work. A two-wheel pulley makes the job easier by reducing the amount of force needed to move the load.

This girl is using a pulley. How does the pulley make her work easier?

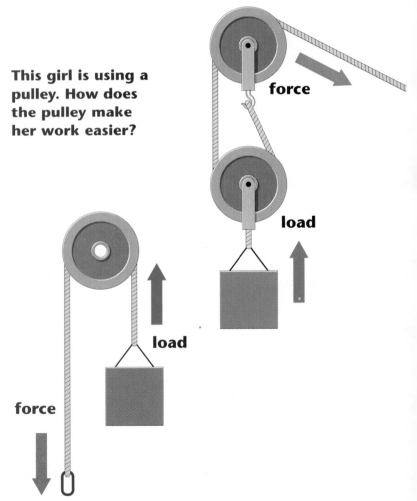

force

load

load

force

A pulley is actually a lever. So is a wheel and axle. Look at the diagrams. The same object is being lifted in each picture, but a different simple machine is doing the work.

You are surrounded by machines. If you don't believe it, take a look around. A spoon is a type of lever, and so is a bottle opener. Even your arms, legs, and fingers are levers!

REVIEW

1. How do machines make work easier?

2. What is a simple machine?

3. What kind of simple machine will help you raise a sail on a sailboat?

4. **COMMUNICATE** Write a paragraph or label a diagram that explains how a wheel and axle is a type of lever.

5. **CRITICAL THINKING** *Evaluate* Give an example of a simple machine. How does this simple machine make work easier?

WHY IT MATTERS THINK ABOUT IT
How many times do you lift things during the day? What sort of things do you lift?

WHY IT MATTERS WRITE ABOUT IT
How do your arms, legs, and fingers help you lift things?

A Music

Can people make music with simple machines? Sure they can! A piano isn't just a musical instrument, it's a machine full of levers!

Press any piano key and you push down on one end of a lever. The other end is inside the piano. It's attached to a small hammer that's covered in soft felt. When the end of this lever goes up, it hits the hammer against the metal strings for that note. The strings begin to vibrate. You hear a musical note!

Take your finger off the key. A pad called a damper touches the strings. They stop vibrating and the sound stops!

A piano has 88 keys and more than 200 strings. Some hammers strike three strings at one time. Short strings make high sounds. Long strings make low sounds.

The first piano was made in 1709 by Bartolomeo Cristofori of Italy. He called the instrument *piano e forte*. That means "soft and loud" in Italian. Before long Cristofori's invention became known as the piano.

Wolfgang Amadeus Mozart was an expert on a piano's levers. Born in Austria in 1756, Mozart wrote some of the world's most important piano music. Ludwig van Beethoven was born in Germany in 1770. He followed in Mozart's footsteps and also wrote great piano music.

DISCUSSION STARTER

1. Which piano part on the outside is a lever? Which part on the inside is a lever?

2. Is playing the piano a form of work? How do you know?

Machine

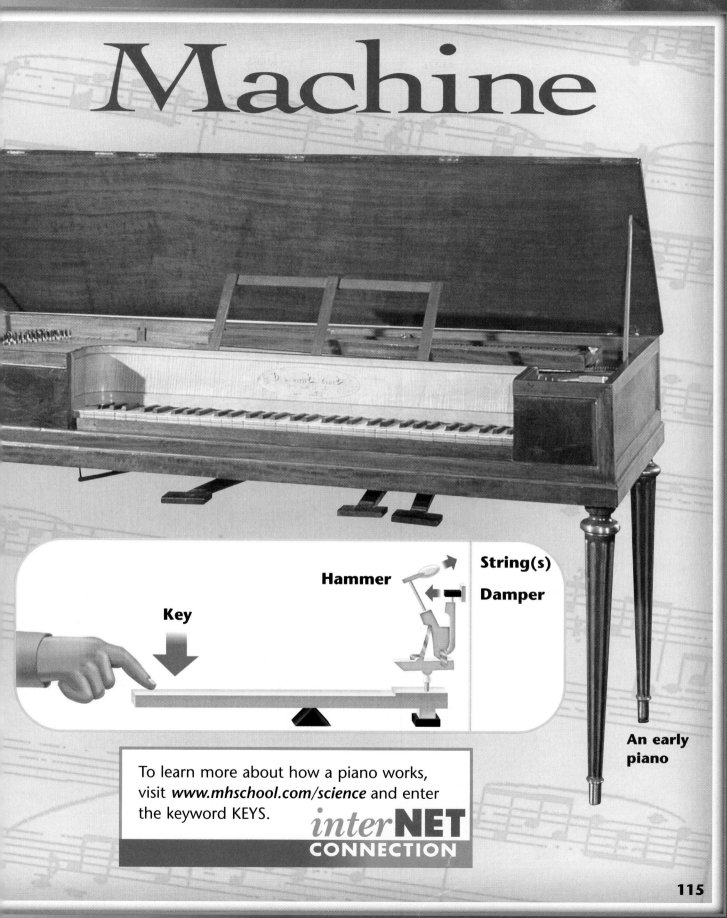

Key

Hammer

String(s)

Damper

An early piano

To learn more about how a piano works, visit *www.mhschool.com/science* and enter the keyword KEYS.

inter**NET**
CONNECTION

WHY IT MATTERS

Simple machines can make small jobs and big jobs less of a chore!

SCIENCE WORDS

inclined plane a flat surface that is raised at one end

wedge two inclined planes placed back to back

screw an inclined plane wrapped into a spiral

compound machine two or more simple machines put together

More Simple Machines

This pyramid, called the Pyramid of the Sun, was built over a thousand years ago. Made from mud, dirt, and large pieces of stone, it stands over 200 feet tall. A thousand years ago there were no bulldozers, tractors, or trucks. Somehow people moved large stones and other material hundreds of feet off the ground. How did they do it?

EXPLORE

HYPOTHESIZE When people built pyramids many years ago, they may have used a ramp to help them move rocks. How can a ramp make work easier? Write a hypothesis in your *Science Journal*. How might you test your ideas?

Investigate How a Ramp Can Make Work Easier

Evaluate how a ramp can make work easier.

PROCEDURES

 Safety: Wear goggles.

1. Lean one end of the wooden board on the chair. Tie one end of the string around the bottom of the spring scale and the other end to the middle of the spiral wire of the notebook.

2. **MEASURE** Measure the pull needed to lift the notebook straight up to the height of the chair's seat. Then measure the distance you pulled the book. Record your measurements in your *Science Journal*.

3. **MEASURE** Measure the pull needed to move the notebook up the board to the seat of the chair. Then measure the distance you pulled the book. Record your measurements.

4. **EXPERIMENT** Adjust the board so it is at a steeper angle. Repeat step 3.

CONCLUDE AND APPLY

1. **INTERPRET DATA** Look at your measurements. Which method of moving the notebook required more force? Which method required moving the notebook a greater distance?

2. **COMPARE** Think about the three methods. What is the advantage of each one? What is the disadvantage?

GOING FURTHER: Apply

3. **EVALUATE** Which method would you use to put a stuffed animal onto a shelf? Which method would you use to put a bike into a truck?

MATERIALS
- 1 meter wooden board
- spring scale
- thin spiral notebook
- 30 cm piece of string
- chair
- meter stick
- safety goggles
- *Science Journal*

117

How Can a Ramp Make Work Easier?

How did the people who built the Pyramid of the Sun lift blocks of stone so high in the air? They may have used ramps. A ramp is an example of an **inclined plane** (in klīnd' plān). An inclined plane is a flat surface that is raised at one end. The Explore Activity shows that inclined planes are simple machines that make work easier.

How does an inclined plane make work easier? Going up a hill, you have two paths. The path that goes straight up is shorter. However, it takes more effort. The ramp is a longer distance, but it takes less effort.

Which way should you go? When the object isn't heavy, you may choose to go straight up. When the object is heavy, you must take the ramp. The stone blocks that the people used to build the Pyramid of the Sun were too heavy to move straight up. Scientists think that they may have moved them on an inclined plane.

Inclined Plane longer distance, less effort

Straight Up shorter distance, more effort

How do ramps make work easier for these people? Where have you seen ramps used in your community?

What Kind of Simple Machine Is a Plow?

A **wedge** (wej) is another simple machine. A wedge is made of two inclined planes placed back to back. A wedge uses force to raise an object up or split objects apart.

An ax is a wedge. When an ax is swung, the downward force of the ax is changed into a sideways force. The sideways force splits the wood apart.

Another example of a wedge is a plow. A plow is a machine used by farmers. As the plow is dragged through the soil, it cuts through the ground. The soil is moved aside.

The downward force of the ax changes to the sideways force that splits the wood.

A plow helps a farmer prepare the ground for planting.

What Is a Screw?

What happens when you wrap an inclined plane around a pole? You have a **screw** (skrü)! A screw is an inclined plane wrapped into a spiral. The ridges of the screw are called threads.

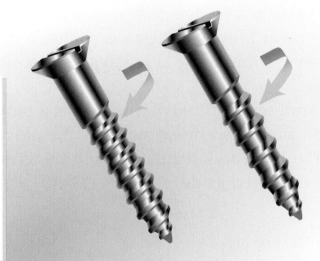

A screw with a longer inclined plane has more threads. A screw with a shorter inclined plane has fewer threads.

READING DIAGRAMS

1. **REPRESENT** Where is the inclined plane on a screw?
2. **DISCUSS** Which screw has a longer inclined plane? How do you know?

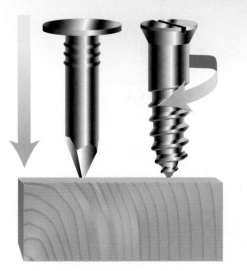

It takes less force to turn a screw than to pound a nail. That is because the screw is moving a longer distance. When you turn the head of the screw once, the spiral part of the screw travels a long way. You apply force over a longer distance, just like any other inclined plane. The longer the distance, the less force you need to do work.

MATH LINK

Skill: Using Numbers

EVALUATING DIFFERENCES

You know that a screw is a simple machine that makes work easier. A screw makes work easier just like any other inclined plane—by letting you use less force over a greater distance. Screws come in many shapes and sizes. Some screws make work easier than others. How can one screw make work easier than another?

The diagram below shows three screws. In this activity you will use numbers to evaluate how each screw is different. Then you will use that information to infer which screw makes work the easiest.

MATERIALS
- *Science Journal*
- ruler

PROCEDURES

1. **MEASURE** What is the width of the head of each screw? What is the length of each screw? Record your measurements in the table in your *Science Journal*.

2. **USE NUMBERS** What is the number of threads on each screw? Record the information in the table.

CONCLUDE AND APPLY

1. **COMPARE** How does the width and length of each screw compare? How does the number of threads on each screw compare?

2. **EXPLAIN** How does the number of threads on each screw relate to the length of its inclined plane?

3. **INFER** Which screw makes the work easiest? How do you know?

What Happens if You Put Two Simple Machines Together?

You can make your work easier by using a **compound machine** (kom′ pound mə shēn′), too. When you put two or more simple machines together, you make a compound machine. A pair of scissors is a compound machine. Part of a pair of scissors is a lever. Part of a pair of scissors is a wedge. Can you tell which part is which?

A water faucet is also a compound machine. Which part of the water faucet is a wheel and axle? Which part is a screw?

A bicycle uses wheels and axles and a lever. There are several sets of wheels and axles. Can you find them all? Can you find the lever?

Brain Power

Design your own compound machine. It should be made of two or more simple machines. What does your compound machine do? How does it work?

Simple and compound machines help you do many of your everyday activities. They help you do things like cut an apple for lunch, wrap a birthday present for a friend, travel from place to place, and wash up before bed!

What compound machine is this girl using? What simple machines make it up?

REVIEW

1. How does an inclined plane make work easier?

2. What is a compound machine?

3. Draw a picture of a knife cutting a banana. In what direction does the knife apply force? In what direction does the banana move?

4. **USE NUMBERS** You have two screws. Each measures 2 inches long and has a 1-inch head. Screw A has 20 threads. Screw B has 30. Which screw will make work easier? How do you know?

5. **CRITICAL THINKING** *Apply* Where is the inclined plane on a screw? Draw or write an explanation.

WHY IT MATTERS THINK ABOUT IT What simple or compound machine have you used today? How did the machine help you?

WHY IT MATTERS WRITE ABOUT IT What if the machine you used today did not exist. How would you have done the work you needed to do? How much harder would the work have been?

READING SKILL Look at page 122. How many compound machines are listed on this page? Choose one of the compound machines. What simple machines make it up? Make a list.

SIMPLE MACHINES on a PLAYGROUND

Push off! Wheeee, you're high in the air. Then down you come. Up and down you go on a simple machine . . . a seesaw! You don't think about working a machine. You're having too much fun!

Can you find the fulcrum of a lever in the picture? Hint: Look under the seesaw. Each person sits on one end of a lever. That lever makes it easy to move up and down.

Did you notice that the ramp is an inclined plane?

This simple machine makes it easy for someone in a wheelchair to play with friends. Without a ramp, it would take several people to lift the wheelchair up the stairs. Rolling up the ramp is easier. A child can do it without help!

DISCUSSION STARTER

Where have you seen ramps? You're going to seesaw with a friend. You both weigh the same. The fulcrum is in the middle. Draw how the seesaw will look when you get on.

To learn more about simple machines, visit **www.mhschool.com/science** and enter the keyword RAMP.

inter**NET** CONNECTION

SCIENCE WORDS

compound
  machine p.122

energy (p.101)

inclined
  plane (p.118)

lever p.109 ✓

machine p.108

pulley (p.112)

✓screw p.120

simple
  ✓machine p.109

wedge p.119

wheel and
  axle p.111

✓work p.100

USING SCIENCE WORDS

Number a paper from 1 to 10. Fill in 1 to 5 with words from the list above

1. An inclined plane wrapped into a spiral is a(n) ___?___ .

2. Pulleys and wheels and axles are both ___?___ .

3. When you use a force to change the motion of an object, you do ___?___ .

4. The simple machine with a fulcrum, load, and force is a(n) ___?___ .

5. A machine with few or no moving parts is a(n) ___?___ .

6–10. Pick five words from the list above. Include all words that were not used in 1 to 5. Write each word in a sentence.

UNDERSTANDING SCIENCE IDEAS

11. How does an inclined plane make work easier?

12. What is the difference between stored energy and energy of motion?

USING IDEAS AND SKILLS

13. **READING SKILL: RECOGNIZE A LIST** Look at the ramps and their measurements. List them in order from longest to shortest.

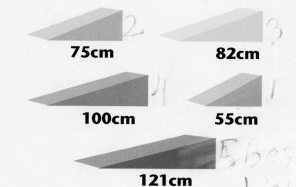

75cm   82cm

100cm   55cm

121cm

14. **USE NUMBERS** Look at your list from question 13. Which ramp makes work easiest? How do you know?

15. **THINKING LIKE A SCIENTIST** You are asked to explain how a lever makes work easier to a class of third-grade students. What will you tell them? Design a poster to help illustrate your ideas.

PROBLEMS and PUZZLES

Whee! Remember the rides at an amusement park? Machines moved you up, down, and around. Use what you've learned about machines and forces to build your own amusement park. You can use materials such as rubber bands, paper plates, milk cartons, and crayons.

SCIENCE WORDS

energy p.101
force p.78
friction p.90
gravity p.80
inclined
    plane p.118
lever p.109
motion p.70
position p.68

pulley p.112
screw p.120
speed p.71
wedge p.119
weight p.81
wheel and
    axle p.111
work p.100

USING SCIENCE WORDS

Number a paper from 1 to 10. Beside each number write the word or term that best completes the sentence.

1. When you squeeze the brakes, the force that slows the bike is ___?___.

2. How fast a car is moving is called its ___?___.

3. An apple falling from a tree is pulled by a force called ___?___.

4. A car that changes position is in ___?___.

5. You can find the pull of gravity on your body by finding your ___?___.

6. The machine made from a wheel and a rope is called a(n) ___?___.

7. You are standing with your leg ready to kick a soccer ball. Your leg has ___?___.

8. When you kick the soccer ball and make it roll, you are doing ___?___.

9. A ramp is a kind of ___?___.

10. A seesaw is an example of a ___?___.

UNDERSTANDING SCIENCE IDEAS

Write 11 to 15. For each number write the letter for the best answer. You may wish to use the hints provided.

11. Which of the following could be the speed of a car?
    a. 30 miles
    b. 30 miles per hour
    c. 30 hours
    d. 30 meters
    (Hint: Read page 71.)

12. The Moon has less matter than Earth. Which is true? You:
    a. are shorter on the Moon
    b. are heavier on the Moon
    c. are heavier on Earth
    d. weigh the same on both
    (Hint: Read page 82.)

13. Very smooth playground slides
    a. decrease friction
    b. decrease speed
    c. decrease motion
    d. decrease weight
    (Hint: Read pages 90–91.)

14. In science, work occurs when a force causes a change in motion. Which is true? Work
    a. takes money
    b. takes a long time
    c. changes an object's size
    d. changes an object's position
    (Hint: Read page 100.)

15. Which simple machine lets a roller skate roll?
    a. a screw
    b. a pulley
    c. an inclined plane
    d. a wheel and axle
    (Hint: Read page 111.)

USING IDEAS AND SKILLS

16. A woman walks one block in two minutes. Another woman walks the same block in eight minutes. Who has the greater speed? Explain.

17. What happens when you hang a weight on a spring scale?

18.  INTERPRETING DATA Look at the graph below. How does the kind of surface that a ball is on affect how far the ball rolls?

19. Give an example of the work you do at home and explain why it is work to a scientist.

THINKING LIKE A SCIENTIST

20.  USE NUMBERS You want to pry a big rock out of your garden. You have a 4-foot board and a 6-foot board. Which board will help you move the rock more easily? Explain.

inter NET
CONNECTION

For help in reviewing this unit, visit **www.mhschool.com/science**

WRITING IN YOUR JOURNAL

SCIENCE IN YOUR LIFE
List three ways you use levers every day. Use the list to write a description of how machines are important to you.

PRODUCT ADS
Advertisements sometimes show people jumping very, very high in a certain type of sneakers. What force are these advertisements ignoring? Explain your answer.

HOW SCIENTISTS WORK
In this unit you learned about machines and how they make work easier. Tell why you think it is important for scientists to do experiments to learn about machines.

Design your own Experiment

Think of a way to make a lever that will lift the front of a chair one inch above the floor. The chair should be touched only by the lever. Review your experiment with your teacher before you carry it out.

PROBLEMS and PUZZLES

Lever-Gram Puzzles

Tell what you think will happen in each lever-gram. Will the lever move? If so, which way?

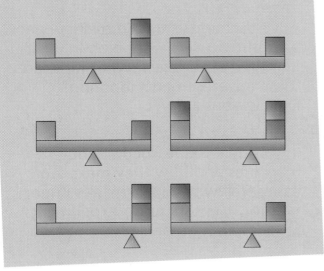

Amanda's Pulley Problem

Amanda can lift 10 kilograms with a single pulley. What kind of pulley system will she need to lift a greater load? Draw a picture of it.

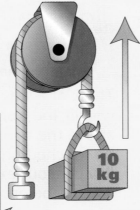

Trucking Troubles!

THE PROBLEM

Brontosaurus Trucks are the biggest trucks on the road! The trucks are so big that drivers complain that their steering wheels are hard to turn. Can you think of a way to make steering a Bronto easier?

HYPOTHESIZE

Decide what you could do to make the steering wheel of a Bronto Truck turn more easily. How would you change the steering wheel? Why do you think your idea would work? Include a drawing of your design.

MATTER AND ENERGY

CHAPTER 5

MATTER

Look around you. You see all sorts of different objects. Can you describe objects so well that another person can identify them? What information would you want to give? In what ways are they different? Can you think of a way they are all the same?

In Chapter 5 you will form generalizations. A generalization is a general rule made from particular facts.

Topic 1
PHYSICAL SCIENCE

WHY IT MATTERS

You can identify objects by describing them.

SCIENCE WORDS

volume how much space matter takes up

mass how much matter is in an object

property a characteristic of something

Rocks, Clocks, Trees, and Bees

Can two things be in the same place at the same time? Take a look at the first picture of the fishbowl. What will happen when other objects are added to the bowl?

Look at the second picture of the fishbowl. What would happen if more objects were put inside the bowl? What would happen if an object were taken out?

EXPLORE

HYPOTHESIZE What will happen when you put different objects in a container of water? Write a hypothesis in your *Science Journal.* How might you test your ideas?

1

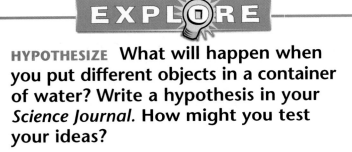

2

MATH LINK

Investigate Which Object Takes Up More Space

Test which object takes up more space by placing different objects in a container of water.

MATERIALS
- 12 oz plastic cup half full of water
- markers (different colors)
- a piece of clay
- classroom objects
- *Science Journal*

PROCEDURES

1. **MEASURE** Find the level of the water. Use a marker to mark the level on the outside of the cup.

2. **PREDICT** What will happen to the level of the water when you place the piece of clay in the cup? Record your prediction in your *Science Journal.*

3. **OBSERVE** Place the clay in the cup. What happens? Use a different color marker to mark the new water level on the outside of the cup. Remove the clay.

4. **PREDICT** Look at the other objects. Which object will make the water level change the most when you put it in the cup? Record your prediction.

5. **EXPERIMENT** Place one object at a time in the cup. Mark the new water level for each object. Use a different color marker for each object.

CONCLUDE AND APPLY

1. **IDENTIFY** What happened each time you placed an object in the cup? Why?

2. **COMPARE AND CONTRAST** How did the different objects affect the water level? Why do you think this happened?

3. **DRAW CONCLUSIONS** Which object takes up the most space? How do you know?

GOING FURTHER: Problem Solving

4. **EXPERIMENT** What do you think will happen to the water level in the cup if you change the shape of the clay?

131

Which Object Takes Up More Space?

As the Explore Activity shows, different things take up different amounts of space. A brick takes up more space than a pencil. A soccer ball takes up more space than a brick. A refrigerator takes up more space than a soccer ball.

What do pencils, bricks, soccer balls, and refrigerators have in common? They are all matter. Matter is anything that takes up space. Bricks, pencils, soccer balls, and refrigerators all take up space. So do mountains, clouds, rocks, and people. How would you describe these things? What other kinds of matter can you name?

Some objects take up more space than others. An object that takes up more space has a greater **volume** (vol′ūm). Volume is how much space matter takes up. The beach ball has a greater volume than the tennis ball. The tennis ball has less volume than the basketball.

beach ball

tennis ball

basketball

132

Describing an object's volume is one way you can describe matter. Another way to describe matter is to describe an object's **mass** (mas). Mass is how much matter is in an object. An object with a large mass feels heavy. An object with a small mass feels light.

A school bus, for example, has more mass than a bike. A bike has more mass than an apple. What has less mass than an apple?

Matter is made up of particles. In some objects the particles are closer together, and in some objects the particles are farther apart. There is more mass in the small book than in the large balloon. The particles in the book are packed together more tightly than the particles in the balloon.

School bus

Bicycle

Apple

The book has more mass than the balloon.

How Do You Measure Mass?

You can measure the mass of an object. One unit used to measure mass is the *gram*. One gram is a small amount of mass. Two paper clips equals about one gram. A nickel is about five grams. You can use the letter g to represent the word gram.

You can measure the mass of larger things in *kilograms*. One kilogram is equal to 1,000 grams. You can represent the word kilogram with the letters kg.

QUICK LAB

MATH LINK

Measuring Mass

HYPOTHESIZE Do objects in your classroom have different masses? Write a hypothesis in your *Science Journal*.

PROCEDURES

1. Estimate the mass of each object. Record your estimates in your *Science Journal*.

2. **MEASURE** Measure the mass of each object. Place the object on one side of the balance. Place paper clips on the other side until the two sides balance. Record the number of paper clips used to balance each object.

3. **USE NUMBERS** What is the mass of each object? (Remember, two paper clips equals about one gram.) Record the mass of each object in the table.

> **MATERIALS**
> * balance
> * small objects
> * 30 paper clips
> * *Science Journal*

CONCLUDE AND APPLY

1. **COMPARE AND CONTRAST** How does your list of estimated masses compare with the measurements you recorded?

2. **PLAN** If you wanted to find the mass of your shoe, how could you do it? How many paper clips would you need?

How Else Can You Describe Matter?

When you look at objects in the world around you, you can describe them in many ways. How would you describe a birthday cake? Would you say that it tastes sweet? When you describe a cake as sweet, you are naming a **property** (pro'pər tē) of the cake. A property is a characteristic of something.

Some properties are common to all types of matter. For example, all matter has volume and mass. Other properties are special to each type of matter. Size, shape, color, and texture are other properties of matter.

Some objects are hard, while other objects are soft. Some objects float in water, while other objects sink. These are more properties you can use to describe matter.

Brain Power

Describe this cake. How many properties did you name?

What are some properties of the objects you see pictured here?

How Are Mass and Weight Related?

You have learned that mass is a measurement of how much matter is in something. How is that like weight? Mass and weight are related. Of two objects, the object with more mass also has the greater weight. For example, an eight-year-old boy has more mass than a cat. A boy also weighs more than a cat.

The weight of an object is the pull of gravity on that object by Earth or any other large body in space. Weight is measured in *newtons*. A newton is the unit used to measure forces.

Gravity is the pulling force between two objects. The pull of gravity between two objects depends on the mass of the objects and how close they are to each other.

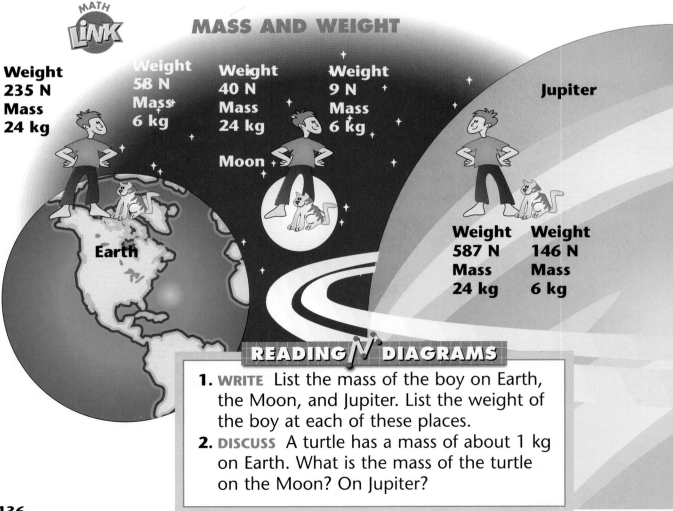

MATH LINK

MASS AND WEIGHT

Weight 235 N
Mass 24 kg

Weight 58 N
Mass 6 kg

Weight 40 N
Mass 24 kg

Weight 9 N
Mass 6 kg

Moon

Earth

Jupiter

Weight 587 N
Mass 24 kg

Weight 146 N
Mass 6 kg

READING N DIAGRAMS

1. **WRITE** List the mass of the boy on Earth, the Moon, and Jupiter. List the weight of the boy at each of these places.
2. **DISCUSS** A turtle has a mass of about 1 kg on Earth. What is the mass of the turtle on the Moon? On Jupiter?

You probably know that the pull of gravity on the Moon is much weaker than the pull of gravity on Earth. That's because the Moon has less mass than Earth. If you were to weigh yourself on the Moon, you would weigh less than you do on Earth. However, you would have the same amount of matter in you, so your mass would be exactly the same!

WHY IT MATTERS

Matter is anything that takes up space and has mass. You can describe matter by naming its properties. You might describe your new sneakers to a friend. Knowing an object's properties is especially important when you need to find an item that you've lost!

REVIEW

1. What would happen if you added several large rocks to a fishbowl filled with water? Why?

2. What is matter?

3. What is your favorite food to eat? Describe some of its properties.

4. **INFER** You have two objects. The mass of one is 5 grams and the mass of the other is 20 grams. Which of these two objects would have the greater weight? How do you know?

5. **CRITICAL THINKING** *Apply* An object has a mass of 20 kg on Earth. Suppose you took the object to the Moon. How would the object's mass change? How would its weight change?

WHY IT MATTERS THINK ABOUT IT
Describe your favorite toy. Why is it your favorite?

WHY IT MATTERS WRITE ABOUT IT
You brought your favorite toy to school. Now it's lost! Write a notice to hang on your classroom bulletin board. What properties of the toy will you describe?

Mass
Measurement

This is the U.S. copy of the one-kilogram cylinder.

Did you know that we measure mass in grams? We do, but how much mass is in one gram? People around the world have to agree on that. If they don't agree, a gram in Norway might have more or less mass than one in China. Then how could scientists compare the results of their experiments?

In 1795 French scientists decided to determine the exact mass of one gram. A gram, they said, was equal to the mass of 1 milliliter of pure water. The water, they added, had to be as cold as melting ice.

Imagine three scientists measuring the mass of pure, icy water. What if one scientist's water is a little colder? What if another's isn't completely pure? The scientists might get three different results!

To keep this from happening, scientists designed a solid metal cylinder. It had the same mass as 1,000 milliliters of pure, ice-cold water. That is, it had the same mass as 1,000 grams, or 1 kilogram.

In 1889 the original cylinder was replaced by a new one. It's the one we still use today.

The cylinder is kept in France. Copies are kept in other countries, including the United States. Now everyone knows exactly how much mass is in one kilogram. A kilogram has as much mass as one of these metal cylinders!

Discussion Starter

1 Why do scientists need to have an exact measurement of the mass in a kilogram?

2 Why do you think scientists used metal for the cylinders?

*inter*NET CONNECTION To learn more about measuring mass, visit www.mhschool.com/science and enter the keyword **MEASURE.**

Topic 2
PHYSICAL SCIENCE

WHY IT MATTERS

There are different forms of matter. These forms can be mixed together in different ways.

SCIENCE WORDS

solid matter that has a definite shape and volume

liquid matter that has a definite volume, but not a definite shape

gas matter that has no definite shape or volume

mixture different types of matter mixed together

solution a type of mixture that has one or more types of matter spread evenly through another

Comparing Solids, Liquids, and Gases

Can you find ten different materials in your classroom? There are many different types of matter in the world. Some matter is solid, like this leaf. What are some properties of solids? Some matter is liquid, like these drops of water. What are some properties of liquids? In your own words, write a definition of a solid and a liquid.

EXPLORE

HYPOTHESIZE How can you tell whether a material is a solid or a liquid? Write a hypothesis in your *Science Journal*. How might you test your ideas?

Design Your Own Experiment

HOW CAN YOU CLASSIFY MATTER?

PROCEDURES

👓 **SAFETY: Wear goggles**

1. **OBSERVE** Observe the Oobleck using only your senses. How does the Oobleck look? What does it feel like? Record all of your observations in your *Science Journal*.

2. **EXPERIMENT** Using the tools given to you, investigate the Oobleck in different ways. What new things do you observe? Record these observations.

3. **CLASSIFY** Look at the observations of Oobleck that you have made. Then review the definitions of solid and liquid that you wrote. Do you think Oobleck is a solid or a liquid? Could it be both? Why?

CONCLUDE AND APPLY

1. **COMMUNICATE** What observations did you make about the properties of Oobleck?

2. **EXPLAIN** How did you decide to classify Oobleck? What observations helped you make your decision?

GOING FURTHER: Problem Solving

3. **HYPOTHESIZE** What do you think Oobleck is made of? How might you find out whether your idea is correct?

MATERIALS

- plastic container of Oobleck
- investigation tools
- newspaper
- safety goggles
- *Science Journal*

141

How Can You Classify Matter?

The Explore Activity demonstrates that some matter has properties of both solids and liquids. Solid and liquid are forms of matter. Three forms of matter are solid, liquid, and gas. Each form of matter takes up space and has mass.

A sneaker is a **solid** (sol'id). A solid is matter that has a definite shape and volume. Definite means that it stays the same. If you put a sneaker into a container, it has the same shape in the container as it had outside the container. Its volume stays the same, too.

Juice is an example of a **liquid** (lik'wid). A liquid is matter that has a definite volume, but does not have a definite shape. A liquid takes the shape of the container it is in.

Another form of matter is **gas** (gas). A gas is matter that has no definite shape or volume. Gases take the shape of whatever container they are in. For example, air is made of gases.

You have learned that matter is made of particles. The particles in matter are very, very small. In a solid, the particles are packed closely together. They form a certain pattern. The pattern gives a solid its definite shape.

The particles in a liquid are close together but they do not form a certain pattern. Particles in a liquid have more energy than particles in a solid. They are able to slide past one another. That is why liquids change their shape.

The particles in a gas have more energy than the particles in a solid or a liquid. They will spread out to fill a large container or squeeze together to fit into a smaller container.

PARTICLES IN DIFFERENT FORMS OF MATTER

Solid   **Liquid**   **Gas**

READING N CHARTS

1. **DISCUSS** Compare the particles in a solid to the particles in a gas.
2. **WRITE** In your own words, describe the particles in a liquid.

How Can Matter Change?

Matter can change and still be the same type of matter. Think about what happens when you slice an orange. The orange may look different, but it is made from the same particles as before it was cut. You can cut an orange into as many small pieces as you want, and it will still be an orange.

Wood is still wood when it is cut.

144

Matter can also change form and still be the same type of matter. You can find water in the form of a solid, a liquid, or a gas. Whether it is a solid, a liquid, or a gas, the particles of water stay the same.

Ice is the solid form of water. The particles in ice are close together. They do not move very much. When ice is heated, it melts. When matter melts it changes from a solid to a liquid. Ice becomes liquid water. When water is in liquid form, the particles have more energy. They move around more freely. When liquid water is warmed, it *evaporates* (i vap′ ə rātz′). Water that evaporates changes from a liquid to a gas. It becomes a gas called water vapor. You cannot see water vapor. The particles of water vapor have more energy than the particles in the solid or liquid water.

THREE FORMS OF WATER

Skill: Communicating

MAKING A TABLE

When you communicate you share information with others. Scientists communicate what they learn from an experiment. They might tell people how they think the new information can be used. You can communicate by talking, or by creating a drawing, chart, table, or graph.

You can communicate what you know about the properties of solids, liquids, and gases. Look at the photograph on this page to help you answer the questions below.

PROCEDURES

1. OBSERVE Look at the photograph. What forms of matter do you see? What properties do these forms have? Record your observations in your *Science Journal.*

2. COMMUNICATE Use your observations to fill in the table in your *Science Journal.*

CONCLUDE AND APPLY

1. DRAW CONCLUSIONS What do solids and liquids have in common? What makes them different?

2. COMMUNICATE Give an example of a solid, a liquid, and a gas. Then write a sentence that tells what you know about the shape and volume of each one.

Can You Mix Different Kinds of Matter Together?

When you mix different types of matter together, you may get a **mixture** (miks'chər). This fruit salad is a mixture of many different types of fruit.

The properties of each type of matter put into a mixture do not change. Each type of fruit in the fruit salad has the same properties in the mixture that it has outside the mixture.

Mixtures can be made of solids, liquids, or gases. Mixtures can also be made with a combination of different forms of matter. Air is a mixture of different gases. Salad dressing is a mixture of liquids like oil and vinegar. Some salad dressings may also have solids like herbs (urbz) or spices mixed in.

Soil is a mixture of solids, such as plant matter, sand, and clay. Air and water also help to make up the soil. Soil is made with three forms of matter!

apple

strawberry

kiwi

Brain Power

When you put milk on your breakfast cereal, you are making a mixture. What two forms of matter have you mixed?

What Is a Different Kind of Mixture?

There are different kinds of mixtures. One kind of mixture is a **solution** (sə lü′shən). A solution is formed when one or more types of matter are spread evenly throughout another kind of matter.

Salt water is an example of a solution. If salt is mixed with water, you will not be able to see the salt anymore. Yet the salt is still there. When the water evaporates, the salt will be left behind.

You wouldn't want to drink salt water, but many of the things people drink are solutions. Tea, coffee, fruit juices, and soft drinks are all solutions.

Solutions are not just made with liquids. Air is a solution of different gases. Dentists make fillings for your teeth out of a solution of metals.

salt water

salt after water has evaporated

You eat many mixtures every day! Foods like salad, spaghetti, and tacos are mixtures. You eat solutions, too. Chocolate milk and tomato soup are two examples of solutions you may eat. Can you think of others?

REVIEW

1. Name three forms of matter and give an example of each.

2. What is the difference between a solid and a liquid? Between a liquid and a gas?

3. Is pizza a mixture or a solution? How do you know?

4. **COMMUNICATE** How can a fish aquarium have a mixture of three forms of matter? Draw a picture and label each state of matter.

5. **CRITICAL THINKING** *Apply* Describe the properties of candle wax. Which form of matter do you think candle wax is? Why?

WHY IT MATTERS THINK ABOUT IT
Describe three kinds of foods you like to eat. Are they foods that you eat for breakfast, lunch, or dinner?

WHY IT MATTERS WRITE ABOUT IT
Choose one of the foods you like to eat. What forms of matter have to be put together to make it? Is the food a mixture? Is it a solution?

READING SKILL Write a paragraph describing any generalizations you've learned about in this lesson.

Making Changes

Do you know what vinegar is? Do you know how it tastes? How it smells? What color it is? Is it a solid, liquid, or gas?

Do you know what baking soda is? Do you know what its properties are?

Let's say that you put a few teaspoons of baking soda into a bowl. Suppose you add a few teaspoons of vinegar to it. What do you think will happen?

What's causing the bubbles?

A Closer Look

When you add salt to water, you get salty water, right? Does that help you figure out what'll happen if you add vinegar to baking soda?

Did you figure out that bubbles would form and the mixture might spill out of the bowl? Bubbles form because a new substance is made. What are the properties of the new substance?

Mixing salt with water is a physical change. It doesn't make a new substance. Mixing vinegar with baking soda is a chemical change. It does make a new substance.

DISCUSSION STARTER

1. What other substances can be mixed to create a new substance?

2. Plan an experiment that can be done with the new substance made from vinegar and baking soda.

To learn more about physical and chemical changes, visit *www.mhschool.com/science* and enter the keyword CHANGES.

*inter*NET
CONNECTION

Topic 3
PHYSICAL SCIENCE

WHY IT MATTERS

All of the matter in the world is made up of the same basic building blocks.

SCIENCE WORDS

metal a shiny material found in the ground

magnetism the property of an object that makes it attract iron

element a building block of matter

atom the smallest particle of matter

compound two or more elements put together

Building Blocks of Matter

Why do you think some objects are attracted to magnets and some are not? Look at the items in the picture. You might buy some items like these for school. What is going to happen when the magnet gets lowered closer to the items? How do you know?

EXPLORE

HYPOTHESIZE Which of the items pictured here will be attracted to a magnet? Write a hypothesis in your *Science Journal.* How might you test your ideas?

EXPLORE ⚡ ACTIVITY

Investigate What Magnets Attract

Test what kinds of objects are attracted to magnets.

MATERIALS
- a magnet
- several objects
- *Science Journal*

PROCEDURES

1. OBSERVE Look at your objects. What properties of the objects do you observe? Record your observations in your *Science Journal.*

2. PREDICT Which of the objects will be attracted to a magnet? Record your predictions.

3. EXPERIMENT Test your predictions. Get a magnet from your teacher. Test each object to see if it is attracted to the magnet. Record the result of each test.

CONCLUDE AND APPLY

1. CLASSIFY Look at the results of your tests. Which objects were attracted to the magnet? Which objects were not? Make two lists. In one list, write the names of the objects attracted to the magnet. In the other list, write those that were not. Title each of the lists.

2. COMPARE AND CONTRAST Read the list of objects that were attracted to the magnet. Can you identify any properties that they all have in common? Write down your thoughts. Now look at the list of objects that were not attracted to the magnet. What kinds of things can you say about these objects? Write down your thoughts.

GOING FURTHER: Apply

3. DRAW CONCLUSIONS What conclusions can you draw about the kinds of things that are attracted to magnets?

What Do Magnets Attract?

As the Explore Activity shows, some objects are attracted to magnets. Other objects are not. Magnets attract some items made of **metal** (met′əl). A metal is a shiny material found in Earth's ground. Many of the items that magnets attract are made from the metals iron and steel. Magnets attract objects made from some other metals, too.

Magnets have the property of **magnetism** (mag′ni tiz′əm). Magnetism is the property of an object that makes it attract iron and some other metals. You can use the property of magnetism to identify objects. For example, junkyards use powerful magnets to lift and sort objects made of metal.

WHAT IS A MAGNET?

1. **A magnet is a piece of material that attracts iron and some other metals. Natural magnets come from a rock called magnetite** (mag′ni tīt′).

2. **Magnetite is not a very strong magnet. The magnets you use are called permanent magnets. Permanent magnets are usually stronger than magnetite.**

3. **Permanent magnets are often made from metals like iron and steel.**

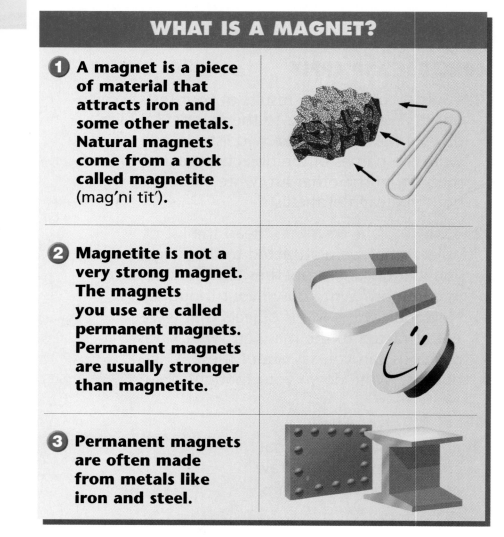

What Are Some Other Uses of Iron and Steel?

Iron is a very useful metal. Iron is often mixed with other materials to make metals with different properties. Steel is a metal made with iron. It is used to build things like buildings, railroads, and bridges.

Iron is also an important part of your diet. You need to eat some iron every day to stay healthy. You can get iron from meats and from dark green vegetables like spinach. You can also get iron from fortified (fōr′tə fĭd′) cereals. Fortified means stronger. Fortified cereal has extra ingredients added to it.

Bowl of Iron

MATERIALS

- 1 package fortified cereal
- plastic sandwich bag
- magnet
- sheet of white paper
- *Science Journal*

HYPOTHESIZE If you read the label of a box of breakfast cereal, you'll probably see iron in the list of ingredients. Does breakfast cereal really contain iron? Write a hypothesis in your *Science Journal.*

PROCEDURES

1. Pour the cereal into a plastic bag. Add the magnet and seal the bag.

2. Shake the bag for several minutes. Carefully remove the magnet. Hold it over a sheet of white paper.

3. **OBSERVE** What do you see when you look at the magnet?

CONCLUDE AND APPLY

PREDICT What would happen if you tried the same experiment using cereal that did not contain iron?

What Are Some Other Metals?

Iron and steel are just two kinds of metals. Other metals include gold, silver, aluminum (ə lü′mə nəm), and copper.

Each metal has its own special properties. Some metals, like steel, are heavy and very hard. Some metals, like copper and aluminum, are light and soft. Metals such as gold and silver are very valuable.

Brain Power

The body of an airplane is covered in aluminum. A bridge is made of steel. What might happen to a bridge made of aluminum? What might happen to an airplane covered in steel?

PROPERTIES OF DIFFERENT METALS

1. Steel is a very strong metal. Try digging a hole without a steel shovel!

2. Copper can be rolled into very thin wires. These wires can be used to make electrical cords. Aluminum foil can be torn into sheets.

3. Gold and silver are used to make beautiful jewelry.

The metals iron, gold, silver, aluminum, and copper are **elements** (el′ə məntz). An element is a building block of matter. There are over 100 different elements. Some elements, like the metals iron and copper, are solids. Some elements are liquids. Some elements, like helium (hē′lē əm), are gases. Each element has its own special properties. Put together in many different ways, elements make up all the matter in the world!

All elements are made up of **atoms** (at′əmz). An atom is the smallest particle of matter. It is too small to see with your eyes. The atoms that make up one element are all alike. They are different, however, from the atoms that make up any other element.

Some balloons are filled with a gas called helium. Helium is lighter than air. The balloons will float away if they aren't held down!

How Can You Put Elements Together?

When you combine the elements iron and oxygen, you get a **compound** (kom'pound) called rust. A compound may form when two or more elements are put together. You have probably seen the compound rust on metal objects left outside.

Remember that when a mixture is formed, different types of matter are mixed together. The properties of the matter in the mixture are not changed. However, the properties of a compound are different from the properties of the elements that make it up.

The compound salt is made up of the elements sodium (sō'dē əm) and chlorine (klōr'ēn). Water is a compound, too. It is made up of the elements hydrogen and oxygen.

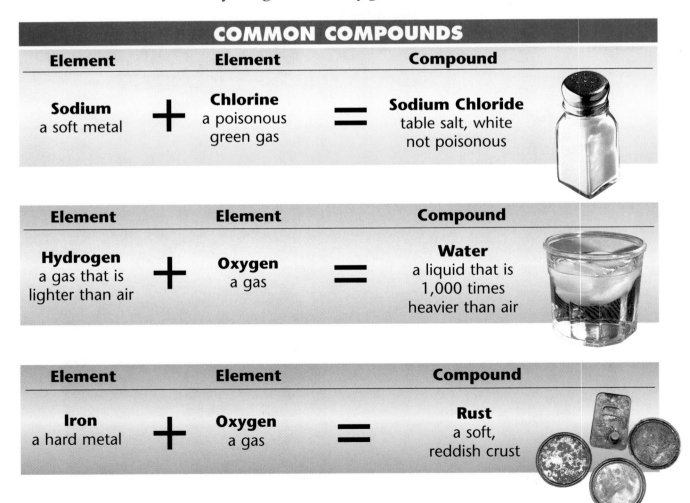

COMMON COMPOUNDS

Element		Element		Compound
Sodium a soft metal	+	**Chlorine** a poisonous green gas	=	**Sodium Chloride** table salt, white not poisonous

Element		Element		Compound
Hydrogen a gas that is lighter than air	+	**Oxygen** a gas	=	**Water** a liquid that is 1,000 times heavier than air

Element		Element		Compound
Iron a hard metal	+	**Oxygen** a gas	=	**Rust** a soft, reddish crust

Everything in the world is made of the same building blocks of matter. Your body is made up of the same elements and compounds as the stars in the sky and whales in the ocean! Although there are over 100 elements, your body contains just about 11 different elements. There are many compounds in your body, too. One very important compound in your body is water.

MATH LINK

Almost $\frac{2}{3}$ of your body is water.

REVIEW

1. What kinds of objects are attracted to a magnet? What kinds of objects are not attracted to a magnet?

2. What is a metal? Why are metals important in your life?

3. What is iron? What are some ways you use iron?

4. **COMMUNICATE** Why are elements called the building blocks of matter?

5. **CRITICAL THINKING** *Analyze* How is a compound different from a mixture?

WHY IT MATTERS THINK ABOUT IT Describe the places you can find water. Why is water an important part of the world?

WHY IT MATTERS WRITE ABOUT IT How do living things use water differently?

SCIENCE MAGAZINE

ELEMENTARY LIST

How many different elements are there? Long ago people thought there were just four: air, water, fire, and earth. Wouldn't they be surprised to know that today there are more than 100?

Is wood an element? Is salt? Wool? Iron? Paper? Plastic? Aluminum? Scientists wanted to know. They heated different substances to a very high temperature for a very long time.

When they heated wood it turned into a hard, black substance—carbon. What do you think happened when the carbon was heated? It got hotter and hotter, but the carbon still was carbon. It was called an element.

When iron is heated, it may melt, but it's still iron. Is it an element?

When scientists heated salt to a high temperature, the salt melted. Heat up the liquid salt and it turns into two new substances: chlorine and sodium.

Sodium's a metal that's so soft it can be cut with a knife.

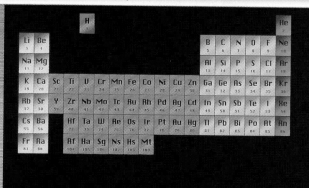

The periodic table above lists 109 elements. It's an orderly way to give information about all the elements we know. As new elements are discovered, they are added to the periodic table.

Chlorine's a gas used to kill germs in swimming pools.

Aluminum is an element. Like all elements, aluminum can't be destroyed. Then why can you tear aluminum foil? The atoms in aluminum foil stick together to form one piece of foil. When you tear foil, you pull the atoms apart! Even though the aluminum has changed, it is still aluminum. All the matter in the universe is made up of atoms from diferent elements.

DISCUSSION STARTER

1. Which elements can you name?

2. Atoms can't be destroyed by heat. Do you think there's another way to break up an atom? Explain.

To learn more about the elements, visit *www.mhschool.com/science* and enter the keyword PERIODIC.

interNET CONNECTION

SCIENCE WORDS

atom p.157

compound p.158

element p.157

gas p.142

liquid p.142

magnetism p.154

mass p.133

metal p.154

mixture p.147

property p.135

solid p.142

solution p.148

volume p.132

USING SCIENCE WORDS

Number a piece of paper 1 to 10. Fill in 1 to 5 with words from the list.

1. The metal iron has the property of ___?___.

2. The amount of space an object takes up is the object's ___?___.

3. Grams are one unit of measurement for ___?___.

4. A shiny material found in Earth is a ___?___.

5. Air is an example of a ___?___.

6–10. **Pick five words from the list above that were not used in 1 to 5, and use each in a sentence.**

UNDERSTANDING SCIENCE IDEAS

11. Is the color yellow a type of matter? How could you test to see if a color is matter?

12. Give an example of a solid, a liquid, and a gas.

USING IDEAS AND SKILLS

13. **READING SKILL: FORM A GENERALIZATION** How can you tell a mixture from a compound?

14. **COMMUNICATE** Describe the differences between solids, liquids, and gases by drawing diagrams of each type of matter. Write a brief explanation of each diagram.

15. **THINKING LIKE A SCIENTIST** Metals are good carriers of heat. They heat up quickly. Do metals also cool off quickly? Write a hypothesis. Describe how you would test your idea.

PROBLEMS and PUZZLES

What Happened? Examine steel wool with a hand lens. Then place it next to a cup of water. Cover them both with a wide-mouth jar or bowl. Wait a day. What happened? How has the steel wool changed? Would it change the same way without the water? Try it.

CHAPTER 6
ENERGY

Energy is all around you. Whenever you see something move, you are seeing the result of some form of energy.

Heat, light, and electricity are forms of energy. What are some ways you use heat, light, and electricity?

 In Chapter 6 you will read several diagrams. A diagram uses pictures and words to show how something works.

WHY IT MATTERS

Knowing what makes heat helps us control how warm things get.

SCIENCE WORDS

temperature how hot or cold something is

degree the unit of measurement for temperature

heat a form of energy that makes things warmer

insulator a material that heat doesn't travel through easily

Heat

Could you fry an egg on the sidewalk? In Oatman, Arizona, they try! Oatman has a sidewalk egg-frying contest every year on the Fourth of July.

Some surfaces, like sidewalks or sand at the beach, can get very hot in the Sun. Other surfaces, like water, stay cooler. Why do you think this happens?

EXPLORE

HYPOTHESIZE **You could measure how hot soil and water get when they are exposed to the same amount of heat. Would one type of matter warm up more than the other? Write a hypothesis in your** *Science Journal*. **How might you test your ideas?**

MATH
LINK

Investigate How Heat Affects Different Materials

Test how hot soil and water get when they are exposed to the same amount of heat.

MATERIALS

- soil
- water
- 2 foam cups
- 2 thermometers
- heat source (sunlight or a lamp)
- *Science Journal*

PROCEDURES

1. Fill one of the cups with water. Place an equal amount of soil in the other cup.

2. MEASURE Using your thermometers, measure how warm the soil and water are. Record your measurements in your *Science Journal*.

3. Estimate how hot the soil and water will get if they are left in a warm place for 15 minutes. Record your estimates, then place the soil and water near a heat source. Make sure they are the same distance from the heat source.

4. MEASURE Record the readings on the thermometers every 5 minutes for 15 minutes.

5. USE NUMBERS Find the difference between the first thermometer reading and the last. To do this, subtract the first measurement you made from the last measurement you made.

CONCLUDE AND APPLY

1. IDENTIFY Which type of matter warmed up more? How do you know?

2. COMPARE AND CONTRAST Were your estimates close to your actual measurements?

GOING FURTHER: Apply

3. INFER Why is it important to place the soil and water an equal distance from the heat source?

Some metals change color as they get hotter. As its temperature rises, a metal may turn red, then orange, then yellow, then white!

Why might you want to heat metal?

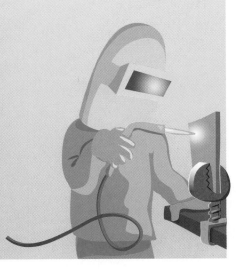

How Does Heat Affect Different Materials?

As the Explore Activity shows, there is a difference in the way heat affects different types of matter. With the same amount of heat, one type of matter may warm up more than another type of matter. You can measure how much each type of matter warms up by using a thermometer.

Thermometers measure **temperature** (tem′pər ə chər). Temperature is a measure of how hot or cold something is. It is measured in **degrees** (di grē′z). A degree is the unit of measurement for temperature. The symbol for degree is °.

What is **heat** (hēt)? Heat is a form of energy. Energy makes matter move or change. Heat is a form of energy that makes matter warmer. Heat can be added to a material to raise the material's temperature.

Some materials need more energy to cause the same change in their temperature than others. For example, it takes more energy to heat water than it takes to heat soil to the same temperature. This is why the soil in the Explore Activity showed a greater change in temperature than the water.

How does temperature affect the things you do each day?

166

HOW DOES HEAT MOVE?

Heat always flows from warmer objects to cooler ones.

Heat flows from the warm air to the cold ice.

Heat flows from the girl's hand to the snowball.

Heat flows from the hot chocolate to the boy's cold hands.

READING N DIAGRAMS

1. **WRITE** Write a sentence that describes how the girl's hands feel. Why do they feel this way?
2. **REPRESENT** You take a popsicle out of the freezer. Draw a picture that shows the direction of heat flow.

How Does Heat Change Matter?

Heat is a form of energy. You can't hold energy in your hand. You can't see energy, either. However, you can see how energy moves or changes matter. In the Explore Activity, the change in matter was the change in temperature.

A thermometer is a glass tube filled with a liquid. When a thermometer is in a warm place, the liquid in the thermometer rises. It rises because the liquid expands when it is heated. Matter that expands gets bigger. It takes up more space.

Remember that when heat is added to matter, the particles in the matter move faster. As the particles move faster, they move farther apart. This movement makes matter expand.

When matter loses heat, the particles in the matter slow down. The slower the particles move, the less energy the matter has. Matter contracts as it cools. Matter that contracts gets smaller. It takes up less space.

Too much heat and too little rain can kill plants. During a heat wave in Texas, all of this farmer's wheat died.

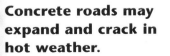

Concrete roads may expand and crack in hot weather.

Expand and Contract

HYPOTHESIZE Do gases expand when heated? Do they contract when cooled? Write a hypothesis in your *Science Journal.*

PROCEDURES

1. Stretch the opening of the balloon over the opening of the bottle.

2. **PREDICT** What will happen when you place the bottle in the bucket of warm water? Test your prediction.

3. **PREDICT** What will happen when you place the bottle in the bucket of cool water? Test your prediction.

CONCLUDE AND APPLY

1. **COMMUNICATE** What happened to the balloon when you placed it in warm water? In cold water?

2. **DRAW CONCLUSIONS** What happened to the air particles in the balloon when the bottle was in the warm water? The cool water?

MATERIALS

- balloon
- 2L plastic bottle
- bucket of warm water
- bucket of cool water
- *Science Journal*

Brain Power

Heat flows from the warm room to the cold popsicle. The particles in the popsicle move faster. The popsicle melts. How can you change the melted popsicle back into a hard popsicle?

169

How Can You Control the Flow of Heat?

Heat moves quickly through some types of matter. For example, some metals are used to make cooking pots. Heat moves quickly from the stove to the metal. The pot gets warm.

Heat doesn't pass quickly through other materials. These materials are called insulators (in′sə lā′tərz). An insulator is a material that heat doesn't travel through easily.

Some materials, like wool, cotton, and air, are good insulators. Other materials, like metals, are not good insulators. These pictures show you some of the ways insulators can be used.

Fluffy goose feathers, called down, make warm winter coats.

Why doesn't a walrus get cold in freezing waters? It has layers of fat under its skin. Fat is a good insulator.

Where does heat come from? Just about everywhere! Remember, heat is energy. Energy changes from one form to another. When machine parts rub together, some of the friction changes to heat. Burning materials like wood creates heat, too. Wood is a fuel. Fuels are materials burned for energy. A car needs gasoline as a fuel. Your body needs food. As your body uses food, it creates heat. That's why your body has a certain temperature.

REVIEW

1. What is temperature?

2. What makes matter expand when it is heated and contract when it is cooled?

3. Name three ways you use insulation.

4. **PREDICT** A cup of water and a cup of sand are left in the Sun for one hour. Will their temperatures change the same amount? How do you know?

5. **CRITICAL THINKING** *Apply* What is energy? How do you know that heat is energy?

WHY IT MATTERS THINK ABOUT IT
Describe a time when you were very hot or very cold. Where were you?

WHY IT MATTERS WRITE ABOUT IT
When you are too hot or too cold, how can you make yourself more comfortable? What insulators might help you?

READING SKILL Look at the diagram on page 167. Write a paragraph that explains what the diagram shows.

COOL IT!

Put a little water on the back of your hand. Some of the heat from your hand warms the water. It begins to evaporate. You feel a coolness on your hand. This process is similar to how most refrigerators work!

How did people keep food cold before there were refrigerators? They used natural ice! Northern ponds and rivers froze in the winter. Workers cut the ice and stored it in underground cellars. The ice was insulated by sawdust and thick walls and roofs. The next summer people delivered the ice to homes in insulated trucks. Customers had special iceboxes that held the ice and food. When winter came, last year's ice was gone, but nature again froze the ponds and rivers.

Liquid evaporates

Insulation

Coolant

Pump

Heat escapes

Energy is needed to move the heat from inside the refrigerator. That's why your refrigerator is plugged into an electric outlet! The electricity runs a motor inside the refrigerator to help it do its job.

DISCUSSION STARTER

1. How does ice keep foods cool?

2. How does a refrigerator make heat flow from a cool place to a warmer one?

A refrigerator doesn't need ice. It uses a liquid that evaporates to pull heat from inside it. The refrigerator has long coils of thin metal. They carry the heat into the room. The room becomes warmer while inside the refrigerator it becomes colder.

To learn more about refrigerators, visit *www.mhschool.com/science* and enter the keyword COOL!

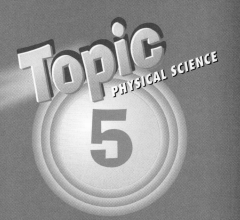

Topic
PHYSICAL SCIENCE
5

WHY IT MATTERS

Light is used in many important ways, including communication.

SCIENCE WORDS

opaque does not allow light to pass through

reflect to bounce off a surface

MATH LINK Light

How fast do you think light travels? Light can travel 186,000 miles in just one second! You depend on light every day. Sunlight in the morning tells you a new day has begun. At school and at home, light allows you to see people and objects. "Lights out!" means it's time for bed. In what other ways do you depend on light?

EXPLORE

HYPOTHESIZE What kinds of materials can light pass through? Write a hypothesis in your *Science Journal.* How might you test your ideas?

Investigate What Materials Light Passes Through

Test these materials to see which ones allow light to pass through.

PROCEDURES

1. EXPERIMENT Hold one material at a time in front of the lighted flashlight. Does the light shine through the material? Record your observations in your *Science Journal.*

2. OBSERVE Blow up your balloon. Look through the balloon. What do you observe now?

3. EXPERIMENT Try changing the other materials in some way. You may want to fold the papers several times to make them thicker, or crumple up the plastic wrap. After you have made a change in the material, test the material again. Record both the change you made and any new observations.

CONCLUDE AND APPLY

1. CLASSIFY Which materials did the light pass through? List them. Which materials blocked the light? Make a separate list of these materials.

2. EXPLAIN What was the effect of the change you made to each material?

GOING FURTHER: Apply

3. IDENTIFY Look at the list of materials that light passed through. What properties do these materials have in common?

What Does Light Pass Through?

Light is a form of energy. Like all forms of energy, light can make matter move or change. There are many different sources of light. Some sources of light are natural sources. Natural light sources include the Sun and other stars, lightning, fire, and some living things. Other light sources, like light bulbs and candles, are made by people.

Light travels in straight lines from its source. The Explore Activity demonstrates that light passes through some materials but not through others. For example, light passes through a glass window, but not through a brick wall. A brick is **opaque** (ō pāk'). Opaque materials do not allow any light to pass through them. Materials that block light create shadows.

Light rays that do not pass through a material **reflect** (ri flekt') off of it. Reflect means to bounce. Light rays that are reflected off of an opaque surface bounce off of it. When light rays reflect off of a surface they change the direction they are traveling.

You see objects because light reflected from the object enters your eyes. A mirror is very smooth and shiny. When light rays are reflected from a mirror, they are reflected in the same direction. When you stand in front of a mirror, you see a face just like yours. This is your reflection.

Rays of light travel from the Sun to Earth.

Brain Power

Try making shadows using several different objects. Why did you choose these objects?

Most objects or surfaces are not as smooth and shiny as mirrors. Light rays that are reflected from surfaces that are dull or rough are reflected in many different directions. You don't see a reflection when light is reflected in many different directions.

Light rays also change direction when they move from one material to another. For example, when light rays pass from air to water or water to air, they bend. Look at the picture of the spoon in the water. The spoon looks bent!

Why does the spoon look bent? Light rays change direction as they pass through the surface of the water and into the air. The bending light rays make the spoon look as if it has bent, too.

The spoon looks bent because the light rays are bent.

HOW DO YOU SEE OBJECTS?

1. Light is a mixture of many different colors. Light bends as it travels through a prism. The colors of light spread out.

2. The color of the object depends on the color of light it reflects. An apple is red because it reflects red light.

3. You see objects because light reflected from the object enters your eyes. A lens in front of the eye bends the light and makes an image. Nerves bring this image to your brain.

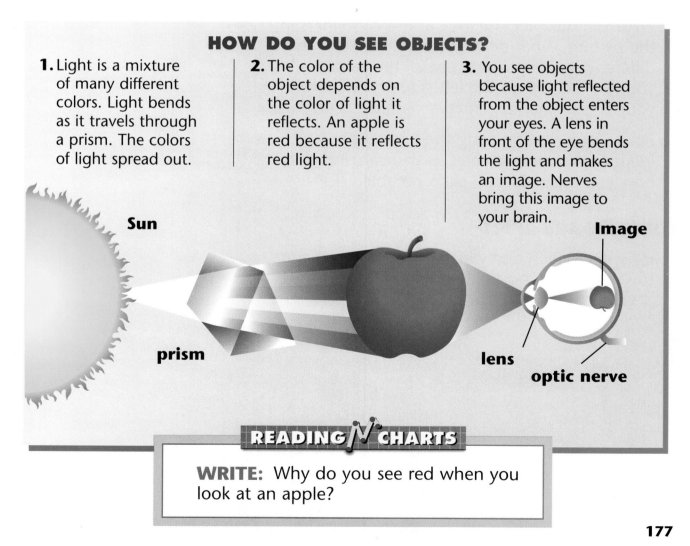

Sun

prism

lens

optic nerve

Image

READING CHARTS

WRITE: Why do you see red when you look at an apple?

SKILL BUILDER

Skill: Using Variables

CONTROLLING AN EXPERIMENT

Variables are things in an experiment that can be changed or controlled. For example, suppose you wanted to answer the question: *What affects how light bends in a liquid?* Here are some variables that could be changed:

• the kind of liquid you use

• the size of the container you use

• the position of the object in the liquid

MATERIALS

• *Science Journal*

PROCEDURES

1. **COMPARE** Take a close look at the containers in the picture. What differences do you see? These differences are variables. List all the variables you can identify on the left side of the table in your *Science Journal*. The first variable is given.

2. **COMMUNICATE** Complete the table. After you identify as many variables as you can, indicate how you could control each variable.

CONCLUDE AND APPLY

IDENTIFY Which one variable would you change to see its effect on the bending of light? Why?

LIGHT CAN CHANGE MATTER

1. A camera is a tool that uses light to make a picture called a photograph. The film inside the camera is coated with chemicals that change when light shines on them.

2. Powerful beams of light, called lasers, can be strong enough to cut steel. Lasers also read special codes of information on items at the supermarket.

3. Light changes plants. Without sunlight, plants could not live and grow.

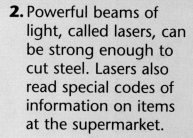

WHY IT MATTERS

Light is everywhere in your world. One important way light is used is for communicating information. Traffic lights tell you when it is safe to cross the street. Light is used to make television programs and movies, too.

REVIEW

1. How does light travel from one place to another?

2. What is an opaque material?

3. How can light change matter?

4. USE VARIABLES You want to know how many marbles will fit into a cup. List the variables in this experiment.

5. CRITICAL THINKING *Apply* Why do you see your reflection when you look in a mirror and not when you look at a book?

WHY IT MATTERS THINK ABOUT IT Describe some different forms of transportation. What form of transportation do you use most often?

WHY IT MATTERS WRITE ABOUT IT Traffic lights help make transportation by foot and by car safer. How is light used to make other forms of transportation safer?

Waves of Energy

How does light get from the Sun to Earth? How does music get from the stage to the audience? They move the same way —in waves!

Light and sound are forms of energy. All waves carry energy, but they may carry it differently. Light and sound travel through different kinds of matter. For example, light waves can't move through walls, but sound waves can. That's why you can hear people talking in another room even though you can't see them. The energy of some waves is destructive. An earthquake produces seismic waves.

Catch a wave. Ask a friend to stand a few feet away from you. Stretch a spring between you. Shake the spring to transfer energy to it. What happens? The spring bounces up and down in waves. When the waves reach your friend, they bounce back to you!

Light waves travel 300,000 kilometers (186,000 miles) per second! They can also travel through a vacuum—a space without matter. That's why light from the Sun and distant stars can travel through space to Earth!

A Closer Look

A spring toy can show how waves travel.

DISCUSSION STARTER

1. How are light and sound alike? How are they different?

2. What causes a shadow?

To learn more about how energy travels, visit *www.mhschool.com/science* and enter the keyword BOUNCE.

PHYSICAL SCIENCE

WHY IT MATTERS

Your life would be very different without electricity.

SCIENCE WORDS

cell a source of electricity

circuit the path electricity flows through

electric current electricity that flows through a circuit

switch opens or closes an electric circuit

Electricity

Why do you think this train set isn't working? Draw a picture of how you think the train set should look when it is put together.

EXPLORE

HYPOTHESIZE You often have to put parts together in a certain way for something to work. How can you put a light bulb, wire, and battery together so that the bulb lights? Write a hypothesis in your *Science Journal*. How might you test your ideas?

Investigate What Makes It Light

Test what makes the bulb light by putting the parts together in different ways.

MATERIALS

- D cell
- small light bulb
- 20 cm wire
- *Science Journal*

PROCEDURES

1. **OBSERVE** Look at the bulb, wire, and cell. How do you think you might put these three things together to make the bulb light? Record any ideas you may have in your *Science Journal*.

2. **EXPERIMENT** Try to light the bulb. Draw a picture of each set-up that you try. Record which ones work and which ones don't.

CONCLUDE AND APPLY

1. **IDENTIFY** How many ways did you find to light the bulb? How many ways did you find that did not light the bulb?

2. **COMPARE AND CONTRAST** How were the ways that worked to light the bulb alike? How were they different from the ways that did not work?

GOING FURTHER: Apply

3. **DRAW CONCLUSIONS** How must the bulb, wire, and cell be put together so that the bulb will light?

What Makes It Light?

The Explore Activity shows a bulb, wire, and **cell** (sel) that can be put together in different ways. A cell is a source of electricity. Just like the train set, these parts have to be put together in a certain way in order to form a system. A system is a group of things that work together.

The bulb, wire, and cell work as an electrical system. The system uses electric energy to light the bulb. How does the system work?

Electricity is a form of energy that travels in a **circuit** (sūr′kit). A circuit is the path electricity flows through. The electricity that flows through a circuit is called **electric current** (i lek′trik kûr′ənt).

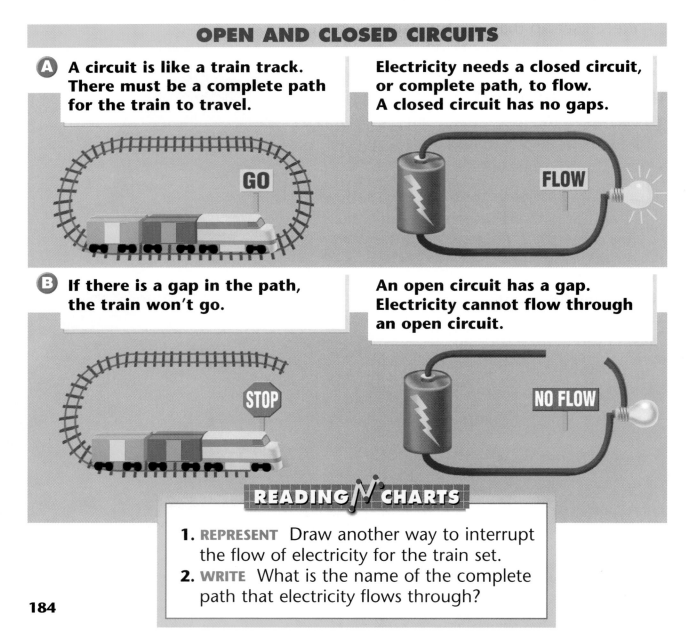

OPEN AND CLOSED CIRCUITS

A A circuit is like a train track. There must be a complete path for the train to travel.

Electricity needs a closed circuit, or complete path, to flow. A closed circuit has no gaps.

GO

FLOW

B If there is a gap in the path, the train won't go.

An open circuit has a gap. Electricity cannot flow through an open circuit.

STOP

NO FLOW

READING N CHARTS

1. **REPRESENT** Draw another way to interrupt the flow of electricity for the train set.
2. **WRITE** What is the name of the complete path that electricity flows through?

Make A Flashlight

MATERIALS
- 2 D cells
- paper tube
- 30 cm wire
- flashlight bulb
- *Science Journal*

HYPOTHESIZE A flashlight is a source of light that uses cells as its source of electricity. How can you put the materials together to make a model of a flashlight? Write a hypothesis in your *Science Journal.*

PROCEDURES

MAKE A MODEL Use the materials provided for you to construct a model of a flashlight.

CONCLUDE AND APPLY

1. EXPLAIN How is your model like a real flashlight? How is your model different?

2. COMMUNICATE Draw a diagram of your model flashlight's circuit. How are you able to turn your circuit on and off?

How Can You Control the Flow of Electricity?

When you want to turn on a flashlight, you use the **switch** (swich). A switch is used to open or close an electric circuit. Pushing the switch one way closes the circuit. It allows electricity to flow in a complete path. The bulb lights up, because the electric current is flowing.

Switch

How Do You Use Electricity?

How many ways do you use electricity at home? Almost everyone uses electric lights. You may also use electricity to heat your home. Electric machines include refrigerators, hairdryers and vacuum cleaners. Radios, computers, and television sets all run on electricity.

Toaster
Electricity changes to heat as it flows through a wire in the toaster.

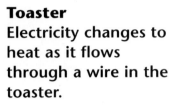

switch

Light Bulb
Electricity makes a thin wire in the bulb so hot that it glows.

switch

Electric Fan
Electricity flows through an electric motor, causing the fan's blades to turn.

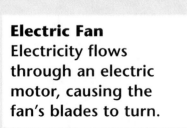

switch

Electricity helps you do all sorts of things. Telephones use electricity to carry sound. You use electricity to cook your food and wash your clothes. You need electricity to watch television and to listen to the radio.

Brain Power

Suppose the electric power is cut off. Could this girl still listen to the radio? How?

REVIEW

1. What is a cell?

2. What is a circuit?

3. What controls the flow of electricity in a circuit? How does it work?

4. **COMMUNICATE** What are some examples of places you would find circuits in your everyday life?

5. **CRITICAL THINKING** *Apply* Draw a diagram that shows the flow of electricity in a flashlight that is turned on.

WHY IT MATTERS THINK ABOUT IT
Describe some of the ways you use electricity every day. How many different ways are there?

WHY IT MATTERS WRITE ABOUT IT
Suppose you spent the summer on an island that had no electricity. What things would you miss doing? What new things might you learn to do?

Making a Difference

SAVING ELECTRICITY

How can you save electricity? Look for places where energy's being wasted. Then… stop wasting it!

- Turn lights off in empty rooms.
- Close the refrigerator door quickly!
- Use a microwave instead of an oven.
- Run the dishwasher only when full.
- Use timers to turn electric coffee pots and other machines on and off.
- Replace old machines that use lots of electricity.
- Let your hair dry naturally!

DISCUSSION STARTER

Saving electricity saves energy. What else does it save?

To learn more about saving energy, visit *www.mhschool.com/science* and enter the keyword SAVE!

SCIENCE WORDS

cell p.184 insulator p.170

circuit p.184 opaque p.176

degree p.166 reflect p.176

electric current p.184 switch p.185

heat p.166 temperature p.166

USING SCIENCE WORDS

Number a piece of paper 1 to 10. Fill in 1 to 5 with words from the list above.

1. A material that heat doesn't flow through easily is called a(n) ___?___.

2. An object that light cannot pass through is ___?___.

3. A thermometer is used to measure ___?___.

4. A complete path for electricity to flow through is called a ___?___.

5. To open or close an electrical circuit, you use a(n) ___?___.

6 –10. Pick five words from the list above. Include all words that were not used in 1 to 5. Write each word in a sentence.

UNDERSTANDING SCIENCE IDEAS

11. Light always flows from light places to dark places. True or false? Explain.

12. A toy car with a good battery falls off a table. Suddenly it won't work. What might be the problem?

USING IDEAS AND SKILLS

13. **READING SKILL: USE A DIAGRAM** Heat is flowing from the living room to the bedroom. Draw a diagram that shows what you know about the temperature in each room.

14. **USE VARIABLES** You want to know whether salt water or fresh water freezes faster. The table shows some variables in this experiment. Fill in the chart. Write how you would control each variable.

Variable	Controlling the variable
Amount of water	
Amount of salt	

15. **THINKING LIKE A SCIENTIST** Do you think paper or cotton balls are a better insulator? Write a hypothesis. Describe how you would test your idea.

PROBLEMS and PUZZLES

Sun Prints Place a rock on black construction paper. Place them together in the Sun for several hours. What happened?

Colored Light What does an apple look like in red light? Blue light? Work with an adult to use different colored light bulbs. How do things look?

SCIENCE WORDS

cell p. 184
compound p. 158
element p. 157
gas p. 142
heat p. 166
liquid p. 142
mass p. 133

opaque p. 176
property p. 135
reflect p. 177
solid p. 142
switch p. 185
temperature p. 166
volume p. 132

USING SCIENCE WORDS

Number a paper from 1 to 10. Beside each number write the word or words that best completes the sentence.

1. Two or more elements put together may form a ___?___.

2. An object's mass or volume is a ___?___ of the object.

3. When matter has a definite shape and volume, it is a ___?___.

4. A quart of milk can fill containers with different shapes. The milk is a ___?___.

5. A building block of matter is a(n) ___?___.

6. To see how hot something is, we measure its ___?___.

7. When ___?___ flows to an ice cube, the ice melts.

8. Air is a mixture of ___?___.

9. A flashlight gets electricity from a ___?___.

10. To turn a light on and off, use a ___?___.

UNDERSTANDING SCIENCE IDEAS

Write 11 to 15. For each number write the letter for the best answer. You may wish to use the hints provided.

11. The amount of space that an object takes up is its
    a. volume
    b. mass
    c. weight
    d. temperature
    (Hint: Read page 132.)

12. Matter that does not have a definite shape or volume is a
    a. solid
    b. gas
    c. solution
    d. liquid
    (Hint: Read page 145.)

13. Salt is made of elements and is an example of a
    a. gas
    b. liquid
    c. mixture
    d. compound
    (Hint: Read page 158.)

14. Heat is a
    a. form of energy
    b. compound
    c. gas
    d. collection of particles
    (Hint: Read page 164.)

15. Light can pass through glass because glass is
    a. a liquid
    b. not opaque
    c. a reflector
    d. a form of energy
    (Hint: Read page 174.)

USING IDEAS AND SKILLS

16. Describe two ways you could find out the volume of a brick.

17.  **COMMUNICATE** Draw a diagram that shows how solids, liquids, and gases are different from each other.

18. What is a magnet? What is one way a magnet can be used?

19. How might you keep lemonade cold at a picnic on a hot day?

THINKING LIKE A SCIENTIST

20. **PREDICT** Two containers in a cold room are filled with warm water. One container is made of metal, and the other container is made of foam. In which container will the water temperature go down faster? Explain why.

WRITING IN YOUR JOURNAL

SCIENCE IN YOUR LIFE
List five ways you use electricity in your home and three ways electricity is used in a grocery store.

PRODUCT ADS
You may have seen advertisements on TV that show people or animals sitting on clouds. What properties of matter have the advertisers ignored?

HOW SCIENTISTS WORK
Scientists study all sorts of things. After scientists make observations and do experiments, they communicate what they have learned. Why is it important for scientists to do this? What are some ways that scientists communicate information?

Design your own Experiment

Plan an experiment that would show if there is electrical energy in a cell. Review your experiment with your teacher before trying it out.

interNET CONNECTION

For help in reviewing this unit, visit *www.mhschool.com/science*

PROBLEMS and PUZZLES

Light in the Tunnel

Tunnel-Craft makes tunnels for children. The Mega Tunnel is 40 feet long and has lights on both ends. However, the middle of the tunnel is very dark. How can you light the middle of the tunnel? List as many ideas as you can. Draw a design of each of your solutions.

Mega Tunnel

PERISCOPE

Look at a model of a periscope. Periscopes are used in submarines and to see around corners. How is the periscope made? How do you think it works? Using the materials given to you, make your own model of a periscope.

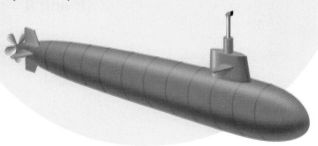

Pattern on the Green

Eddie hooked up 25 bulbs in a pattern on the front lawn. Each bulb has its own cell and wire.

1. Copy the pattern Eddie's bulbs make on a sheet of paper. Number the bulbs as shown.

2. Look at the cells, bulbs, and wires below. Which bulbs will light up? Record the numbers. Color the same numbers on your pattern yellow.

3. Which bulbs below will not light up? Record the numbers. Color the same numbers on your pattern blue.

4. What letter do you see?

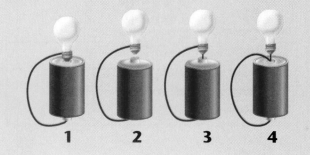

CHAPTER 7
TRAVELING AROUND THE SUN

You see the Sun and the Moon on most days. The Sun warms you up. It also provides energy for other living things on Earth. Sometimes the Moon is so bright it does not seem like night. What else do you know about the Moon and the Sun?

In Chapter 7 you will read for cause and effect. Cause and effect helps you to understand both what happens and why it happens.

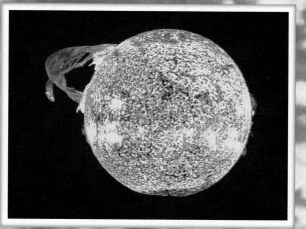

WHY IT MATTERS

Day and night and the seasons affect the things you do each day.

SCIENCE WORDS

rotate to turn around

axis a real or imaginary line through the center of a spinning object

revolve to move in a circle around an object

orbit the path an object follows as it revolves

Earth and the Sun

Have you ever seen the Sun seem to come up and turn night into day? A dark sky brightens with just a peek of the Sun. What about when the Sun seems to go down? Shades of orange, yellow, red, and pink paint the sky. Before you know it, day becomes night. What do you think causes night and day?

EXPLORE

HYPOTHESIZE **The Sun gives us plenty of light during the day. Where does it go at night? Write a hypothesis in your *Science Journal.* How might you test your ideas?**

194

EXPLORE ACTIVITY

Investigate What Causes Night and Day

Use a model to investigate what causes night and day.

MATERIALS
- globe
- 2 to 5 medium self-stick notes
- flashlight
- *Science Journal*

PROCEDURES

1. MAKE A MODEL Write "I live here" on a self-stick note. Place it over the United States on the globe. Pick another place on the opposite side of the globe. It can be where a friend lives. Write "My friend lives here" and place it on the globe.

2. In a darkened room, one person will hold the globe, or Earth. Another person will hold the flashlight, or the Sun. The third person will record the results.

3. OBSERVE Shine the light on the globe at the place where you live. Is it day or night where you live? Is it day or night where your friend lives?

4. EXPERIMENT Think of two different ways to make it night where you live. Use the globe and the flashlight to show both of your ideas. Record your observations in your *Science Journal*.

CONCLUDE AND APPLY

1. EXPLAIN What was the first way you made day turn into night? The second way?

2. COMPARE AND CONTRAST How do your group's ideas compare with other groups?

GOING FURTHER: Apply

3. IDENTIFY Which example do you think best explains what you know about day and night? Why?

195

What Causes Night and Day?

The Explore Activity uses a model. The model showed that the turning of Earth can cause daytime and nighttime. The model also showed that the movement of the Sun around Earth can cause daytime and nighttime.

A long time ago, people thought that Earth stood still while the Sun traveled around it each day. It's easy to see why people once thought the Sun moved. Every day we see the Sun seem to come up and go down.

Today we know that the Sun does not move around Earth. Earth **rotates** (rō' tātz). To rotate means to turn. As Earth rotates there is daylight where Earth faces the Sun and darkness where Earth is turned away from the Sun. By turning the globe, you can see how different parts of Earth move from "night into day," and from "day into night."

It takes 24 hours for Earth to make one complete rotation. One complete rotation is one day. A day is made up of the hours of light and the hours of dark.

THE ROTATING EARTH

morning   evening

Each day, the Sun appears to move across the sky. This is because Earth rotates. As Earth rotates, you see the Sun rise in the east and set in the west.

What Is Earth's Position in Space?

Have you ever seen a basketball spinning on a player's fingertip? Think of a line drawn from the player's fingertip to the top of the ball. The line would be straight up and down. The ball spins around this line. This imaginary line is called an **axis** (ǝk'sis). An axis is a real or imaginary line through the center of a spinning object.

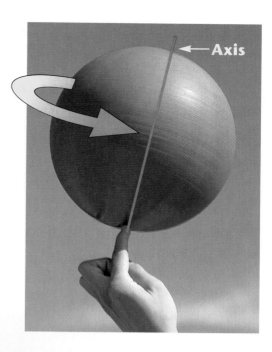

Earth also spins on an axis. As you can see in the illustration, Earth's axis is not straight up and down. It is slightly tilted. At the north end of Earth's axis is the North Pole. At the south end is the South Pole.

EARTH ROTATES ON A TILTED AXIS

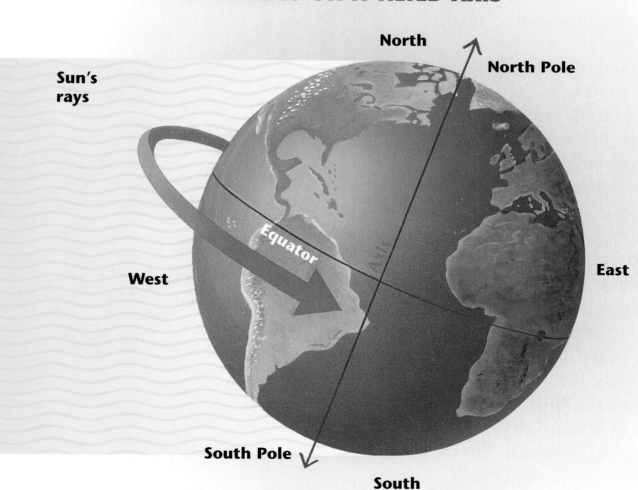

197

What Is a Year?

Rotation is only one way in which Earth moves.
Earth also **revolves** (ri volv′z). An object that moves in a circle around another object revolves. Earth travels in a oval path around the Sun.

Earth revolves in a certain way. It travels in an **orbit** (ôr′bit). An orbit is the path that an object follows as it revolves. It takes $365\frac{1}{4}$ days for Earth to make one complete revolution around the Sun. One complete revolution is one year.

Seasons

In many parts of the world, the year is made up of four seasons: Winter, spring, summer and fall. Why do we have seasons? The answer has to do with Earth's tilted axis. Having a tilted axis means that Earth slants a little as it revolves around the Sun.

Look at the diagram. Notice that as Earth revolves around the Sun, its axis is always tilted in the same direction. Earth is always tilted in the same direction, but as Earth travels around the Sun, the part of Earth tilted towards the Sun changes. For part of the year, the north end of the axis slants toward the Sun. During another part of the year, the North Pole slants away from the Sun.

When the North Pole is tilted towards the Sun, the Sun's rays strike that part of Earth more directly. It is then summer in this part of Earth. When the North Pole is tilted away from the Sun, the Sun's rays strike that part of Earth at an angle. It is then winter in this part of Earth.

Summer (begins June 21–22)

Earth's orbit

EARTH REVOLVES AROUND THE SUN

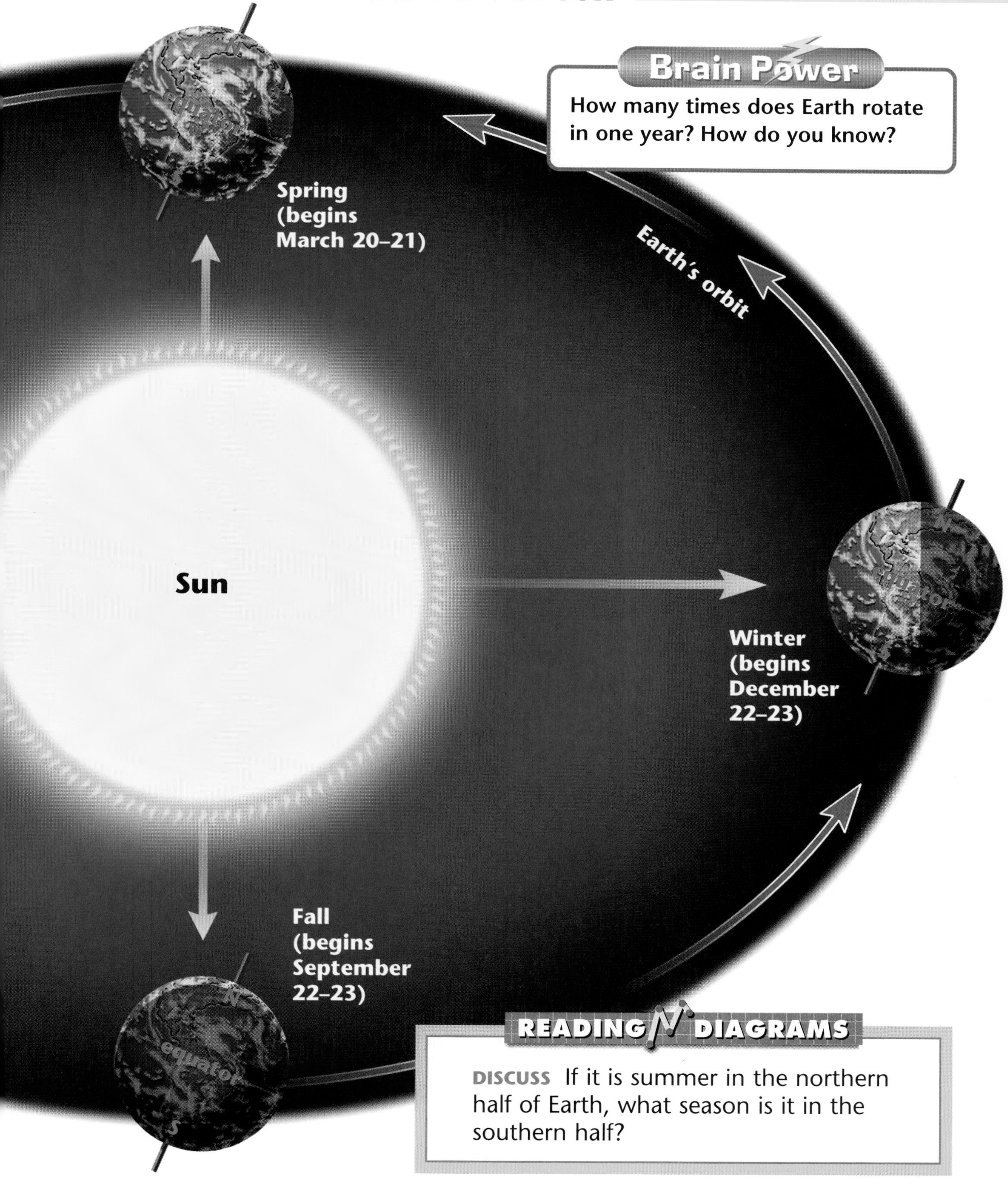

N
equator
Spring (begins March 20–21)
Earth's orbit
Sun
N
equator
Winter (begins December 22–23)
Fall (begins September 22–23)
N
equator
S

Brain Power

How many times does Earth rotate in one year? How do you know?

READING DIAGRAMS

DISCUSS If it is summer in the northern half of Earth, what season is it in the southern half?

June

December

morning   evening

How Does the Sun's Path in the Sky Change?

As the seasons change, so does the way the Sun appears to travel across the sky each day. In summer, your part of Earth is slanted toward the Sun. The Sun's path appears higher in the sky. In winter, your part of Earth is slanted away from the Sun. The Sun's path appears lower in the sky.

MATH LINK

QUICK LAB

Sundial

HYPOTHESIZE How can you measure the Sun's changing path in the sky? Write a hypothesis in your *Science Journal*.

PROCEDURES

MATERIALS
- pencil
- paper taped to cardboard
- marker
- clay
- *Science Journal*

1. At 9 A.M. on a sunny day, go outside with your materials. Working on the ground, use the clay to anchor the pencil to the center of the paper.

2. **MEASURE** Use the marker to draw a line straight through the middle of the pencil's shadow. Label the line with the time of day. Measure the pencil's shadow again at 12 P.M. and 3 P.M. Label the paper with the date.

3. **REPEAT** Once a month, measure the pencil's shadow three times a day. Label each paper with the date you make your measurements.

CONCLUDE AND APPLY

1. **COMPARE AND CONTRAST** How does the position of the pencil's shadow change throughout one day? Is the Sun high or low in the sky when the shadows are the longest?

2. **INFER** During which month is the Sun's path highest in the sky? Lowest? How do you know?

The way Earth moves affects the way we lead our lives. Just think of all the things you do during the day and throughout the year. You probably have a favorite season. Do you enjoy swimming to cool you off on a hot summer day? How about riding a sled down a snowy hill?

Autumn is a time of falling leaves and changing colors.

REVIEW

1. Where is the Sun when it is nighttime on Earth?

2. How long is a day? Describe the motion of Earth that makes up one day.

3. What is an axis?

4. **INFER** What would happen to the seasons if Earth's axis were not tilted?

5. **CRITICAL THINKING** *Evaluate* How would your life be different if you lived in the southern half of Earth?

WHY IT MATTERS THINK ABOUT IT Describe your favorite season. What activities do you enjoy during this time of the year?

WHY IT MATTERS WRITE ABOUT IT Suppose Earth made one complete rotation every 12 hours. How long would a day be? How would you fit your activities into this kind of day?

Star Time

Two bright stars mark Orion's shoulders, and three stars form his belt.

A Closer Look

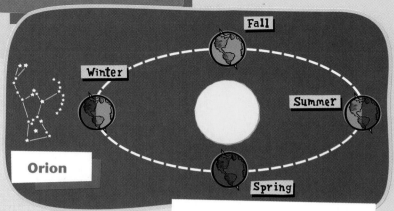

Could you tell time without a clock or calendar? Ancient people had to, because there were no clocks or calendars!

Ancient farmers needed to keep track of time. They had to know when to plant their crops. Their lives depended on planting at the right time to get the food they needed. How did they do it? They used the stars!

The farmers carefully studied the skies. They noticed that groups of stars formed shapes, or constellations. They saw that different constellations were visible at different times of the year. For thousands of years, people used those constellations to predict the seasons.

Orion, the Hunter, is a constellation. Let's say that it's winter in the Northern Hemisphere and you study the night sky. If you observe Orion every night from the same spot—like your bedroom window—you'll notice that Orion seems to move across the sky! What's really happening? Earth is revolving around the Sun, so you're the one who's moving past Orion!

In early spring, Orion disappears from the night sky. Perhaps ancient farmers used this as a sign to start planting their crops. As winter approaches, Orion returns.

As Earth revolves around the Sun, Orion comes into view in winter and disappears from view in spring.

Discussion
Starter

1 Why are the stars a reliable way to tell time and predict the seasons?

2 How could ancient travelers have used the constellations to set their courses?

*inter***NET** CONNECTION To learn more about stars and seasons, visit *www.mhschool.com/science* and enter the keyword **STARS.**

WHY IT MATTERS

The Moon is Earth's closest neighbor in space, but it is very different from Earth.

SCIENCE WORDS

satellite an object that orbits another, larger object in space

phase apparent change in the Moon's shape

crater a hollow area in the ground

Exploring the Moon

How did the Moon look the last time you saw it? Although the Moon is in the sky each day, it doesn't always look the same. Sometimes the Moon is a full circle, and sometimes it is a thin slice. Why does the Moon seem to change shape? How does it happen?

EXPLORE

HYPOTHESIZE You know that the Moon does not always look the same. Can a sphere look like a different shape without actually changing its shape? Write a hypothesis in your *Science Journal.*

Investigate How the Moon's Shape Changes

Use a model to investigate how a sphere can appear to change its shape.

MATERIALS
- lamp
- white volleyball
- *Science Journal*

PROCEDURES

1. OBSERVE Look closely at the ball from your seat. Draw the ball in your *Science Journal*.

2. Next turn off the classroom lights. Turn on the lamp and shine it on one side of the ball. Draw the shape of the ball where the light is hitting it.

3. COMMUNICATE Share your drawing with the rest of the class.

4. INFER Compare all the drawings. What do you think caused the different shapes?

CONCLUDE AND APPLY

1. COMPARE How did the ball look when you first observed it? How did it look in the darkened room?

2. COMPARE How did your drawing compare with those of your classmates?

GOING FURTHER: Apply

3. DRAW CONCLUSIONS How did the round ball appear to be a different shape without really changing its shape?

How Does the Moon's Shape Change?

The Explore Activity showed that a sphere, like the ball, can appear to have different shapes. The position of the ball and the position of the light made the ball seem to change shape.

The Moon, like a ball, is a sphere. Just like a ball, the shape the Moon appears to be depends on its position. The Moon changes position as it revolves around Earth in an orbit. The Moon is a **satellite** (sat′ə līt′) of the Earth. A satellite is anything that orbits another larger object in space.

PHASES OF THE MOON

As the Moon orbits Earth, one side is always lit. As the Moon changes position, different parts of its lighted side are seen from Earth.

Sun's rays light the Moon

New Moon

READING N DIAGRAMS

1. **WRITE** When can you see half-moon shapes?
2. **DISCUSS** How much light do the full Moon and the half Moon reflect? Draw a picture of each to show what it might look like outdoors.

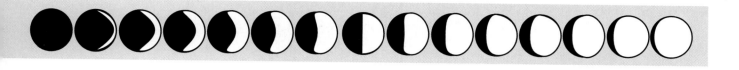

As the Moon orbits Earth, your view of it changes. Your changing view of the Moon is called the Moon's **phases** (fāzəz). The Moon's phases are the apparent changes in the Moon's shape. The Moon passes through all of its different phases once about every 29 days. Then the phases repeat. The four main phases of the Moon are new Moon, first quarter, full Moon, and last quarter.

Have you seen the Moon in each phase shown in the picture? In which phase was the Moon last night?

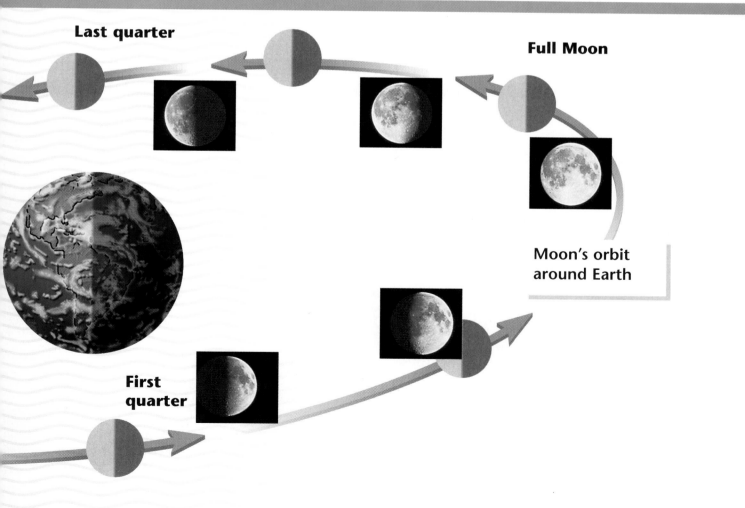

Last quarter

Full Moon

Moon's orbit around Earth

First quarter

207

What Is the Moon Like?

Take a good look at a full Moon. Do you see its rocky surface? In most places the Moon's surface is covered by a layer of dust. The Moon has high mountain peaks, large flat plains, and trillions of **craters** (krā'tərz). A crater is a hollow area, or pit, in the ground.

Some of the Moon's craters may have been formed by ancient volcanoes. Most, however, were caused by chunks of rock or metal from space that crashed into the Moon. Some of the Moon's craters are very large. Others are quite small.

The Moon does not give off any light of its own. It appears to shine because of the light it reflects. We see the Moon because it reflects the light of the Sun.

You may be surprised to learn that the Moon is both very hot and very cold. On the side of the Moon facing the Sun, it is much hotter than it is any place on Earth. On the side facing away from the Sun, it is much colder than it is any place on Earth.

LINK SCIENCE

Direct Rays of the Sun

Sun

Moon

Reflected light

The Moon reflects light from the Sun to Earth.

Earth

Large and small craters cover the Moon's rocky surface.

Skill: Predicting

USING PATTERNS

Rachel observed the Moon on different days over one month. She drew her observations on this calendar. There were some days she did not observe the Moon. Can you predict the shape of the Moon on the days she did not observe?

MATERIALS
- markers
- *Science Journal*

PROCEDURES

1. OBSERVE Study the drawings Rachel made of her observations of the Moon.

2. Look for similar shapes and patterns of the Moon.

CONCLUDE AND APPLY

1. PREDICT What do you think the Moon's shape was on Wednesday, September 9th? Compare it to the shape of the Moon on the 8th and the 11th. Draw your prediction.

2. COMPARE AND CONTRAST What was the Moon's shape on Friday, September 25th? Compare it to the shape of the Moon on the 24th and the 26th. Draw the shape of the Moon.

3. PREDICT Draw the shape of the Moon you would expect to see on the 29th. What helped you decide on that shape?

4. COMMUNICATE What helps you predict Moon shapes? What do you need to know to predict the shape of tomorrow's Moon?

SEPTEMBER calendar showing Moon observations for each day.

How Are Earth and the Moon Different?

Both Earth and the Moon are spheres that rotate and revolve. They also receive light from the Sun. In most ways, however, Earth and the Moon are quite different.

Earth is almost four times as wide as the Moon. The Moon has less mass than Earth. Since the Moon has less mass than Earth, it has less gravity. The Moon's gravity is about $\frac{1}{6}$ of Earth's gravity. If you weigh 60 pounds on Earth, you would weigh only 10 pounds on the Moon!

Craters cover most of the Moon's surface. Earth has few craters. Most objects from space burn up before they reach Earth. An object from space can create a lot of friction when it enters the air surrounding Earth. Friction creates heat—so the object burns up. Earth's air and water also cause craters on Earth to erode, or wear away. The Moon has no air.

Water is found in many places on Earth. It is in the air, rivers, lakes, and seas. Water is also found in the ground. The Moon has no liquid water. Water is needed by all living things. Since the Moon has no air or liquid water, scientists believe there is no life on the Moon. Astronauts were able to visit the Moon because their spacesuits provided air and protection from the heat.

The U.S. *Apollo 11* astronauts landed on the Moon on July 20, 1969.

Brain Power

Astronauts visiting the Moon left footprints. How long do you think these footprints will last? Explain.

Earth provides you with things you need to survive, like water, air, and temperatures that aren't too hot or too cold. The Moon is Earth's nearest neighbor in space. Yet the Moon does not have what you need to survive. It is very hot in some places and very cold in others. The Moon doesn't have any liquid water or air.

This girl is working with spacecraft equipment at the United States Space Camp in Huntsville, Alabama.

REVIEW

1. What shape is the Moon? Why does it appear to change shape?

2. Explain what the term "a phase of the Moon" means. Identify the four main phases.

3. Why does the Moon appear to shine?

4. PREDICT Last night it was a new Moon. What will the next main phase be?

5. CRITICAL THINKING *Evaluate* Why is there no life on the Moon?

WHY IT MATTERS THINK ABOUT IT
Suppose you are an astronaut standing on the Moon. You look up, straight down, and behind you. How would what you see be different from what you see on Earth?

WHY IT MATTERS WRITE ABOUT IT
Describe what you think it would be like to live on the Moon. What things would you need that the Moon does not provide? How would you get those things?

READING SKILL Why does the Moon have craters? Write a paragraph that explains the cause and the effect.

MOON TIME

Iroquois Calendar

Have you ever used the Moon to keep track of time? For thousands of years, other people have. They watched a full Moon slowly change into a half moon, then into a sliver. They noticed that the same shapes reappeared every 29 or 30 days. They thought the different shapes were a great way to tell time!

Different cultures around the world had lunar, or Moon, calendars. The Babylonians, Egyptians, Chinese, and Jews divided the year into 12 months. (The word *month* comes from the word *moon*.) This made a year no more than 360 days. That was a problem, because it takes Earth $365\frac{1}{4}$ days to orbit the Sun! The seasons started on a set day and month. With a lunar calendar, the year ended five days early!

Science, Technology, and Society

Different cultures solved the problem differently. The Babylonians added two months seven times within every 19-year period. The Jews added 7 months during every 19-year period. The Egyptians added five days to the end of the year. The Chinese added an extra month every now and then!

Native American Iroquois used a turtle shell as a calendar. It was also based on the Moon. A year had 13 months, each marked on the turtle's shell. Every month had 28 days, marked on the outside of the shell. Each month had a special Iroquois name.

Jewish Calendar

Roman Calendar

DISCUSSION STARTER

1. Why is the Moon a good way to keep track of time?

2. How many days were in the Iroquois year? Would this match the seasons? Why or why not?

To learn more about telling time by the Moon, visit *www.mhschool.com/science* and enter the keyword CALENDAR.

*inter*NET CONNECTION

WHY IT MATTERS

The positions of Earth, the Sun, and the Moon can result in some exciting sights in the sky!

SCIENCE WORDS

eclipse when one object passes into the shadow of another object

solar eclipse when the Moon's shadow blocks the Sun

lunar eclipse when Earth's shadow blocks the Moon

Earth, Sun, and Moon

There is a colorful hot-air balloon high in the sky. Up there it looks like it's the same size as a toy balloon. How can something so big look so small? To find out, try this:

Put a pencil on the floor. Stand back and close one eye. Use your thumb and finger to "measure" the pencil. Then lean down and compare your measurement with the real size of the pencil. What happened? Why?

EXPL RE

HYPOTHESIZE The Sun and the Moon appear to be the same size in the sky. One is actually larger. Why do you think they look the same size? Write a hypothesis in your *Science Journal*.

Investigate the Sizes of the Sun and the Moon

Use a model to investigate why the Sun and the Moon appear to be the same size in the sky.

MATERIALS

- notched index card
- meter tape or stick
- 1-inch styrofoam ball, 2-inch styrofoam ball, 3-inch styrofoam ball
- *Science Journal*

PROCEDURES

1. MEASURE Place the 1-inch and 3-inch balls in a line across a table 10 cm from the edge. Bend down so that your eyes are at table-top level. Look at the balls through the notch in the index card. How do their sizes compare? Write your observations in your *Science Journal*.

2. EXPERIMENT Place the 1-inch ball at the edge of the table. Move the 3-inch ball back on the table until it appears to be the same size as the 1-inch ball.

3. PREDICT Where would you have to place the 2-inch ball so that its size appears to be the same as the other balls? Test your prediction.

CONCLUDE AND APPLY

1. EXPLAIN What did you observe as each ball moved farther from your eyes?

2. IDENTIFY Where did you place the 2-inch ball so that it seemed to be the same size as the others?

GOING FURTHER: Apply

3. INFER The Sun and the Moon appear to be the same size in the sky. The Sun is much farther from Earth than the Moon. Are the Sun and the Moon really the same size? Why does it look that way?

Are the Sun and the Moon the Same Size?

The Explore Activity shows that the farther away an object is, the smaller it looks. The Sun and the Moon are both very large. Since they are so far away, they look like they are the size of basketballs in the sky.

The Moon and the Sun also seem to be about the same size, but they are not. The Sun is enormous. It is nearly 400 times wider than the Moon. Just like the balls in the Explore Activity, the Sun and the Moon appear to be the same size because the Sun is so much farther away from Earth than the Moon.

MATH LINK

Brain Power

How could you draw a circle that represents the size of the Sun compared to the Moon and Earth shown below? You would need a square piece of paper that is 600 cm on each side! You might make a square this size with tape on the classroom floor. A circle drawn just inside this square would be the right size.

1 This circle represents the size of the Moon.

2 The size of Earth is shown by this circle.

QUICK LAB

It's Farther Than You Think!

HYPOTHESIZE How can you model the distance from Earth to the Sun? Write a hypothesis in your *Science Journal.*

PROCEDURES

1. Make signs with the construction paper. Write "Earth" on one sign, "Moon" on another, and "Sun" on the third.

2. MEASURE Have one person hold the sign labeled "Earth." Another person will hold the Sun sign 75 m away from the Earth sign. Have someone hold the Moon sign 19 cm away from the Earth sign.

3. OBSERVE Look at the distances between the Sun, Earth, and the Moon. Change positions so everyone gets a chance to observe the model.

CONCLUDE AND APPLY

COMPARE How do the Sun and the Moon compare in their distance from Earth?

Sun

MATERIALS
- construction paper, $4\frac{1}{2}''$ x 6"
- markers
- meter tape
- *Science Journal*

NATIONAL GEOGRAPHIC

FUNtastic Facts

If you traveled at a speed of 100 miles an hour, it would take you 3 days to circle the Moon. It would take 10 days to circle Earth. It would take 3 years to circle the Sun! Why? How fast does a rocket travel in space?

217

Does the Moon Have a Shadow?

The Moon is always orbiting Earth. Together, Earth and the Moon are always orbiting the Sun. As the Moon and Earth orbit the Sun, their positions change. Sometimes the Moon passes between Earth and the Sun. When this happens the Moon blocks the light from the Sun. The Moon's shadow falls on Earth. A shadow is a dark area made when light rays are blocked by a person or an object.

The Moon always has a shadow. However, you see its shadow only when it falls on Earth during an **eclipse** (i klips′). An eclipse occurs when one object passes into the shadow of another object.

The photo above shows the movement of the Moon across the Sun during a solar eclipse.

Sun

Moon

Earth

Moon's shadow

Moon's orbit

As the Moon passes between the Sun and Earth, a **solar eclipse** (sō′lər i klips′) occurs. The word *solar* means sun.

218

Even though the Moon is much smaller than the Sun, it can completely hide the Sun. This is because from Earth, the Moon and the Sun appear the same size. To see the Sun completely covered by the Moon you must be in the part of Earth where the Moon's shadow falls.

Sometimes the Earth is between the Moon and the Sun. At these times the Moon passes into Earth's shadow. A **lunar eclipse** (lü′nər i klips′) occurs when the Full Moon moves into Earth's shadow. The word *lunar* means moon. To see a lunar eclipse you must be on the side of Earth facing the Moon.

When Earth is directly between the Moon and the Sun, a lunar eclipse occurs.

Earth →

Earth's shadow

Moon

READING ⋀ DIAGRAMS

1. **DISCUSS** How are the Sun, the Moon, and Earth lined up during a lunar eclipse?
2. **REPRESENT** What might it be like outdoors during a solar eclipse?

What Is a Partial Solar Eclipse?

When the Sun, the Moon, and Earth line up just right, a total solar eclipse occurs. During a total solar eclipse, the Moon completely blocks out the Sun. The part of Earth in the Moon's shadow gets so dark that some animals think it's night.

Sometimes, Earth, the Sun, and the Moon are just slightly out of line with each other. At these times only part of the Moon's shadow falls on Earth. When only part of the Sun is blocked by the Moon, a partial solar eclipse occurs. The word partial means not complete. During a partial solar eclipse, part of the Sun is blocked by the Moon. Part of the Sun is visible.

There are total and partial eclipses of the Moon, too. During a partial lunar eclipse, part of the Moon is darkened by Earth's shadow. There is a part of the Moon that is brightly visible. The Moon doesn't become completely dark in most lunar eclipses.

An eclipse is an exciting event. If either the Sun or the Moon were a different size than it is, or a different distance from Earth, eclipses wouldn't happen as they now do.

REVIEW

1. If the Moon were closer to Earth than it is, would it appear larger or smaller? How do you know?

2. How do the Moon and the Sun compare in size? Why do they appear to be the same size?

3. How is a solar eclipse different from a lunar eclipse?

4. COMMUNICATE Draw a picture to show the difference between a total eclipse and a partial eclipse.

5. CRITICAL THINKING *Analyze* If the Moon were much smaller than it is, could a total solar eclipse occur? Why or why not?

WHY IT MATTERS THINK ABOUT IT What if the Sun and Earth were farther apart? How might the Sun look in the sky?

WHY IT MATTERS WRITE ABOUT IT If the Sun or the Moon were a different size, eclipses would not occur as they do now. What else might be different?

EXPLAINING

Ancient people were fascinated by eclipses. No one knew why they happened. Different cultures made up stories to try to explain eclipses.

In China, a solar eclipse was first described in 2134 B.C. The Chinese thought a dragon was eating the Sun. To scare away the dragon, people made lots of noise. Then in the 1800s, the Chinese navy began to shoot guns at the dragon during eclipses!

Tales from other cultures also included a wild animal that caused eclipses. The Vikings and some Native Americans told of a dog or wolf that bit or attacked the Sun or Moon. Other ancient people told of an attacker that was a snake or jaguar. When the Moon was red, some ancient people thought it was bleeding.

Ancient people in the Far North told a different tale. They said the Sun and Moon left the sky during eclipses to see how everything was going on Earth!

On the South Pacific island of Tahiti, people used to smile during an eclipse. They liked seeing the Moon and Sun together. People believed that the Moon and Sun were making more stars!

Language Arts Link

ECLIPSES

DISCUSSION STARTER

1. Why did people make up stories about eclipses?

2. Why do you think ancient people thought wild animals caused eclipses?

To learn more about eclipses, visit *www.mhschool.com/science* and enter the keyword ECLIPSE.

*inter*NET
CONNECTION

SCIENCE WORDS

axis p.197

crater p.208

eclipse p.218

lunar eclipse p.219

orbit p.198

phase p.207

revolve p.198

rotate p.196

satellite p.206

solar eclipse p.218

USING SCIENCE WORDS

Number a paper from 1 to 10. Fill in 1 to 5 with words from the list above.

1. A real or imaginary straight line through the center of an object around which the object turns is the ___?___.

2. Anything that orbits another larger object in space is a ___?___.

3. When the Sun is blocked by the Moon, there is a ___?___.

4. The path an object follows as it revolves is an ___?___.

5. When the reflected light from the Moon is blocked by Earth, there is a ___?___.

6–10. Pick five words from the list above that were not used in 1 to 5 and use each word in a sentence.

UNDERSTANDING SCIENCE IDEAS

11. Why do we have day and night on Earth?

12. What would you see during a solar eclipse?

USING IDEAS AND SKILLS

13. **READING SKILL: CAUSE AND EFFECT** Explain the cause of a lunar eclipse.

14. **PREDICT** If the Moon was in its first quarter last night, what would the next main phase be?

15. **THINKING LIKE A SCIENTIST** What if the Moon had air and liquid water? What might this mean?

PROBLEMS and PUZZLES

Land of the Midnight Sun
Some boys and girls live where they have almost 24 hours of daylight in the summer and almost 24 hours of darkness in the winter. Where do you think they live?

CHAPTER 8

THE SUN AND ITS PLANETS

In addition to the Sun, Earth, and the Moon, there are other bodies in space. You may know some of them already. On a clear night, you may see some of these bodies. As you learned in the last chapter, Earth and the Moon orbit the Sun. In this chapter you will learn about other bodies that orbit the Sun.

In Chapter 8, you will have many opportunities to summarize what you have read. Summarizing will help you to remember the most

WHY IT MATTERS

The Sun's energy affects you every day.

SCIENCE WORDS

star a hot sphere of gases that gives off energy

planet a satellite of the Sun

sunspot a dark area on the Sun's surface

corona outermost layer of gases surrounding the Sun

fuel something burned to provide heat or power

Here Comes the Sun

What difference would it make if the Sun were larger or smaller than it is? Every day you see how the Sun brightens the sky. Even though the Sun is far away, you can see and feel its energy. How does the energy from the Sun affect Earth?

EXPLORE

HYPOTHESIZE Each day Earth receives light and heat from the Sun. How does this affect Earth's temperature? Write a hypothesis in your *Science Journal*.

MATH LINK

Investigate How the Sun's Energy Affects Earth

Use a model to explore how the Sun's energy affects Earth's temperature.

MATERIALS

- lamp with light bulb, 60 watt
- aluminum can
- thermometer
- black paper
- meter stick
- tape
- *Science Journal*

PROCEDURES

1. MAKE A MODEL Cover the can with black paper. The can represents Earth. Place the thermometer in the can, and set the can on a table 20 cm from the lamp. The lamp represents the Sun.

2. COLLECT DATA Read the temperature inside the can. Record the number in your *Science Journal*.

3. COLLECT DATA Turn on the lamp. Record the temperature of the can every two minutes for 10 minutes.

CONCLUDE AND APPLY

1. IDENTIFY What was your first temperature measurement? What was the temperature after 10 minutes?

2. EXPLAIN Was the temperature of the can still increasing after 10 minutes? How do you know?

3. INFER Why did the temperature of the can stop increasing? Where do you think the energy from the lamp is going?

GOING FURTHER: Problem Solving

4. EXPERIMENT Suppose the can were twice as far from the lamp. How warm do you think it would get in 10 minutes? Write your prediction. Test it.

How Does the Sun's Energy Affect Earth?

The Sun is a **star** (stär). A star is a hot, glowing sphere of gases that gives off energy. Energy is what makes things move, heat up, or change in other ways. The Sun's energy reaches Earth in the form of heat and light. Earth is warmed by the Sun each day. Earth gets heat from the Sun and also *radiates* heat out into space. Radiate means to spread around. The Explore Activity shows that when objects reach a certain temperature, they give off as much heat as they get.

The Sun is only a medium-sized star. It looks larger than any other star because it is the closest star to Earth. We see other stars as tiny points of light in the night sky. Even stars larger than the Sun appear very small. This is because these stars are much farther away.

The Sun has a lot of mass. Since the Sun is so massive, the pull of its gravity is strong. The Sun's gravity pulls Earth toward the Sun. Earth is a **planet** (plan' it). A planet is a satellite of the Sun. Earth is just one of nine planets orbiting the Sun. The Sun's gravity pulls on each of the planets. The motion of each planet keeps the planet from falling into the Sun.

Sun ←

Brain Power

The Sun is very far away, but you still see its light and feel its heat. What does this tell you about the amount of energy the Sun gives off?

How Hot and Bright Is the Sun?

The Sun is very hot and bright because its gases have a lot of energy. It is hundreds of times hotter on the Sun than it is any place on Earth. You should never look directly at the Sun. It is far too bright and may injure your eyes.

Scientists have found that the Sun is hotter in the center than at its surface. Some parts of the surface are not as hot as others. These cooler parts appear as **sunspots** (sun'spot'z). A sunspot is a dark area on the Sun's surface. Many sunspots are larger than Earth. The number of sunspots changes from time to time. There may be fewer than 10 or more than 100.

The surface of the Sun is surrounded by thin, hot gases. These gases are a beautiful reddish-pink color. During a total solar eclipse, you can see the Sun's **corona** (kə rō'nə). The corona is the outermost layer of the thin gases around the Sun. *Corona* means "crown" in Spanish.

Sunspot

Sunspots look small, but many are larger than Earth!

Can you see the crown shape of the Sun's corona?

The distance across the Sun is more than 100 times the distance across Earth.

Earth

229

How Do We Use the Sun's Energy?

Light and heat from the Sun are Earth's main sources of energy. This energy is always available. The Sun will produce light and heat for billions of years.

Much of the energy we use comes from **fuels** (fu'əlz). A fuel is something burned to provide heat or power. Have you ever built a campfire? Wood is a fuel. When you burn wood, you release energy. The energy came from the Sun and was stored in the trees.

Coal, oil, and gas are other fuels. They were formed from plants and animals that lived long ago. These plants and animals used the Sun's energy, just as living things use it today. When we burn these fuels today, we are using stored energy that originally came from the Sun.

LIFE LINK SCIENCE

Our food supply depends on the Sun. Green plants need sunlight to grow and make food. Many animals eat plants. Other animals eat plant-eating animals. Both plants and animals provide food for people.

READING DIAGRAMS

DISCUSS Why is our food supply dependent on the Sun's energy?

What Is a Solar Storm?

Giant storms occur on the Sun. They often occur at the sunspots, where gases explode into hot, bright flares. Flares give off lots of energy. Solar flares are called solar storms.

At times fiery ribbons and loops of gases rise from the Sun's surface and move into its corona. They are called prominences (prom'ə nənsəz). Prominences are like giant fireworks, and all of them are larger than Earth. They may shoot off at speeds of more than 500 miles in a single second. Some stretch out nearly 1,000,000 miles into space.

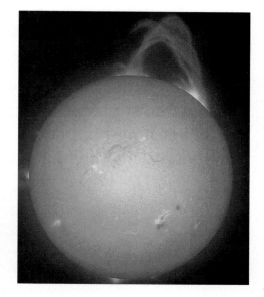

Solar flares can make compasses show wrong directions on Earth.

Compare the Sun and the Moon

HYPOTHESIZE How are the Sun and the Moon alike? How are they different? Write a hypothesis in your *Science Journal.*

MATERIALS
• *Science Journal*

PROCEDURES

1. With your partner, list as many facts as you can about the Sun and the Moon.

2. **IDENTIFY** Separate the things that are similar about the Sun and the Moon from the things that are different.

CONCLUDE AND APPLY

COMMUNICATE Organize your facts into a chart comparing the Sun and the Moon. Illustrate your chart.

When the Sun is shining, you are probably outside enjoying many different activities. A sunny day puts most people in a good mood. Energy from the Sun is stored in plants and trees. Without the Sun there would be no life on Earth.

Do you enjoy spending time outside on a sunny day?

REVIEW

1. What would happen to Earth if it did not move around the Sun?

2. What is the Sun like?

3. What causes solar storms?

4. **COMMUNICATE** Where does much of the energy we use on Earth come from? Draw a diagram to illustrate your answer.

5. **CRITICAL THINKING** *Apply* Suppose the Sun were closer to Earth than it now is. What effect would this change in distance have on Earth?

WHY IT MATTERS THINK ABOUT IT
How would Earth be different if it received more sunlight than it already does?

WHY IT MATTERS WRITE ABOUT IT
How would more hours of daylight affect some of the things you do each day? What would you like about longer days? What would you dislike about them?

SUN POWER

Need energy? Then look to the Sun. It offers free energy and you can even store some for a "rainy day!"

Some of the Sun's energy is stored in fuels. Food is fuel for our bodies. Vegetables use the Sun's energy to grow. Some energy is passed on to us as we eat them.

The Sun's energy is also stored in gasoline and coal. The stored energy in gas can make a car move. The stored energy in coal can provide heat.

Solar cells use the Sun's energy to make electricity. Small solar cells run watches or calculators. Unlike chemical batteries, solar cells can easily recharge themselves in light!

DISCUSSION STARTER

1. Why is solar power useful in outer space?

2. Could solar cells be used to power machines in a mine? Explain.

To learn more about solar energy, visit **www.mhschool.com/science** and enter the keyword SOLAR.

*inter*NET CONNECTION

WHY IT MATTERS

Each of the nine planets orbiting the Sun is very different from Earth.

SCIENCE WORDS

solar system the Sun and all the objects that orbit the Sun

atmosphere a layer of gases surrounding a planet

telescope tool that gathers light to make faraway objects appear closer

lens a curved piece of glass

Looking at the Inner Planets

Long ago people gazing at the night sky saw something strange happen. A few of the points of light seemed to wander among the other points. What were these "wanderers?" They were planets.

The photographs show the planet Venus and several stars as they appear in the night sky at different times. What changes do you see?

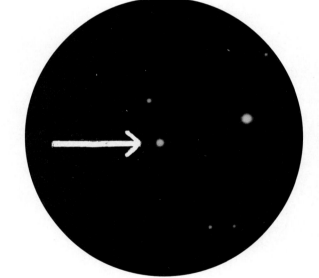

EXPLORE

HYPOTHESIZE You know that the Moon appears to change shape as it moves around Earth. You can observe other changes in the night sky, too—like the position of the planets. Why don't you see the planets in the same place every night? Write a hypothesis in your *Science Journal*.

Investigate How Planets Move

Use a model to investigate the motion of the planets.

PROCEDURES

1. MAKE A MODEL The class will be divided into two groups. The first group will model the motion of the planets around the Sun. The second group will observe. Then the second group will model and the first group will observe.

2. OBSERVE Listen to the student who is modeling Earth. He or she will share with the class what can be seen from Earth in the night sky. Record your observations in your *Science Journal*.

CONCLUDE AND APPLY

1. COMPARE Which planets were visible from Earth the first time you modeled the motions of the planets? Which planets were visible from Earth the second time?

2. EXPLAIN How did Earth's motion affect which planets could be seen from Earth? How did the motion of the other planets affect which planets could be seen from Earth?

3. DRAW CONCLUSIONS Why does the position of the planets in the night sky change?

GOING FURTHER: Apply

4. PREDICT What would happen if you had moved faster around the Sun? If you had moved more slowly?

MATERIALS

- sign for each planet
- 2 signs for the Sun
- *Science Journal*

How Do Planets Move?

The Explore Activity showed how planets orbit the Sun. The model that was made was a model of the **solar system** (sō'lər sis'təm). The solar system is a system made up of the Sun and all of the objects that orbit the Sun.

Earth is one of nine planets that orbit the Sun. Each planet is a different size. Some are smaller than Earth, and some are larger. Each planet rotates on an axis and revolves around the Sun at a different distance. Here is the order of the planets from the Sun: Mercury, Venus, Earth, Mars, Jupiter, Saturn, Uranus, Neptune, and Pluto. This sentence may help you remember the order: My Very Excellent Mother Just Served Us Nine Pizzas.

Some of the planets close to Earth can be seen in the night sky. As these planets move in their orbits, and Earth moves in its own orbit, the position of the planets in the night sky changes.

Stars and planets look very much alike in the night sky. How can you tell them apart? Stars give off their own light. As the light from a star comes through Earth's air, it appears to twinkle.

Like the Moon, planets have no light of their own. They reflect sunlight. If you observe the night sky, you can see the planets change position. (Look back at the pictures on page 234.) The name *planet* comes from a word meaning "wanderer."

Outer Planets

Uranus

Pluto

Neptune

THE NINE PLANETS REVOLVE AROUND THE SUN

Inner Planets
Sun
Earth
Mercury
Venus
Mars
Jupiter
Saturn

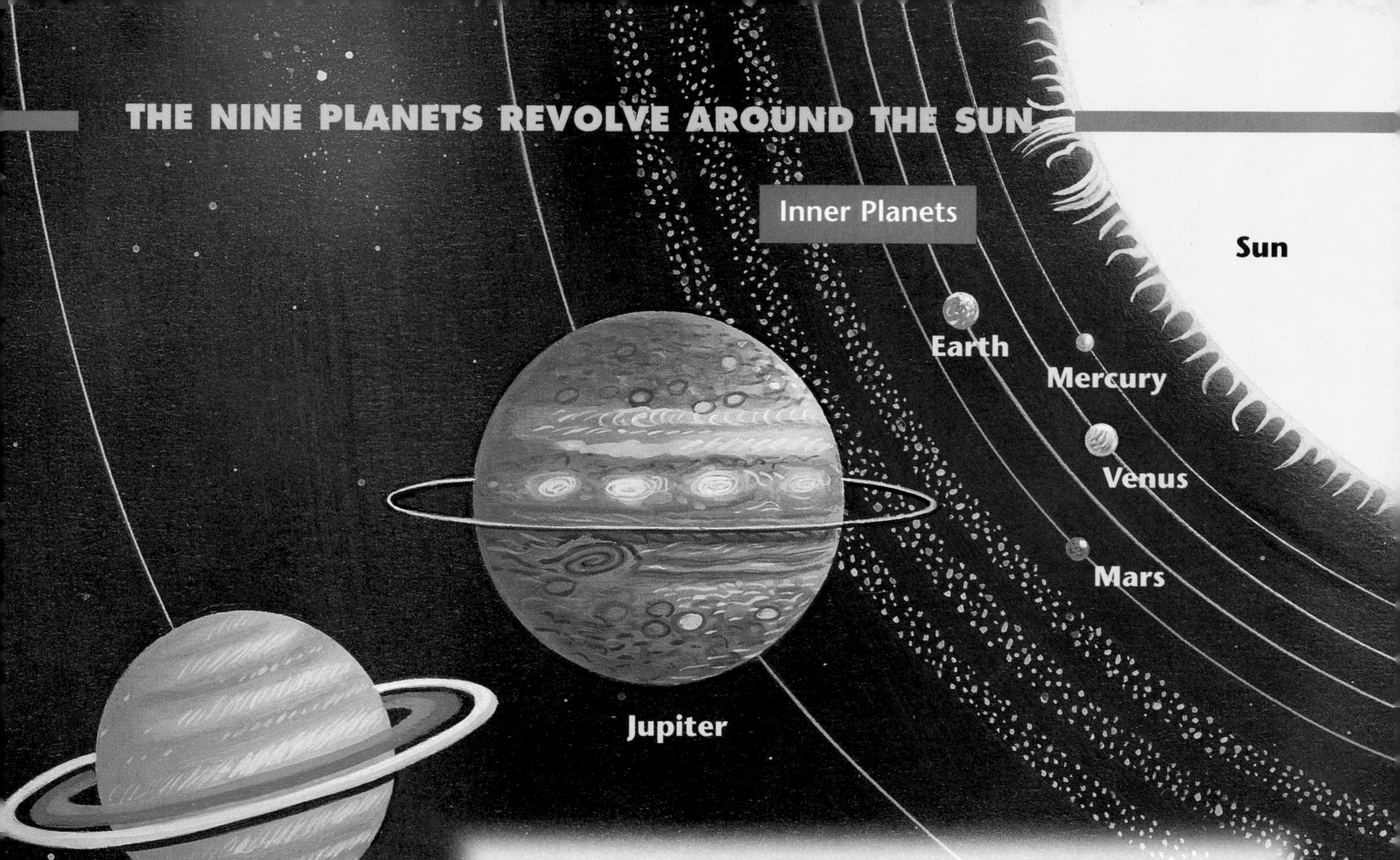

Planets appear to wander through the sky. Each planet moves in a different orbit, and at a different speed. The planets are always moving and changing positions.

The planets are divided into two groups: the inner planets and the outer planets. The inner planets are the four planets closest to the Sun: Mercury, Venus, Earth, and Mars. The other five planets are known as outer planets.

The inner planets are similar in several ways. They are all rather small and made up of solid, rock-like materials. The inner planets are closer to the Sun than the outer planets. The inner planets are also much warmer.

READING DIAGRAMS

1. WRITE Which planets are closest to Earth? Which planets are farthest from Earth?

Mercury is the closest planet to the Sun.

What Is It Like on Mercury and Venus?

Mercury, the planet closest to the Sun, is less than half the size of Earth. It takes Mercury 88 days to orbit the Sun. Mercury does not have much of an **atmosphere** (at'məs fir'). An atmosphere is a layer of gases that surrounds most planets. Not only does Mercury not have much air, it also does not have any water. Mercury is very hot on the side facing the Sun. It is very cold on the side facing away from the Sun.

No one has visited Mercury, but scientists have sent space probes to visit the planet. A space probe is a spacecraft designed to gather information in space. Photographs taken by the space probes show that Mercury's surface is covered with craters.

Venus is the second planet from the Sun. Venus is only slightly smaller than Earth. It has been called Earth's twin because of its size, but Venus is very different from Earth!

It takes about 225 days for Venus to complete its orbit around the Sun. Like Mercury, Venus has no water. However, Venus does have an atmosphere. Its atmosphere is made up mostly of carbon dioxide. This gas makes the air very thick. It traps heat, making Venus the hottest planet in the solar system.

Space probes have visited Venus many times. Photographs of the surface show features such as mountains and canyons.

What Is It Like on Earth and Mars?

Earth is the third planet from the Sun. It is the only planet known to have living things. Earth's atmosphere keeps it from getting very hot or very cold. Earth has water. Earth also has oxygen in its atmosphere. These things help support life.

Do you remember that Earth completes one revolution around the Sun every 365 days? The Moon is Earth's only satellite.

Mars, the fourth planet from the Sun, has two moons. Mars is about half as wide as Earth, and it takes about two years to orbit the Sun.

Mars has a thin atmosphere made up mostly of carbon dioxide. Strong winds create large dust storms. With its reddish surface, Mars is known as "the red planet." Craters and volcanoes that are no longer active cover most of its surface. One of the volcanoes is the highest known mountain in the solar system. It is more than 15 miles high!

Mars has some water, but most of it is frozen ice.

This photo shows the view of Earth from the surface of the Moon.

How Do We Learn About Space?

The Sun, the Moon, and planets are very far away. How do scientists learn about them? One tool they use is a **telescope** (tel′ə skōp′). A telescope is a tool that gathers light to make faraway objects appear larger, closer, and clearer. Telescopes gather light with mirrors and **lenses** (lenzəz). A lens is a curved piece of glass.

Make a Letter Larger

HYPOTHESIZE How does the shape of lenses change how objects look? Write a hypothesis in your *Science Journal.*

PROCEDURES

1. Lay the newspaper flat and cover it with wax paper. Tape the wax paper down over the newspaper.

2. **OBSERVE** Put a small drop of water over a printed letter. How does the print look under the water drop?

3. **EXPERIMENT** Put water drops of different sizes over other letters. Look at the shape of each letter.

MATERIALS
- dropper
- water
- paper cup
- newspaper
- wax paper
- masking tape
- *Science Journal*

CONCLUDE AND APPLY

1. **COMPARE** Are big drops and small drops of water shaped the same? How does the size of the drop affect the way the print looks?

2. **INFER** How do you think the curved lens in a telescope might be like the drop of water on the wax paper?

The solar system is Earth's "family" in space. Since early times people have wanted to know more about the other planets. Today, telescopes and space probes tell us more about them. Do you like to look at the stars and planets at night? Now you know how to tell which objects are stars and which are planets!

Brain Power

Besides telescopes, what other uses of lenses can you think of?

With a telescope, you can observe the stars and some planets.

REVIEW

1. What is the solar system?

2. Name the nine planets in the solar system. Why do we see them in different places at different times?

3. People sometimes say that Venus is Earth's twin. Is this a good way to describe Venus?

4. **COMMUNICATE** How are Mercury and Mars different?

5. **CRITICAL THINKING** *Evaluate* How would life be different without the telescope?

WHY IT MATTERS THINK ABOUT IT
Describe the four inner planets. How are they similar? How are they different?

WHY IT MATTERS WRITE ABOUT IT
What if you were to go on a trip through space? What tools would you take with you? What would you see as you pass by Mercury, Earth, Venus, and Mars?

EYES ON MARS

Look up at the sky on a clear night. Even without a telescope, you can spot Mars. It's a bright, red point of light. With powerful telescopes, scientists can see Mars's mountains, large plains, and polar ice caps.

For years people have wondered if there was life on Mars. Space exploration has let us see Mars up close and personal and look for signs of life.

Science, Technology, and Society

In 1964, the U.S. launched the space probe *Mariner 4*. It was the first to fly by and send back to Earth images of Mars. Since then, space probes have sent back thousands of pictures of the red planet. None showed signs of life, but scientists were surprised to see giant volcanoes and dry canyons. Did the canyons mean that water had once flowed on Mars?

In 1976, the U. S. celebrated its 200th birthday and landed two spacecraft on Mars. Both *Viking 1* and *2* took pictures of the rocky plains around the landing sites. Again, there was no evidence of life on Mars.

On July 4, 1997, the U.S. spacecraft *Pathfinder* landed on Mars. Aboard was *Sojourner,* a robot on wheels that could travel to rocks and report what they were made of. Scientists on Earth could choose a rock and send *Sojourner*

to make a close-up examination. The *Pathfinder* mission showed that Mars once had the water that could have made life possible!

The U.S. plans a Mars mission every two years. Will they find life? Stay tuned!

DISCUSSION STARTER

1. Why would finding water on Mars prove that there is or was life on the planet?

2. How was *Pathfinder* different from other space missions?

To learn more about Mars, visit *www.mhschool.com/science* and enter the keyword ONMARS.

*inter*NET
CONNECTION

WHY IT MATTERS

There is still much to be learned about the solar system.

SCIENCE WORDS

asteroid a small chunk of rock or metal that orbits the Sun

comet a body of ice and rock that orbits the Sun

Looking at the Outer Planets

What has a great red spot, 16 moons, and could swallow up hundreds of Earths? It's the fifth planet from the Sun and the largest planet in the whole solar system. It's the giant planet Jupiter! It's sometimes hard to get a good idea of how much larger one object is than another. Models can help.

EXPLORE

HYPOTHESIZE **How might you use a model to compare the volumes of Jupiter and Earth? Write a hypothesis in your** *Science Journal.*

Design Your Own Experiment

MATH LINK

WHAT IS THE VOLUME OF JUPITER?

PROCEDURES

1. If Earth had the volume of a bean, Jupiter would have the volume of the bowl.

2. **MAKE A MODEL** How can you estimate how much larger the volume of the bowl is than the volume of the bean?

3. **COMMUNICATE** Write your plan in your *Science Journal.* Share your plan with your teacher.

4. **EXPERIMENT** Try your plan.

MATERIALS
- 2 lb. bag of beans
- plastic bowl
- small cup
- *Science Journal*

CONCLUDE AND APPLY

1. **USE NUMBERS** How much greater is the volume of the bowl than the volume of the bean?

2. **DRAW CONCLUSIONS** How much greater is the volume of Jupiter than the volume of Earth?

GOING FURTHER:
Apply

3. **INFER** How do the spaces between the beans in the bowl affect your estimate?

What Is the Volume of Jupiter?

The Explore Activity compared the volumes of Jupiter and Earth. Volume is the amount of space something takes up. You probably found that it would take more than 1,000 Earths put together to make a planet as large as Jupiter.

Scientists have measured the volumes of Earth and Jupiter, too. They have found that Jupiter's volume is 1,500 times greater than Earth's!

Jupiter is an outer planet. You learned that the outer planets are the five planets farthest from the Sun. In order, they are Jupiter, Saturn, Uranus, Neptune, and Pluto.

What Is Jupiter Like?

Jupiter is the largest planet in our solar system. It is the fifth planet from the Sun. The distance across Jupiter is 89,000 miles. Giant Jupiter takes about 12 years to orbit the Sun. It has 16 moons that scientists know about.

Jupiter is made up mostly of gases. It has a thick, cloudy atmosphere that hides its surface. The top of the atmosphere is very cold. Inside, Jupiter is hotter than the surface of the Sun. A photograph of Jupiter from space shows colorful bands of gases. One of Jupiter's special features is the Great Red Spot. Scientists think that the Great Red Spot is caused by a large, permanent storm. Jupiter is also surrounded by a thin ring of dust.

The Great Red Spot on Jupiter has been whirling around for 300 years!

Skill: Inferring

USING OBSERVATIONS TO EXPLAIN AN EVENT

Why does Jupiter's ring shine? In this activity you will make a model to show what happens when light shines on dust particles. You can use what you observe to suggest an explanation of why Jupiter's ring shines. When you suggest an explanation for an event based on observations you have made, you are inferring. To infer means to form an idea from facts or observations.

MATERIALS
- flashlight
- newspaper
- plastic bottle of cornstarch
- safety goggles
- *Science Journal*

PROCEDURES

 SAFETY: Wear goggles.

1. Place the flashlight on the edge of a table. Cover the area below the table with newspaper. Darken the room.

2. **OBSERVE** Turn on the flashlight. What do you see? Record your observations in your *Science Journal*.

3. **OBSERVE** Holding the opened bottle of cornstarch below the beam of light, quickly squeeze the bottle. What do you see?

CONCLUDE AND APPLY

1. **COMPARE** How did the beam of light appear when you first observed it? How did it appear after you squeezed the cornstarch into it?

2. **INFER** Jupiter's ring is made up of dust particles. Why do you think Jupiter's ring shines?

247

Uranus is called the "sideways planet" because it rotates on its side.

What Are Saturn and Uranus Like?

Saturn is the second-largest planet in the solar system. It is the sixth planet from the Sun. Saturn is 74,500 miles across. Like Jupiter, Saturn is made up mostly of gases. Its thick atmosphere is very cold at the top. Looking from outer space, colorful bands of clouds can be seen. Saturn has 18 known moons! There may be even more.

Saturn is known for its beautiful rings. It has thousands of them! These rings are made up of pieces of ice and rock of all different sizes. It takes Saturn $29\frac{1}{2}$ years to complete one revolution around the Sun.

Uranus, the seventh planet from the Sun, is surrounded by a bluish fog. Uranus is so far away that it is difficult to see, even with a telescope. Like Jupiter and Saturn, Uranus is made up of gases.

Uranus is about 32,190 miles across, and it takes 84 years to orbit the Sun. It has at least 17 moons. Telescopes and photographs show that Uranus has 10 rings. It also has a very tilted axis.

Saturn is known for its thousands of beautiful rings. They are made up of different-sized bits of ice and rock that orbit the planet.

What Are Neptune and Pluto Like?

Neptune, the eighth planet from the Sun, is only slightly smaller than Uranus. It takes Neptune 165 years to orbit the Sun. Neptune has eight moons.

Neptune is another "gas giant." Its gases give it a blue-green color. The form and atmosphere of Neptune is similar to Uranus. It is very cold in its upper atmosphere, but very hot at its center. The planet had a Great Dark Spot, similar to Jupiter's Great Red Spot. It was caused by a large storm. Neptune also has an unusual white cloud. Like Jupiter, Saturn, and Uranus, it has rings.

Pluto is the ninth and farthest planet from the Sun. Only about 1,300 miles across, it is the smallest planet in the solar system. It takes Pluto more than 247 years to orbit the Sun. Pluto has one large moon.

Pluto is made up of a mixture of rocky materials and frozen gases. It has a thin atmosphere. Little is known about Pluto because it is so very far away.

Neptune is over 2 billion miles from Earth.

The distance across Pluto's moon is $\frac{1}{2}$ the distance across Pluto

Brain Power

You have learned many features of each of the outer planets. What features do they have in common? Make a chart that explains how the outer planets are alike and different.

What Other Objects Are in the Solar System?

Asteroids (as'tə roid'z) and **comets** (kom'itz) are also part of the solar system. An asteroid is a small chunk of rock or metal. A comet is a body of ice and bits of rock. Both asteroids and comets orbit the Sun.

Asteroids are like "little planets," and they come in all shapes and sizes. They range from a few miles across to several hundred miles across. There are thousands of asteroids. Most are found in the large space between Mars and Jupiter. This part of space is called the asteroid belt.

Comets move around the Sun in long, narrow orbits. They can be small or very large. When a comet passes close to the Sun, it becomes very warm. Some of its ice changes into gases. The solar wind pushes the gases out into a long tail. When a comet passes close to Earth, you can see its tail across the sky.

The appearance of Halley's Comet was first recorded more than 2,200 years ago. When will it appear next? Read page 252 to learn more.

More has been learned about the solar system in the last 50 years than ever before. There is still a lot that is not known, especially about the outer planets. New discoveries will be made by future astronauts and space scientists. Maybe you will be one of them!

Someday you may want to study the solar system.

REVIEW

1. How does the volume of Earth compare with the volume of Jupiter?

2. Why do Saturn's rings shine?

3. Name the other four outer planets. Choose one and describe its features.

4. **INFER** You know what causes the phases of Earth's Moon. Do you think there are phases of the moons of other planets? Explain.

5. **CRITICAL THINKING** *Apply* Suppose the outer planets were farther away from the Sun. How would this affect the planets' orbit around the Sun?

WHY IT MATTERS THINK ABOUT IT
Do you think you might like to be an astronaut or space scientist? What special skills would you need?

WHY IT MATTERS WRITE ABOUT IT
What would it be like to live in a space colony? Write a description of what you think life would be like there. Where might you go on vacation?

READING SKILL Write a summary of the features the outer planets have in common.

COMET
COME-BACK

This is a famous early picture of Halley's Comet. It is a tapestry that shows the comet in 1066.

Ever heard of "Halley's comet?" It's named for astronomer Edmond Halley. He was only 25 years old when he first saw the comet in 1682. He believed it was the same one people had reported in 1531 and 1607. Using Isaac Newton's laws of gravity, Halley predicted the comet would return in 1758 or 1759.

Astronomers eagerly awaited the comet. It appeared in 1758, as Halley had predicted. It crosses Earth's orbit about every 76 years.

Before there were cameras, people recorded Halley's comet in paintings. The first photos were taken in 1910. When the comet appeared in 1985, five spacecraft observed it. Perhaps when it comes in 2061, people on spacecraft will go for a closer look!

DISCUSSION STARTER

1. What helped Halley figure out when the comet would reappear?

2. What year did the Halley's comet appear between 1758 and 1910?

To learn more about Halley's comet, visit *www.mhschool.com/science* and enter the keyword HALLEY.

*inter*NET
CONNECTION

SCIENCE WORDS

asteroid p.250

atmosphere p.238

comet p.250

corona p.229

fuel p.230

planet p.228

solar system p.236

star p.228

sunspot p.229

telescope p.240

USING SCIENCE WORDS

Number a paper from 1 to 10. Fill in 1 to 5 with words from the list above.

1. A dark area on the Sun's surface is a __?__.

2. A small chunk of rock or metal that orbits the Sun is a(n) __?__.

3. A satellite of the Sun is called a __?__.

4. Something burned to provide heat or power is a __?__.

5. A tool that gathers light to make faraway objects appear larger, closer, and clearer is a __?__.

6–10. **Pick five words from the list above that were not used in 1 to 5 and use each word in a sentence.**

UNDERSTANDING SCIENCE IDEAS

11. In what form does the Sun's energy reach Earth? Why is the Sun's energy important to Earth?

12. What is the order of the planets from the Sun by distance?

USING IDEAS AND SKILLS

13. **READING SKILL: SUMMARIZE** Write a summary of important facts about Mars.

14. **INFER** How does the distance of a planet from the Sun affect the time it takes to orbit the Sun?

15. **THINKING LIKE A SCIENTIST** How might Earth be different if it received less energy from the Sun?

PROBLEMS and PUZZLES

Sun Block Danger! The Sun's rays can damage your eyes. One way to view the Sun carefully is to make a pinhole in a piece of black paper. Lay white paper on the ground. Move the black paper over the white paper until the Sun's image is clearly cast through the pinhole.

SCIENCE WORDS

asteroid p.250

√atmosphere p.238

√axis p.197

√comet p.250

√crater p.208

fuel p.230

√lunar eclipse p.219

orbit p.198

√phases p.207

√planets p.228

√satellite p.206

solar eclipse p.218

√sunspots p.229

√telescope p.240

USING SCIENCE WORDS

Number a paper from 1 to 10. Beside each number write the word or words that best completes the sentence.

√**1.** The path that the Moon takes as it travels around Earth is its ___?___. orbit

√**2.** Earth spins around an imaginary line called a(n) ___?___.

√**3.** When a meteorite slams into the Moon, it makes a hollow area called a(n) ___?___.

√**4.** A new moon and a full moon are two of the Moon's ___?___.

√**5.** When the Moon moves between Earth and the Sun, there is a(n) ___?___. Solar eclypse

√**6.** Mercury, Mars, and Pluto are three of the nine ___?___.

√**7.** Dark areas on the Sun are called ___?___.

√**8.** The tool that makes faraway objects seem closer is a(n) ___?___.

√**9.** The blanket of gases around a planet is called the planet's ___?___.

√**10.** Bodies of ice that orbit the Sun and have tails are called ___?___.

UNDERSTANDING SCIENCE IDEAS

Write 11 to 15. For each number write the letter for the best answer. You may wish to use the hints provided.

11. There are days and nights because
 a. the Sun rotates
 b. Earth revolves around the Sun
 c. Earth rotates
 d. the Moon revolves around the Sun

(Hint: Read page 196.)

12. Unlike Earth, the Moon
 a. has no gravity
 b. has no air
 c. has craters
 d. is a sphere

(Hint: Read page 210.)

13. A lunar eclipse happens when
 a. the Moon moves into Earth's shadow
 b. there is a new moon
 c. the Sun is between Earth and the Moon
 d. there is a new year

(Hint: Read page 219.)

14. How can you tell if an object in the night sky is a planet?
 a. It is bigger than any star
 b. It is red
 c. It twinkles at night
 d. It seems to move in the sky

(Hint: Read page 234.)

15. Halley's Comet orbits the Sun about once every
 a. 1,000 years
 b. 76 years
 c. 10 years
 d. day

(Hint: Read pages 250 and 252.)

USING IDEAS AND SKILLS

16.  **PREDICT** What would be different about summer and winter if Earth's axis were straight up and down instead of tilted?

17. Explain why there is no wind on the Moon.

18. Draw a diagram of a solar eclipse. Label the parts of your diagram.

THINKING LIKE A SCIENTIST

19. **INFER** You can see the gases that make up the tail of a comet when the comet passes near Earth. However, a comet's tail does not glow. How, then, are you able to see a comet's tail?

20. In what ways have you observed the Sun's energy in your everyday life?

WRITING IN YOUR JOURNAL

SCIENCE IN YOUR LIFE
List different kinds of fuel that come from plants. How do people use these fuels?

PRODUCT ADS
Name several things that you see advertised and sold in the summer but not in the winter. Pick one thing used in summer and tell why it is not used in the winter.

HOW SCIENTISTS WORK
Scientists use tools to help them observe things better. What tool discussed in this unit has helped scientists to understand planets? How has it helped?

Design your own Experiment

Earth is about four times wider than the Moon. How might you model the sizes of Earth and the Moon? Think safety first. Review your model with your teacher before you make it.

For help in reviewing this unit, visit www.mhschool.com/science

PROBLEMS and PUZZLES

Big Tilt

The tilt of Earth causes the four seasons. What would happen if Earth became even more tilted? The diagram shows what an "extra tilt" would look like. How do you think an extra tilt would affect Earth? Would an extra tilt cause summer to be cooler and winter warmer? Summer to be hotter and winter colder? No change? Explain your answer.

Earth's tilt now

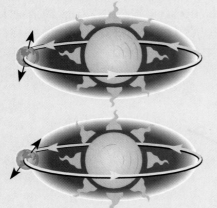

Extra tilt

Space Probe

Earth is sending a probe into space. You are part of the mission. Your job is to make a space capsule to send with the probe. The capsule contains information about Earth for anyone who finds the probe. You can write information for the space capsule or you can place real objects into a container. The capsule should include:

- where Earth is in the solar system
- who lives on Earth
- pictures of life forms from Earth
- important objects from Earth
- information about who you are

Solar System Mobiles

Use cardboard, markers, and yarn to make solar system mobiles that you can hang in your classroom. Draw, color, and cut out a model of each member of the solar system. Attach an information card below each model. Write information on the card.

Hang your models in order. Put the Sun in the center of the solar system.

Saturn: The Ringed Planet
6th planet from the Sun
Distance from the Sun: about 890 million miles
Distance across: 75,000 miles
One rotation: about 11 hours
One revolution: almost 30 years
Moons: at least 18

ROCKS AND RESOURCES

CHAPTER 9
THE CHANGING EARTH

Rocks are everywhere. They are on mountains and beaches. They are on the bottoms of rivers and at the bottom of oceans. Rocks have been around for a long time. Do rocks change? Has Earth's land always looked the way it does now?

In Chapter 9, you will read for cause and effect. Cause and effect helps you to understand both what happens and why it happens.

WHY IT MATTERS

Rocks have many different uses.

SCIENCE WORDS

mineral a substance found in nature that is not a plant or an animal

landform a feature on the surface of Earth

plain a large area of land with few hills

valley an area of land lying between hills

plateau a flat area of land that rises above the land that surrounds it

Looking Under Your Feet

What was Earth like when dinosaurs roamed the land? Clues are right under your feet. The clues are rocks. Big ones like boulders. Little ones like grains of sand. Hard ones. Soft ones. Some that sparkle. Others that are dull or gray. Each kind of rock tells a different story.

EXPLORE

HYPOTHESIZE **What makes up rocks? Are all rocks alike? Write a hypothesis in your *Science Journal*. How might you test your ideas?**

Investigate How Rocks Are Alike and Different

Observe different rocks to infer how they are alike and different.

MATERIALS

- several different rocks
- hand lens
- *Science Journal*

PROCEDURES

1. OBSERVE Touch each rock. How does it feel? Record your observations in your *Science Journal*.

2. OBSERVE Look at each rock. Write or draw what you see. Write about any lines or patterns you observe.

3. COMPARE Now use your hand lens to look at each rock again. Write about what you see with the hand lens that you could not see before.

CONCLUDE AND APPLY

1. COMPARE AND CONTRAST Did any rocks feel the same? Did any rocks have similar lines or patterns?

2. IDENTIFY When you observed the rocks with a hand lens, did you observe any quality that all the rocks have in common?

3. INFER Are the rocks made of one material or more than one material? How can you tell?

GOING FURTHER: Apply

4. CLASSIFY Based on your observations, what are some ways the rocks could be grouped together to show their similarities or differences?

How Are Rocks Alike and Different?

The Explore Activity demonstrates that rocks are not all alike. In fact, there are many different kinds of rocks. Rocks are found in different sizes, shapes, and colors. Some rocks are smooth. Other rocks are rough.

Although rocks look and feel different from each other, all rocks are made of the same material. All rocks are made of **minerals** (min'ər əlz). A mineral is a substance found in nature that is not a plant or an animal. Minerals are the building blocks of rocks.

Some rocks, like granite (gran'it), are made up of many different minerals. Other rocks, like limestone (līm'stōn'), are made up of mostly one mineral. Minerals make a rock look and feel the way it does. Some minerals are hard. Other minerals are soft.

There are over 3,000 minerals and about 600 kinds of rocks.

mica
(mī'kə)

feldspar
(feld' spär')

quartz
(kworts)

Granite is made up of many different minerals.

Limestone is made up mostly of the mineral calcite.

260

QUICK LAB

Mineral Scratch Test

HYPOTHESIZE Which of these minerals do you think is the hardest: quartz, calcite, or mica? Write a hypothesis in your *Science Journal.*

PROCEDURES

1. PREDICT What do you think will happen if you scratch each mineral with your fingernail? The penny? The iron nail? Write your predictions in your *Science Journal.*

2. OBSERVE Test your predictions. Scratch each mineral with your fingernail, the penny, and the iron nail. Record your observations.

CONCLUDE AND APPLY

1. INTERPRET DATA List the minerals you tested in order of hardness, from softest to hardest. How did you determine the order?

2. COMMUNICATE Use your observations to create a chart that describes the three minerals you tested. Include drawings of the minerals.

MATERIALS

- large pieces of quartz, calcite, and mica
- penny
- iron nail
- *Science Journal*

Brain Power

Eyeglasses can be made with either plastic or glass lenses. Glass lenses have the mineral quartz in them. Plastic lenses are light, but can be scratched more easily. What might be the advantage of quartz-glass lenses?

How Are Rocks Formed?

All of Earth's rocks are formed in one of three ways.

Some rocks are formed when melted rock below the surface of Earth cools and hardens. Granite is formed in this way. Sometimes the melted rock flows out onto Earth's surface, where it cools and hardens more quickly. Rocks such as basalt (bə solt') and obsidian (ob sid'ē ən) form in this way.

Other rocks are formed when bits of soil, mud, and rock in the bottoms of rivers, lakes, and oceans pile up over time. As the layers build up, the materials on the bottom of the pile begin to change. The layers at the bottom of the pile get cemented together, forming solid rock. Rocks such as conglomerate (kən glom'ər it), sandstone (sand'stōn'), and shale (shāl) are formed this way.

Limestone is another kind of layered rock. It is made up of shells, skeletons of tiny sea animals, and hardened parts of small sea plants.

Basalt

Limestone

Sometimes rocks get squeezed and heated below Earth's surface. When this happens, the rock's properties change. It becomes a new kind of rock. This is a third way new rocks are formed.

All three kinds of rocks can be changed over and over again. They form, break up, and reform. Old rocks become new rocks. The chart below gives some examples.

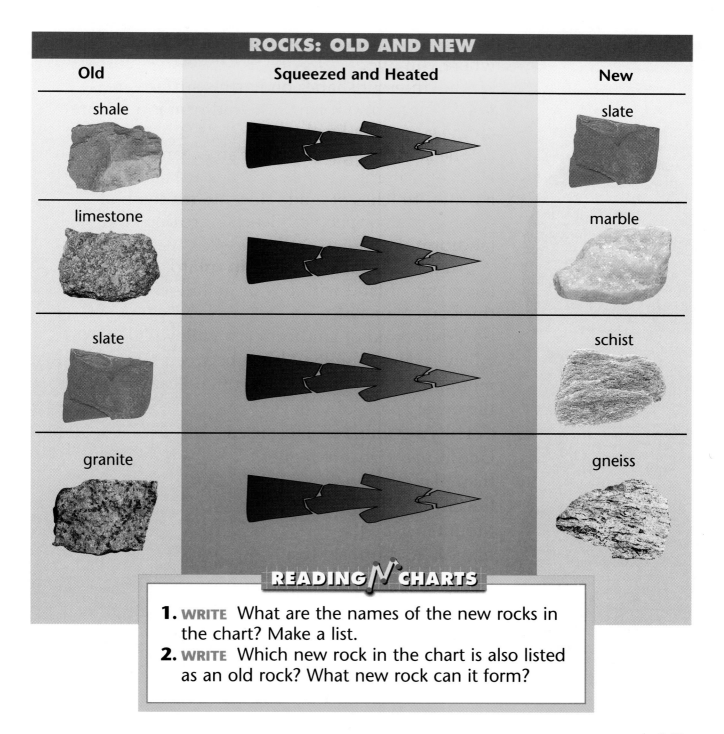

ROCKS: OLD AND NEW

Old	Squeezed and Heated	New
shale		slate
limestone		marble
slate		schist
granite		gneiss

READING /N/ CHARTS

1. **WRITE** What are the names of the new rocks in the chart? Make a list.
2. **WRITE** Which new rock in the chart is also listed as an old rock? What new rock can it form?

What Is Earth's Surface Like Where You Live?

Earth is an enormous ball with an outer "crust" of rock. In some places the rock is exposed, like on the side of a mountain. In other places the rock might be covered by soil, sand, buildings, pavement, or water.

The surface of a ball is smooth, but the surface of Earth is not smooth at all! It has many different shapes. What shape does Earth's surface have where you live?

The different shapes on Earth's surface are **landforms** (land'formz'). A landform is a feature on the surface of Earth.

The land along the edge of an ocean or other body of water is a beach. Beaches are flat and narrow stretches of land. They are made up of sand, gravel, or pebbles. Beaches are one kind of landform.

Another landform is a **plain** (plān). A plain is a large area of land with few or no hills. Plains have thick layers of soil.

A third kind of landform is a **valley** (val'ē). A valley is an area of land lying between hills or mountains. Rivers or streams often flow through the lowest parts of valleys.

Hills are rounded and raised landforms. They are higher than plains and valleys, but lower than mountains. Mountains are the highest landforms. Most mountains have large areas of exposed rock. In some places the rock may be covered by a thin layer of soil.

Beach

Valley

Plains

Whether you walk up a mountain or down into a valley, you are walking over rock. Rocks are always under your feet, but sometimes they are over your head, too! People use rocks to build many of the bridges, buildings, statues, and walls that you see every day.

This landform is a plateau (platō′). A plateau is a flat area of land that rises above the land that surrounds it.

REVIEW

1. Name and describe three landforms. What lies under each of these landforms?

2. What are rocks made of?

3. Name one mineral and describe its characteristics.

4. **COMMUNICATE** Describe three ways rocks are formed.

5. **CRITICAL THINKING** *Evaluate* How are mountains, hills, and plateaus alike? How are they different?

WHY IT MATTERS THINK ABOUT IT
What kinds of rocks have you seen in your community? Describe their colors, sizes, and shapes.

WHY IT MATTERS WRITE ABOUT IT
How are rocks used to make structures in your community? Describe some structures made from rock that you've seen. Where did you see them?

Stone SYMBOLS

Statues on Easter Island

Stonehenge

Geography Link

Pyramids

Great Wall

Long ago, people began building with rock. Many old structures stand today as monuments. They help us learn about ancient cultures.

Stonehenge is one of the world's oldest monuments. It was built in England about 5,000 years ago. Huge sandstone blocks and smaller rocks are arranged in circles. The largest rocks weigh 50 tons! Ancient people may have used Stonehenge to mark the movements of the Sun.

About 4,500 years ago, the people of Egypt built large stone pyramids as tombs for their kings. Millions of limestone blocks were used for the pyramids. Pyramids point to the sky. Egyptians may have thought the pyramids helped their kings reach heaven!

The Great Wall of China was built more than 2,000 years ago to keep out invaders. It's made mostly of granite and brick. At about 6,400 kilometers (4,000 miles) in length, the Great Wall is the longest structure ever built!

Giant statues stand on Easter Island, west of Chile. They were carved from volcanic rock more than 1,000 years ago. Hundreds of statues have been found, some as tall as 22 meters (66 feet). They may have been monuments to people who had died.

Discussion Starter

1 Name a stone monument in our country.

2 Which American monuments do you think will best tell future people about our culture?

*inter*NET **CONNECTION** To learn more about stone monuments, visit www.mhschool.com/science and enter the keyword **STATUES.**

Topic 2
EARTH SCIENCE

WHY IT MATTERS

You can see changes to Earth's surface all around you.

SCIENCE WORDS

weathering the process that causes rocks to crumble, crack, and break

erosion occurs when weathered materials are carried away

glacier a large mass of ice in motion

Slow Changes

How can a chunk of rock be turned into a soaring tower? How can a giant boulder be changed into a beautiful bridge? Is it magic? No! Something else is at work. How do you think these features were formed?

EXPLORE

HYPOTHESIZE Chalk is a kind of rock made up of the mineral calcite. How do you think the chalk got its shape? What are some ways you could change its shape? Write a hypothesis in your *Science Journal.* How might you test your ideas?

Investigate How Rocks Change

Investigate how rocks can change. Test what happens to chalk when you write on sandpaper.

PROCEDURES

1. OBSERVE Look at your piece of chalk and your sandpaper. Write down what they look and feel like in your *Science Journal*. List as many properties of each one as you can.

2. PREDICT What will happen when you draw with the chalk on the sandpaper? Write down your prediction.

3. Draw with your chalk on the sandpaper. You might draw a picture or write some words.

4. COMPARE Look at your chalk. How does the way it looks and feels now compare to before? Look at your sandpaper. How does the way it looks and feels now compare to before?

CONCLUDE AND APPLY

1. DESCRIBE What happened to the piece of chalk? What happened to the sandpaper?

2. EXPLAIN Which material changed the most? Why do you think this happened?

GOING FURTHER: Apply

3. INFER Strong winds sometimes carry sand as they blow over rocks. How might the wind and sand change the rocks over time?

MATERIALS

- 3 pieces of chalk (different colors)
- piece of sandpaper
- *Science Journal*

How Do Rocks Change?

All rocks are eventually broken up. One process that helps to break up rocks is **weathering** (weth′ər ing). Weathering is the process that causes rocks on Earth's surface to crumble, crack, and break. Things such as chemicals, water, temperature changes, plant roots, ice, and wind can cause the weathering of rocks. Weathering is usually a very slow process.

The Explore Activity demonstrates how a piece of chalk changes shape when it is rubbed on a rough surface. Wind carrying sand and pebbles can blast the surface of rocks, wearing the rocks down over time.

Water causes the weathering of rocks on beaches and riverbeds. Over time, these rocks also change shape and break down. When water gets into spaces in and around rocks and then freezes, rocks are broken open. Plant roots can do this, too.

Chemicals (kem′i kəlz) can also change rocks. Chemicals are all around you. They are in the air and water. When rocks are exposed to chemicals, the minerals in the rocks soften. Then the rocks change shape.

Ice can break rocks apart.

270

HOW A CAVE FORMS

Water runs down through cracks in limestone.

Chemicals in the water soften the minerals in the rock. A small opening forms.

The space gets larger. A cave has formed.

READING  DIAGRAMS

1. **DISCUSS** What softens the minerals in the rock?
2. **WRITE** What is the large space in the rock called?

QUICK LAB

Changing Chalk

HYPOTHESIZE Vinegar is a kind of chemical. What will happen when chalk is put in vinegar? Write a hypothesis in your *Science Journal*.

MATERIALS

- apron
- safety goggles
- piece of chalk
- small jar
- vinegar
- *Science Journal*

PROCEDURES

SAFETY: Wear Goggles.

1. Put on your apron and safety goggles. Place the chalk in the jar and pour in just enough vinegar to cover the chalk.

2. **OBSERVE** After a few seconds, describe what you see. Record your observations in your *Science Journal*.

CONCLUDE AND APPLY

EXPLAIN Why did the chalk change? How do you know?

Glaciers form when more snow falls than can melt away. As the snow piles up, it eventually begins to move.

This large pile of rocks formed when gravity pulled rocks down a hillside.

What Happens to Weathered Materials?

Weathered materials don't stay put. They are moved around by **erosion** (i rō′zhən). Erosion occurs when weathered materials are carried away. Erosion, like weathering, is usually a slow process. Ice, water, gravity, and wind all help to move weathered materials around.

Erosion happens all around us. Rivers and streams carry weathered materials over great distances. Gravity can pull weathered materials down hills and mountains. Winds pick up and move large amounts of soil and sand.

Glaciers (glā′shərz) cause erosion, too. A glacier is a large mass of ice in motion. If a glacier is up high, it will move to lower land. If it is on flat land, it will begin to spread. As glaciers move over the land they pick up weathered materials and rocks. These materials become stuck in the glacier, scraping the ground.

Skill: Forming a Hypothesis

WHICH MATERIALS SETTLE FIRST?

What happens to the material that is carried away by erosion? In this activity, you will put pebbles, sand, soil, and water in a jar. After you shake the jar, you will let it sit for several hours. How will the materials in the jar look after several hours? Write down what you think the outcome will be. This is your hypothesis. A hypothesis is an answer you propose to a question that can be tested.

MATERIALS

- a large plastic jar with lid
- measuring cup
- pebbles
- sand
- soil
- water
- *Science Journal*

PROCEDURES

1. Put one cup of each of the materials (pebbles, sand, and soil) in the jar and fill the jar with water. Put the lid on the jar and shake it.

2. OBSERVE Write a description of what your jar looks like in your *Science Journal*. Draw a picture of the jar and the materials.

3. OBSERVE Let the jar sit for several hours, then observe the contents again. How does the jar look now?

CONCLUDE AND APPLY

1. COMPARE How did the jar look when you first observed it? How did it look several hours later? Was your hypothesis correct?

2. DESCRIBE Which material in the jar settled first? Last? How do you know?

3. INFER A fast-moving stream may carry pebbles, sand, and soil. As the water slows down, which material will settle out first? Which material will be carried the greatest distance?

273

How Do Things in Your Neighborhood Change?

No matter where you live, you can observe some of the changes brought about by weathering and erosion. As plants grow, their roots may break apart sidewalks, or roads. Changes in temperature, and the action of chemicals, water, and ice also cause sidewalks and pavement to bend, crack, and crumble. What other examples of changes caused by weathering and erosion have you observed in your community?

What caused the words on this grave marker to disappear?

Brain Power

Tree roots pushing up from below have caused this sidewalk to break. The tree has changed its environment. In what other ways do living things change their environment to meet their needs?

274

Weathering and erosion are always at work. You can see the changes they cause all around you. People make changes to Earth's surface, too. Farmers move rocks and soil to prepare fields for planting. Hikers clear trails in the woods. Families plant gardens and children pick up rocks to collect. Homes, towns, and cities are built.

Rocks are not the only materials affected by weathering. This weathered house was once a solid wooden structure covered by paint.

REVIEW

1. How do rocks change?

2. How is weathering different from erosion?

3. Name three things that cause weathering. Name three things that cause erosion.

4. **HYPOTHESIZE** Devil's Tower, shown on page 268, is the "neck" of an ancient volcano. Why are the rocks that once surrounded this feature no longer there? State a hypothesis.

5. **CRITICAL THINKING** *Evaluate* Water can cause both weathering and erosion. What properties does water have? How do these properties help water to cause so much change?

WHY IT MATTERS THINK ABOUT IT Think about your schoolyard. What evidence of changes have you observed there? What changes were made by people?

WHY IT MATTERS WRITE ABOUT IT How might your schoolyard look ten years from now? Twenty years from now?

ERASING

Soil is very important, especially on farms. Crops need rich soil to help them grow. Wind and rain can wash away, or erode, farm soil. Farmers try to slow erosion and protect their farmland.

Contour (kon'tùr) farming protects the soil, too. Crops are planted in rows around hills. Each row soaks up rainwater as it runs down the hill.

Terrace (ter'is) farming protects the soil. "Shelves" are cut into the sides of a hill. The flat shelves hold rainwater better than a steep hillside!

Cover crops can help save soil. These crops aren't for harvesting. They're planted in empty fields. Their roots hold the soil in place during storms.

EROSION

Rows of trees can be planted between crop fields. The trees help break the force of the wind. Gentle winds don't carry as much soil away as strong winds.

During the 1930s the Great Plains were very dry. Dust storms carried away loose soil. Now farmers plant trees and terrace hillsides to keep the soil in place.

In Texas, people fight erosion in two ways. They reseed the prairies and terrace the farm-land in hilly fields.

DISCUSSION STARTER

1. What ways of controlling erosion have you seen in your community?

2. Compare and contrast contour farming and terrace farming.

To learn more about erosion, visit *www.mhschool.com/science* and enter the keyword WEAROFF.

*inter*NET CONNECTION

WHY IT MATTERS

It's important to be prepared for fast changes to Earth's surface.

SCIENCE WORDS

hurricane a violent storm with strong winds and heavy rains

earthquake a sudden movement in the rocks that make up Earth's crust

volcano an opening in the surface of Earth

Fast Changes

How is a storm like a broom? Can you solve this riddle? Sometimes land can change in just a few hours. One day it's here. Another day it's somewhere else. You may think it's gone altogether. However, it has just been moved around.

Think about what you know about weathering and erosion. What kinds of changes might this storm cause?

EXPLORE

HYPOTHESIZE A hurricane is a powerful storm. A drizzle isn't a storm at all. Each dumps water on land. Which kind of rainfall causes the most erosion? Write a hypothesis in your *Science Journal.* How might you test your ideas?

Design Your Own Experiment

HOW CAN LAND CHANGE QUICKLY?

PROCEDURES

1. Mix some rocks and soil together. You can smooth the rocks and soil or shape them into a hill, but don't pack them down. Draw how your "land" looks in your *Science Journal.*

2. MODEL How can you use cups A and B to model a gentle rain and a heavy rain? How can you use the pencils to help you?

3. EXPERIMENT How is your land affected by a gentle rain? How is your land affected by a heavy rain?

4. COLLECT DATA Make a table to record your results. Use your data to answer the questions below.

MATERIALS

- 2 paper cups, labeled A and B
- 2 trays, labeled A and B
- 2 different-sized pencils
- measuring cup
- soil and rocks
- water
- *Science Journal*

CONCLUDE AND APPLY

1. COMPARE What happened to the two trays? In which tray did the most change take place?

2. DRAW CONCLUSIONS Which kind of rainfall causes the most erosion? How do you know?

GOING FURTHER: Problem Solving

3. EXPERIMENT How could you test the effects of wind on land?

How Can Land Change Quickly?

Weathering and erosion usually take place slowly over long periods of time. The Explore Activity demonstrates that a heavy rainstorm can cause erosion quickly. Heavy rainstorms speed up the weathering and erosion of land.

When weathering and erosion happen quickly, there are sudden changes to Earth's surface. There are several events that can speed up the weathering and erosion of Earth's land. One of these events is a **hurricane** (hur'i kān').

A hurricane is a violent storm with strong winds and heavy rains. Hurricanes are the largest and most powerful of all storms. They begin over the oceans. Hurricane winds move in a circular pattern at speeds of 75 miles an hour or more!

Brain Power

Hurricanes are just one kind of violent event that cause sudden changes to Earth's surface. Can you think of any others?

Most hurricanes die out far from land. Hurricanes that move toward land act like giant bulldozers. Strong winds and giant waves damage or destroy almost everything in their paths. Coasts can be changed—often in minutes. Flooding occurs. Houses, roads, bridges, and cars may be swept away. Trees are uprooted. Lives are often lost.

Hurricane damage

QUICK LAB

MATH LINK

Weather Adds Up

HYPOTHESIZE Some cities have a lot of rain each year. Other cities only have a little. In which kind of city will a stone monument change more quickly? Write a hypothesis in your *Science Journal*.

PROCEDURES

1. INTERPRET DATA Look at the table. What is the difference in winter temperatures between the two cities? Write the number in your *Science Journal*.

2. INTERPRET DATA Which city has more rainfall?

CONCLUDE AND APPLY

DRAW CONCLUSIONS A stone monument was moved to New York City from Egypt. The monument has changed very quickly in New York. Why do you think this has happened?

MATERIALS
• *Science Journal*

COMPARING WEATHER IN NEW YORK AND CAIRO

	New York City, USA	Cairo, Egypt
Average Temperature in Winter	32°F	56°F
Average Rainfall Each Year	107 cm	0 to 10 cm

What Other Events Cause Sudden Changes to Earth's Surface?

Another event that causes sudden changes to Earth's surface is an **earthquake** (urth'kwāk'). An earthquake is a sudden movement in the rocks that make up Earth's crust. Earthquakes are caused by forces deep within Earth. The forces cause the rocks to break. The breaking rock makes the ground shake.

Some earthquakes are so weak they can hardly be felt. Others are very strong. Strong earthquakes cause landslides, great destruction, and loss of lives. People may be left homeless when houses are destroyed. Cities may lose electricity and water as power and water lines break. Food supplies may run low if transportation is interrupted. Fires may also break out.

Landslides often happen when earthquakes do. They also occur when heavy rains or melting snow loosen rocks, soil, sand, and gravel. Then mud, sand, and boulders tumble down from mountains and hills. Buildings may be damaged, swept away, or buried.

earthquake damage

landslide damage

HOW A VOLCANO FORMS

Lava and other materials flow out onto the surface of Earth during a volcanic eruption.

The materials pile up around the opening, forming a volcanic mountain, or volcano.

READING ✎ DIAGRAMS

1. **WRITE** What flows out of a volcano?
2. **REPRESENT** How would the volcano look after another eruption?

Sudden changes to Earth's surface are also caused by **volcanoes** (vol kā'nōz). A volcano is an opening in the surface of Earth. Melted rock, gases, pieces of rock, and dust are forced out of this opening. The word *volcano* is also the name of the landform that is built up around this opening. Melted rock that flows out onto the ground is called lava (lä'və).

Volcanoes may not erupt for hundreds of years and then erupt again. A large disaster happened in Italy about 2,000 years ago when Mt. Vesuvius (və sü'vē əs) erupted. Many people died from breathing deadly gases. Three entire cities were buried under lava, ash, and volcanic rocks. Hundreds of years later, the remains of these cities were discovered.

What Is the Dust Bowl?

Terrible dust storms spelled disaster for many people living in the Great Plains of the United States in the 1930s. This area of the country became known as the Dust Bowl.

Farmers in the Great Plains dug up millions of acres (ā'kərz) of land in order to grow crops. For many years there was plenty of rain. There were also very good harvests.

Then, in 1931, a long, dry period began. Crops did not grow and the soil dried out. Without plants to hold the soil in place, the dry soil began to blow away with the wind. Thick, black clouds of dust were carried hundreds of miles across the plains. When the dust settled, it buried fences, houses, and farm buildings.

As the dust storms continued over the next several years, more and more farmers had to move away. Finally, eight years later, the rains returned. A hard lesson had been learned. Farmers had learned to plant crops that would protect the soil from erosion.

Sudden events like hurricanes, earthquakes, landslides, and volcanic eruptions can cause a lot of damage. People cannot prevent these events from happening, but they can prepare for them. Weather forecasters can predict when hurricanes will move toward land. Scientists can predict where earthquakes and volcanic eruptions are likely to occur.

REVIEW

1. How can land change quickly?

2. Name two things that work to change the shape of the land when hurricanes hit the coast.

3. What is a volcano?

4. **COMMUNICATE** What caused the dust storms of the 1930s? Draw a diagram to explain. Label your diagram.

5. **CRITICAL THINKING** *Apply* Describe some of the ways people are affected when strong earthquakes occur where they live.

WHY IT MATTERS THINK ABOUT IT Describe the emergency drills you have at your school. How should you act in an emergency?

WHY IT MATTERS WRITE ABOUT IT Why is it important to know what to do in the case of an emergency?

READING SKILL How does a volcano form? Write a paragraph that explains the cause and the effect.

PREDICTING HURRICANES

When Christopher Columbus arrived in the New World, he was met by Native Americans. They told him about storms they called hurricanes. They said the storms brought great winds, heavy rains, and giant waves. They never knew when a hurricane would form or where it would strike land!

Today modern tools help weather forecasters predict when and where a hurricane will strike. This information gives people time to board up their windows and find a safe place to stay.

Brave pilots fly planes into the center, or eye, of a hurricane. Instruments on the planes measure the hurricane's size and strength, and what direction it's moving.

Science, Technology, and Society

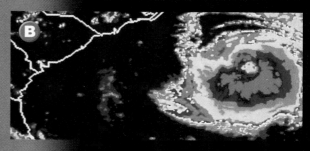

A

B

C

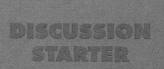

DISCUSSION STARTER

1. What tools are used to predict a hurricane?

2. How would you prepare for a hurricane?

A Weather satellites are always orbiting Earth. They take pictures of weather patterns around the world. Satellite pictures can show hurricanes forming and crossing the Atlantic Ocean.

B Radar sends out radio signals that bounce back off raindrops. The radar screen can show a hurricane's heavy rains when they are still very far away.

C Denise Stephenson-Hawk is a scientist who studies the atmosphere. She uses models to learn how conditions in the atmosphere, oceans, and land may be used to predict the weather.

To learn more about predicting weather, visit *www.mhschool.com/science* and enter the keyword STORMY.

*inter*NET CONNECTION

SCIENCE WORDS

earthquake p.282

erosion p.272

glacier p.272

hurricane p.280

landform p.264

mineral p. 260

plain p.264

plateau p.265

valley p.264

volcano p.283

weathering p.270

USING SCIENCE WORDS

Number a paper from 1 to 10. Fill in 1 to 5 with a word from the list above.

1. An opening in Earth's crust through which melted rock and other materials are forced out is a ___?___.

2. All rocks are made up of ___?___.

3. The process that causes rocks to crack, crumble and break is ___?___.

4. A flat area of land that rises above the land that surrounds it is called a ___?___.

5. A sudden movement in the rocks that make up Earth's crust is called an ___?___.

6–10. Pick five words from the list above that were not used in 1 to 5 and use each in a sentence.

UNDERSTANDING SCIENCE IDEAS

11. Beaches often have laws against walking on sand dunes. Why do you think this is so?

12. How does a glacier cause erosion?

USING IDEAS AND SKILLS

13. **READING SKILL: CAUSE AND EFFECT** On a walk you see an old, crumbling stone wall. Why is the wall falling apart?

14. **HYPOTHESIZE** How do you think the three landforms shown below are related? Write a hypothesis.

Mesa

Plateau

Butte

15. **THINKING LIKE A SCIENTIST** You find a rock near your school. How could you test how hard it is?

PROBLEMS and PUZZLES

Lava Flow Can you make a model of a volcano? Wear goggles. Fill half a bottle with warm water. Add a few drops of liquid detergent and vinegar. Add a teaspoon or two of baking soda and stand back!

WHAT EARTH PROVIDES

You walk on it. You run on it. Your school is built on it. Earth is your home! Have you ever thought about all the things that Earth provides? What kinds of things do you take from Earth? What do you put back in their place?

In Chapter 10 you will read for the order, or sequence, of events. Knowing the sequence of events helps you to understand and remember them.

WHY IT MATTERS

Rocks and soil are necessary to your community.

SCIENCE WORDS

natural resource
a material on Earth that is necessary or useful to people

renewable resource
a resource that can be replaced or used over and over again

Rocks and Soil: Two Resources

Would these plants exist if there were no soil? Tall trees reach into the sky. Little garden plants brush your ankles. Tall or short, these plants have something in common. They have roots. Roots reach into the soil to soak up water and minerals. Have you ever looked closely at soil?

HYPOTHESIZE You know that soil is important for growing plants. What is in soil? Write a hypothesis in your *Science Journal*. How might you test your ideas?

Investigate What Is in Soil

Examine a soil sample to find out what is in soil.

MATERIALS

- small amount of soil
- piece of white paper
- hand lens
- *Science Journal*

PROCEDURES

1. Spread out your soil sample on the piece of white paper.

2. OBSERVE Look at the soil closely. What do you see? Are there different colors? Different size particles? Write your observations in your *Science Journal.*

3. OBSERVE Smell your soil. How does it smell? Feel your soil. How does it feel? Are there different textures? Write down a description of your soil based on how it looks, feels, and smells. Be sure to wash your hands after touching the soil.

4. COMPARE Using your hand lens, examine your soil again. What do you see that you didn't see before? Record your new observations.

CONCLUDE AND APPLY

1. COMMUNICATE What did you see in your soil?

2. IDENTIFY Was there anything in the soil that surprised you? What was it?

GOING FURTHER: Apply

3. HYPOTHESIZE Think about what you saw in your soil. How do you think those things got into the soil?

Why Are Rocks and Soil Important?

Rocks and soil are **natural resources** (nach′ər əl rē′sors′əz). A natural resource is a material on Earth that is necessary or useful to people.

How are rocks useful to people? You know that rocks are important building materials. Crushed limestone is used in making cement. Some roads are covered with sand or gravel. Sand is also an important ingredient in glass. Clay and sand are used in making bricks. Weathered rocks are part of the soil. If there were no rocks, there would be no soil.

Soil is the part of the ground that plants grow in. Without soil, there would be no plants on the land. People and animals need plants for food.

Deer like to eat small branches and leaves from trees or bushes.

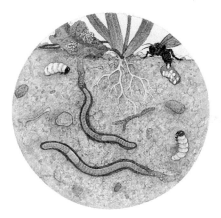

What materials make up soil?

What Is in Soil?

The Explore Activity shows that soil is made up of several different materials. Soil is a mixture of tiny rock particles, minerals, and decayed plant and animal material. Growing plant roots, worms, and insects make spaces for air and water.

There are usually two layers of soil. The top layer, called topsoil, is made up of very small particles that are dark in color. Topsoil has a lot of minerals and decayed plant and animal material. These things are necessary for plant growth. Topsoil holds water well, which is also necessary for plant growth.

A layer of soil called subsoil lies below the topsoil. Subsoil is made up of bigger particles and is lighter in color than topsoil. It does not have decayed plant and animal material, but it does hold water and has some of the minerals needed by plants. Below the subsoil is solid rock.

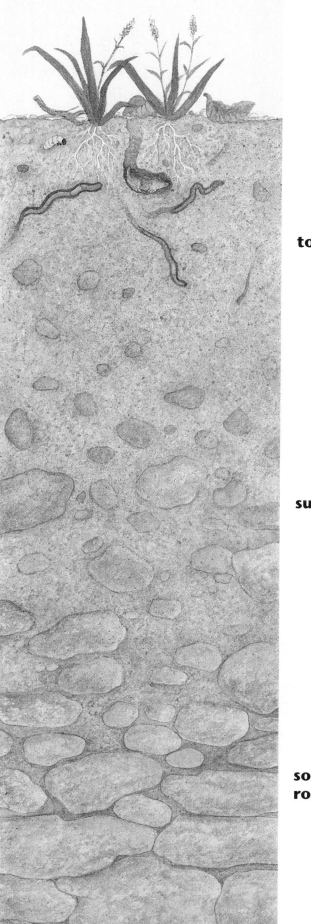

topsoil

subsoil

solid rock

293

Are There Different Kinds of Soils?

There are many different kinds of soils. Different soils have different types of rock and minerals in them. Some soils have more water in them than others. Some soils might have more plant and animal material in them, too.

Different kinds of soils are found in different parts of the world. There are several kinds of soils found in the United States. In some areas, the soil has a lot of clay. Other soils are very sandy. Loam (lōm) is a kind of soil that has a good mixture of clay and sand.

In some places, soil layers are very thick. Lots of plants grow in places with a thick soil layer. In dry and windy places soil layers are much thinner. Layers of soil on mountains are thin because gravity pulls the soil downhill.

The type of soil in a particular place affects what kinds of plants can grow there.

This soil is sandy.

Plants grow well in loam.

This soil has a lot of clay in it.

Skill: Measuring

MATH
LiNK

FINDING THE VOLUME OF A WATER SAMPLE

The amount of water that soil can hold is an important property of soil. In this activity, you will measure the amount of water held by two soil samples. Sometimes you measure something to find out an object's size, weight, or temperature. In this activity, you will measure the volume of a sample of water. You can use a calculator to help.

PROCEDURES

1. MEASURE Using the measuring cup, measure 1 cup of potting soil into a paper cup with holes. Pack the soil down. Label the cup. Measure 100 mL of water in the graduated cylinder.

2. EXPERIMENT Hold the paper cup with potting soil over a paper cup without holes. Have your partner pour the water slowly into the cup of soil. Let the water run through the cup for two minutes. If there is still water dripping out, place the cup of soil inside an empty cup.

3. MEASURE Pour the water that ran out of the cup into the graduated cylinder. Read and record the volume of water in the graduated cylinder. Write the number in your *Science Journal*.

4. EXPERIMENT Repeat steps 1–3 with the sandy soil.

CONCLUDE AND APPLY

1. INTERPRET Which soil held more water? How do you know?

2. APPLY Which type of soil would be best for use in a garden? Which sample would be best for use on a soccer field?

MATERIALS

- 4 paper cups, 2 with holes
- measuring cup
- water
- sandy soil
- potting soil
- graduated cylinder
- watch or clock
- calculator (optional)
- *Science Journal*

Soybeans are planted as a cover crop on this field.

Why Is It Important to Conserve Natural Resources?

Some natural resources are **renewable resources** (ri nü'ə bəl rē'sors'əz). A renewable resource is a resource that can be replaced or be used over and over again. Soil is an example of a renewable resource.

However, the erosion of soil happens quickly when soil is left unprotected. Soil is unprotected when forests are cut down and when farmland is left bare. You read about how this happened in the Dust Bowl on page 284.

Although soil is renewable, it takes many, many years for it to form. For this reason, it is important to conserve soil. To conserve something means to protect it and use it wisely. Good farming practices, like contour farming and planting cover crops, help conserve the soil.

Brain Power

Some Native American peoples only took a plant for use if they could find several others just like it. Why do you think they did this?

The next time you take a walk, take a good look around you. How does the land look where you live? The way the land looks depends on what rocks and soil are at Earth's surface. The area where you live feels like home to you. Rocks and soil are part of what makes your home special.

REVIEW

1. What is a natural resource?

2. Why is soil a natural resource?

3. In what ways do soils differ?

4. **MEASURE** Every time you water your classroom plant, water drips onto the floor. How can you find out how much water the plant is losing?

5. **CRITICAL THINKING** *Apply* You know that soil is important to plants. Do you think plants are important to soil? Explain.

WHY IT MATTERS THINK ABOUT IT
Describe the area of the country where you live. Why do you like it?

WHY IT MATTERS WRITE ABOUT IT
Identify the rocks and soil in your neighborhood. Describe how they are important.

George Washington Carver:

The FARMERS' FRIEND

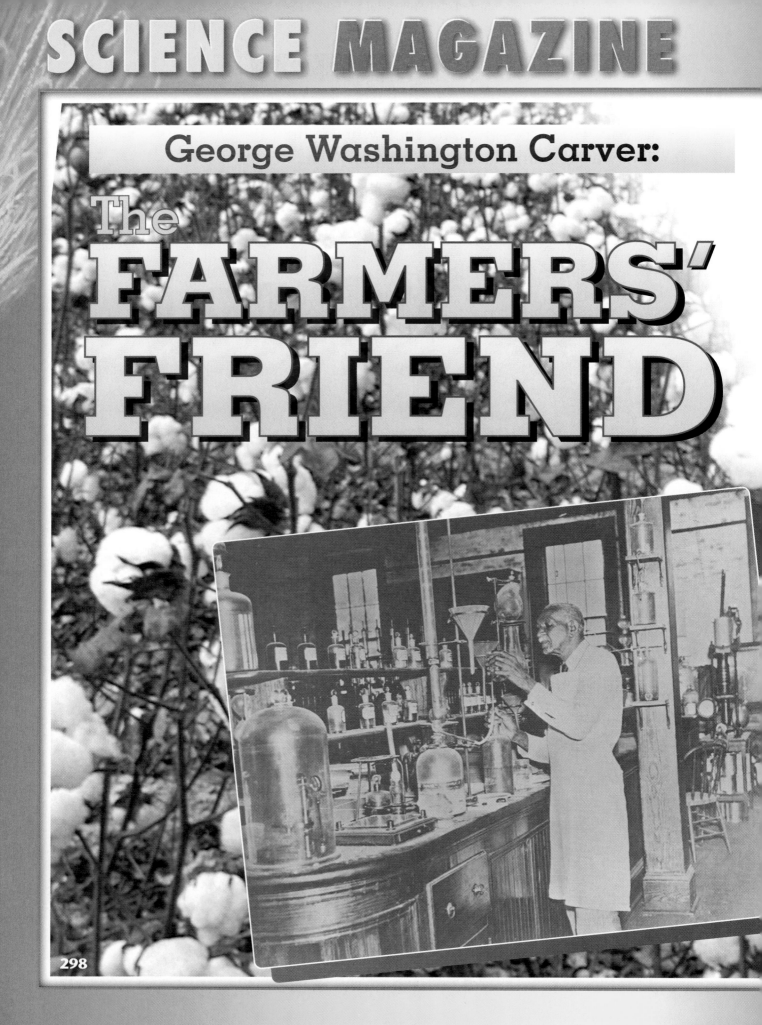

History of Science

Next time you eat a peanut, think of George Washington Carver: He's the man who made the peanut famous!

Carver was born in slavery in Missouri in 1861. Even at a young age, he was very interested in plants.

At age 12, Carver went away to get an education. By 1896 he had earned two college degrees. Then he got a job at the Tuskegee Institute in Alabama. His goal was to help poor Southern farmers.

Most Southern farmers grew only cotton. The plant took all the nitrogen (nĭ′trə jən) out of the soil. Carver suggested that they plant cotton one year and a different crop the next year. He wanted the farmers to use peanuts, soybeans, and sweet potatoes. Why? As these plants grow, they put nitrogen back into the soil!

Carver developed more than 300 products from peanuts alone! These included milk, coffee, flour, and soap. He also developed more than 100 products from sweet potatoes, including flour, rubber, and glue!

Soon many companies bought the new crops and made the new products. More and more Southern farmers rotated their crops with cotton. In time, their cotton grew better, too.

George Washington Carver received many honors. He was most proud of helping the farmers. They began to earn more money. Best of all, their farmland could support generations of farmers in the future.

DISCUSSION STARTER

1. Why did Carver work to develop products made from peanuts and sweet potatoes?

2. How did Carver prove that soil is a renewable resource?

To learn more about Carver's work, visit **www.mhschool.com/science** and enter the keyword CARVER. *inter*NET CONNECTION

WHY IT MATTERS

Earth provides many different resources.

SCIENCE WORDS

nonrenewable resource
a resource that cannot be reused or replaced in a useful amount of time

Other Natural Resources

Are diamonds a natural resource? Diamonds are hard to find. They are hidden below Earth's surface. They must be mined, or dug up, before they can be used. It takes a lot of work to mine diamonds! It takes even more work to prepare a diamond so that it can be used.

Do you think diamonds are a renewable resource?

EXPLORE

HYPOTHESIZE Some natural resources, such as diamonds and metals, are hard to find. What effect do you think mining these resources might have on Earth's land? Write a hypothesis in your *Science Journal*. How might you use a model to test your ideas?

Investigate How Mining Affects Land

The cookie in this activity represents an area of land. The chocolate chips in the cookie are the resource. Experiment to find out what you must do to get the resource.

MATERIALS
- chocolate chip cookie
- 4 toothpicks
- paper towel
- *Science Journal*

PROCEDURES

1. OBSERVE Place your cookie on the paper towel. Draw how your cookie looks in your *Science Journal*. Label your drawing.

2. MODEL Using your toothpicks, try to remove the resource (chocolate chips) from the land (cookie) without damaging the land. Before you begin, discuss with your partner how you will mine the resource.

3. EXPERIMENT Mine all the resource from your land. Draw how your cookie looks now.

CONCLUDE AND APPLY

1. COMPARE How does your cookie look after you removed all the chocolate chips?

2. DRAW CONCLUSIONS What happens when you can't find any more chips? How can you get more?

3. INFER What might be some problems people face in trying to mine resources from Earth?

GOING FURTHER: Problem Solving

4. How can damage to mining areas be repaired?

How Does Mining Affect Land?

The Explore Activity demonstrates that some resources take a lot of work to find. When one area of land has been mined of all of a resource, you must go to another place to find more. Mining often damages land.

Diamond

Diamonds take billions of years to form. Not only do they take a long time to form, but a lot of work is needed to find them. Diamonds are an example of a **nonrenewable resource** (non'ri nü'ə bəl rē'sors'). A nonrenewable resource is a resource that cannot be reused or replaced in a useful amount of time.

Many of the fuels we use for energy are also nonrenewable resources. Coal, oil, and natural gas are fuels. This means they can be used for energy.

Wood stove

About 200 years ago, most people in the United States burned wood for fuel. One hundred years ago, coal provided almost all the energy used in the United States. Today, oil and natural gas are the fuels used for most of our energy needs.

Coal, oil, and natural gas are nonrenewable resources. Coal is a hard, dark brown or black substance that is found in layers in the ground. It formed from the remains of plants that lived long ago.

HOW COAL FORMS

1 Most coal was formed millions of years ago, when swamps covered large parts of Earth. Plants growing in the swamps died and sank to the bottom.

2 Layers of decayed plants formed a soft material called peat. The peat sank deeper and deeper. Eventually, the peat was buried beneath layers of mud and sand.

3 Thick layers of rock eventually covered the top of the peat. Gradually, over a long period of time, the peat changed into coal.

READING DIAGRAMS

1. WRITE List the steps that must occur for plant material to form coal.

2. DISCUSS What is peat?

How Are Natural Gas and Oil Used?

Oil and natural gas are fuels that have many uses. Both oil and natural gas are used for heating buildings and homes. Natural gas is also used for cooking food on gas stoves. Oil is made into gasoline, which powers cars and other vehicles. Oil is a thick, brown or black substance found in rocks below Earth's surface. Natural gas is often found in the same places that oil is found.

Both oil and natural gas formed from the remains of plants and animals that lived millions of years ago.

Before oil and natural gas can be removed from the ground, a well must be drilled. Then the oil and gas can be pumped to the surface.

Energy Survey

HYPOTHESIZE Do you think more people in your class have a gas stove or an electric stove? Write a hypothesis in your *Science Journal.*

MATERIALS
• *Science Journal*

PROCEDURES

COLLECT DATA Conduct a survey of your classmates. Who has an electric stove? Who has a gas stove? Record the information in your *Science Journal.*

CONCLUDE AND APPLY

1. **IDENTIFY** How many people have electric stoves? How many people have gas stoves?

2. **COMMUNICATE** Make a bar graph that shows the results of your survey.

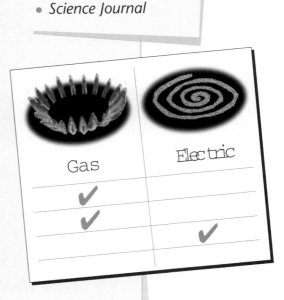

Gas	Electric
✔	
✔	
	✔

What Kind of Resources Are Water and Air?

All living things need water. Water can be used over and over again, but it is never used up. Water is a renewable resource.

Almost all water is found in Earth's oceans. Ocean water is salt water. Fresh water is found in glaciers, rivers and lakes.

Air is a mixture of gases. Air, like water, is necessary for living things. It is also a renewable resource. When plants make food they release oxygen into the air.

WHY IT MATTERS

Like all living things, you need water and air to survive. People use coal, oil, and natural gas as fuels. You can survive without fuel, but your life would be very different and much less comfortable.

REVIEW

1. What is a nonrenewable resource?

2. How do we use coal, oil, and natural gas?

3. What kinds of resources are water and air? How do you know?

4. **COMMUNICATE** Draw a picture that shows the many ways that people use water and air.

5. **CRITICAL THINKING** *Evaluate* Wood is a fuel. Do you think wood is a renewable or nonrenewable resource? Explain.

WHY IT MATTERS THINK ABOUT IT
Why is water an important resource in your neighborhood.

WHY IT MATTERS WRITE ABOUT IT
Gasoline is a fuel that powers cars, buses, and trucks. How would your life be different if there were no gasoline?

READING SKILL How does coal form? Draw a diagram that shows the sequence of events.

POSITIVELY PLASTIC

What comes in every color of the rainbow and can be found in almost every home in America? Something that's made of plastic!

We use plastic wrap to protect our foods. We put our garbage in plastic bags or plastic cans. We sit on plastic chairs, play with plastic toys, drink from plastic cups, and wash our hair with shampoo from plastic bottles! We know how useful it is, but exactly what is it?

Plastic doesn't grow in nature. It's made by mixing certain things together. We call it a produced or manufactured material. Plastic was first made in the 1860s from plants, such as wood and cotton. That plastic was soft and burned easily.

The first modern plastics were made in the 1930s. Today plastics are made from oil and natural gas. It's true! Most clear plastic starts out as thick, black oil. That plastic coating inside a pan begins as natural gas.

Over the years, hundreds of different plastics have been

developed. Some are hard and strong. Some are soft and bendable. Some are clear. Some are many-colored. There's a plastic for almost every need. Scientists continue to experiment with plastics. They hope to find even more ways to use them!

DISCUSSION STARTER

1. Most plastics don't rot. What's good about that?

2. What problems occur because plastics don't rot?

To learn more about plastics, visit **www.mhschool.com/science** and enter the keyword MADE.

*inter***NET**
CONNECTION

Topic
EARTH SCIENCE
6

WHY IT MATTERS

Conserving resources means making sure there are enough of them for the future.

SCIENCE WORDS

pollution what happens when harmful substances get into water, air, or land

reduce to make less of something

reuse to use something again

recycle to treat something so it can be used again

Conserving Earth's Resources

What has made the water dirty in this picture? Living things need clean water. People use water for drinking, cleaning, and cooking. Plants need clean water in order to grow. Dirty water can cause sickness and even death in animals and people. Do you think this water is safe to use?

EXPLORE

HYPOTHESIZE One way we use water is to keep ourselves clean. When you wash your hands, where do the dirt and grime go? Do they stay in the water? Write a hypothesis in your *Science Journal.* How might you test your ideas?

Investigate What Happens
When Materials Get into Water

Explore what happens when materials are put into water.

PROCEDURES

 SAFETY: Wear goggles.

1. OBSERVE Pour some water into your jar and add a spoonful of the oil. How does the water look? Where is the oil? Record your observations in your *Science Journal.*

2. OBSERVE Shake the jar. Set the jar down and watch it for a few minutes. What happens? Can you scoop the oil out with your spoon?

3. EXPERIMENT Add a few drops of liquid soap to the jar and shake the jar again. What happened to the oil? Can you clean the oil out now?

CONCLUDE AND APPLY

1. DESCRIBE What happened when you shook the jar with the oil and water in it?

2. IDENTIFY Where did the oil and soap go when you shook the jar a second time?

GOING FURTHER: Apply

3. INFER Where do you think dirt and grime go when you wash a car or dirty dishes?

MATERIALS
- small jar with lid
- water
- oil
- plastic spoon
- liquid soap
- safety goggles
- *Science Journal*

309

What Happens When Materials Get into Water?

As we use Earth's water, air, and land, we add materials to them. For example, when you wash your hands, you rinse soap and dirt into the water. Water is cleaned naturally by flowing through layers of rock in the ground.

The Explore Activity shows that a problem may develop when too many materials get into the water. This problem is **pollution** (pə lü'shən). Pollution occurs when harmful substances get into the water, air, or land. When these resources become polluted they become unsafe to use.

Some pollution happens naturally. Polluted water happens naturally when too much sand or soil settles in a lake. Then the lake isn't a good place for fish and plants to live. Volcanic eruptions and forest fires pollute the air with dust, gas, and ashes.

Forest fire

Human actions cause pollution, too. People add things like soap and *fertilizers* (fur'tə li'zər) to water. A fertilizer is used to help plants grow. Fertilizers can soak through the ground and into water supplies.

Cleaning Water

HYPOTHESIZE **Can you clean water by letting it flow through rocks? Write a hypothesis in your *Science Journal*.**

PROCEDURES

SAFETY: Wear goggles.

1. **MODEL** Place the funnel inside the bottom half of the plastic bottle. Put a layer of gravel in the funnel and cover it with a layer of sand.

2. **MODEL** Mix a cup of water with a little soil and some crushed leaves. Draw a picture of the water in your *Science Journal*. Slowly pour the mixture into the funnel.

CONCLUDE AND APPLY

1. **DESCRIBE** How does the water look when it filters through to the bottom half of the bottle?

2. **INFER** Where is the soil?

MATERIALS

- plastic funnel
- bottom half of plastic bottle
- gravel
- sand
- measuring cup
- water
- spoonful of soil
- dead leaf
- cup
- safety goggles
- *Science Journal*

Smog hangs over the city of Los Angeles. Smog is fog that has been polluted by smoke.

Mario Molina studies the effects of chemicals called *fluorocarbons* on Earth's atmosphere. The results of his research have been used to create laws that help to control pollution.

What Other Materials Pollute Earth's Land and Air?

Cars, airplanes, and factories add gases and chemicals to the air. Rain carries materials in the air to Earth. This polluted rain water flows into rivers, lakes, and oceans, and soaks into the ground.

In some places, land is polluted by enormous amounts of trash. As Earth's population grows, more trash is produced.

There are many people and other living things on Earth. All living things need to use Earth's resources. There are several things people can do to help conserve the resources that all living things need.

One way for people to conserve resources is to **reduce** (ri düs′) the amount of things they use. To reduce something is to make less of it. You can reduce trash by buying products that come in less packaging. You can use both sides of notebook paper before throwing it out. You can reduce the amount of water you use by turning off the faucet while you brush your teeth.

ONE PERSON'S TRASH EACH YEAR

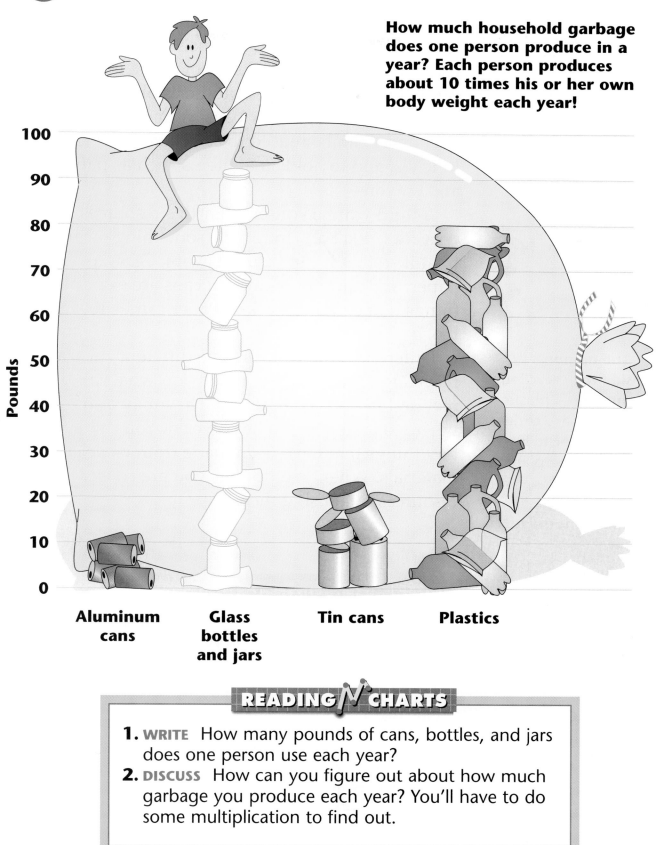

How much household garbage does one person produce in a year? Each person produces about 10 times his or her own body weight each year!

Pounds

100
90
80
70
60
50
40
30
20
10
0

Aluminum cans   Glass bottles and jars   Tin cans   Plastics

READING N' CHARTS

1. **WRITE** How many pounds of cans, bottles, and jars does one person use each year?
2. **DISCUSS** How can you figure out about how much garbage you produce each year? You'll have to do some multiplication to find out.

What Other Things Can You Do to Conserve Resources?

Another way for people to conserve resources is to **reuse** (rē ūs′) things. To reuse something is to use it again. You can make an old sock into a puppet for your younger brother's birthday. Or you can reuse plastic grocery bags as trash bags. Plastic containers can be reused to store leftovers, to pack lunches, and to hold small items such as paper clips and crayons.

A third way to conserve Earth's resources is to **recycle** (rē sī′kəl). To recycle something means to treat it so that it can be used again. Glass, plastic, paper, and aluminum and tin cans are examples of things that can be recycled. Paper can be recycled, too.

Different communities have different rules about recycling. These rules may tell you what can be recycled in your community. They may also tell you where to take items to be recycled. You can even buy things that have been made from recycled materials. When you do this, you are conserving resources by reusing them!

DID YOU KNOW?

The numbers inside the recycling symbol on a plastic container are codes. The number tells the recycling plant what type of material the container is made from.

Take a survey of plastics in your house. Can you find an example of each type?

Brain Power

How could you reduce the amount of trash thrown away in your classroom?

As the number of people in the world increases, the need for resources also increases. People can help conserve resources. When you work to conserve resources, you are working to make sure there are enough of them for the future.

This person is recycling.

REVIEW

1. What happens when too many materials get into water?

2. What is pollution?

3. How can water, air, and land become polluted?

4. **IDENTIFY** Name three ways to reuse a plastic container.

5. **CRITICAL THINKING** *Apply* You are given the job of Resource Monitor in your classroom. Write a description of what you would do to make sure the class resources are used wisely.

WHY IT MATTERS THINK ABOUT IT
Estimate the amount of trash you throw away each day. What kinds of things do you throw away?

WHY IT MATTERS WRITE ABOUT IT
What can you do to reduce the amount of trash you throw away? What can you reuse? What can you recycle?

Pollution at Paint Creek

Is Paint Creek polluted? Nine kids who lived near the creek wanted to find out. The kids, ages six to ten, were part of a group in a Ypsilanti (ip'sə lan'tē), Michigan, summer program.

Kids in the program chose several tests to help answer their question.

The kids created data sheets to record their findings. Was the creek polluted? After checking all the data, the kids didn't agree on an answer. They did agree that they learned a lot about pollution and about working together! They also agreed it was fun to have their story and picture in the local newspaper!

DISCUSSION STARTER

1. What tests did the group decide to use?

2. What did the group learn from the project?

Test 1
Water temperature
Healthy water in a stream like Paint Creek should be cool, about 17°C or 63°F.

Test 2
Water speed
Water moves faster in a healthy stream.

Test 3
Number of insects
The more insects, the better. They're fish food!

Test 4
Water quality
How the water looks, smells, and feels. The group decided they better not taste it!

To learn more about checking water pollution, visit **www.mhschool.com/science** and enter the keyword CREEK.

*inter**NET*** CONNECTION

SCIENCE WORDS

natural
  resource p.292
nonrenewable
  resource p.302
pollution p.310

recycle p.314
reduce p.312
renewable
  resource p.296
reuse p.314

USING SCIENCE WORDS

Number a paper from 1 to 10. Fill in 1 to 5 with words from the list above.

1. A material on Earth that is necessary or useful to people is a ___?___.

2. A resource that cannot be reused or replaced in a useful amount of time is a ___?___.

3. When too many materials get into water, there is ___?___.

4. When you ___?___ something, you find a way to use it again.

5. A resource that can be used over and over again is a ___?___.

6–10. Pick five words from the list above. Include all words that were not used in 1 to 5. Write each word in a sentence.

UNDERSTANDING SCIENCE IDEAS

11. How does water become polluted?

12. If polluted water can be made clean again, why is it important not to pollute it?

USING IDEAS AND SKILLS

13. **READING SKILL: SEQUENCE OF EVENTS** How is soil formed?

14. **MEASURE** Look at the graduated cylinder. How much water does it hold?

15. **THINKING LIKE A SCIENTIST** You want to know if a lake near your school is polluted. How might you test the lake to find out?

PROBLEMS and PUZZLES

Growth Spurt How is soil different from sand? Experiment. Fill a can with soil and a second can with sand. Plant bean seeds in each can. What happens after one week? Two weeks? Why did you get these results?

UNIT 5 REVIEW

SCIENCE WORDS

earthquake p.282
erosion p.272
glacier p.272
hurricane p.280
mineral p.260
natural resource p.292
nonrenewable resource p.302
plain p.264
pollution p.310
recycle p.314
reduce p.312
renewable resource p.296
reuse p.314
valley p.264
volcano p.283
weathering p.270

USING SCIENCE WORDS

Number a paper from 1 to 10. Beside each number write the word or words that best completes the sentence.

1. Rocks are made up of ___?___.

2. The landform that makes up the low area between hills is a ___?___.

3. The wearing away of rock by ice, water, or wind is ___?___.

4. A huge mass of ice and snow that moves is called a(n) ___?___.

5. A sudden movement of Earth's crust that can cause the ground to shake is a(n) ___?___.

6. Lava pours out of the hole of a ___?___.

7. Materials from Earth that are useful or necessary are ___?___.

8. Coal is a ___?___ because it cannot be reused or replaced in a useful amount of time.

9. Smoke from a fire can cause air ___?___.

10. You can ___?___ plastic bags so that the plastic can be used again.

UNDERSTANDING SCIENCE IDEAS

Write 11 to 15. For each number write the letter for the best answer. You may wish to use the hints provided.

11. What tells you that a rock is soft?
    a. The rock scratches easily.
    b. The rock is very heavy.
    c. The rock is gray and white.
    d. The rock is smooth.
    (Hint: Read page 261.)

12. Weathering makes rocks
    a. larger
    b. break apart
    c. melt
    d. harder
    (Hint: Read pages 270–272.)

13. Hurricanes often cause
    a. earthquakes
    b. rocks to break
    c. soil to be washed away
    d. caves to form
    (Hint: Read pages 279–280.)

14. Natural gas and oil are
    a. renewable resources
    b. minerals
    c. nonrenewable resources
    d. formed by glaciers
    (Hint: Read page 302.)

15. Treating old materials to make them into new products is
    a. recycling
    b. pollution
    c. weathering
    d. reusing
    (Hint: Read pages 313–314.)

USING IDEAS AND SKILLS

16. In what ways can rocks be different from each other? Give three examples.

17. Name two renewable resources and describe how people use them.

18. **MEASURE** Your kitchen sink has a leaky faucet. How can you find out how much water is wasted each day?

19. Describe two ways that an earthquake might be dangerous to people.

THINKING LIKE A SCIENTIST

20. **HYPOTHESIZE** You visit a lake that was once clear and full of fish. The lake water now looks dirty and the fish are all gone. What do you think happened?

WRITING IN YOUR JOURNAL

SCIENCE IN YOUR LIFE
List some things that people recycle. Explain how you might make recycling easier for people to do.

PRODUCT ADS
The labels of some laundry soaps tell you that the soaps break down into harmless materials. Why is this a good characteristic for something that will be put into water?

HOW SCIENTISTS WORK
In this unit you have learned that weathering and erosion can change landforms. Scientists use their skills of observation and measuring to study these changes. Why do you think it is important to understand how landforms change?

Design your own Experiment

Would clay or sand be washed away more easily by rain? Design an experiment to find out. Review your experiment with your teacher before trying it out.

inter **NET**
CONNECTION

For help in reviewing this unit, visit *www.mhschool.com/science*

PROBLEMS and PUZZLES

Be a Rockhound at Home

You don't have to go outside to start a rock and mineral collection. You can find rocks and minerals in your house or apartment. Here are some examples to get you started:

table salt (halite)

pencil lead (graphite)

pumice (volcanic rock)

You can store and display your collection in egg cartons or in reusable plastic bags and containers.

A Dune on the Move

Dunes are mounds of sand made by the wind. The wind picks up the sand from the side of the dune that is not steep. Then it leaves the sand on the steeper side. See if you can put the pictures in the correct order.

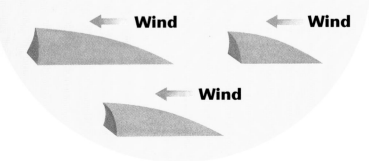

The Garbage Problem

Food garbage is a part of the things people throw away. Is there a way this garbage can be reused or recycled? Find out!

Line a shoebox with plastic. Poke several holes through the box and the plastic on each side. Fill the box about half full with crushed dead leaves. Add two handfuls of soil and 1/2 cup of water. Do this again, then mix the materials with your hands. The mixture should be damp, but not wet. Add more soil or water if you need to.

Next mix in two or three tablespoons of food garbage—vegetable peelings, eggshells, or coffee grounds. Don't include meat scraps, milk, or cheese! Put about 150 red worms in the box and cover it with the lid.

For best results, you will need to keep this project going for at least 10 days. Check the box each day. Add water and soil if needed. Add more kitchen scraps as they disappear. What changes take place?

WHERE LIVING THINGS LIVE

CHAPTER 11

GETTING ALONG

Wherever you live on Earth, there are many different living things sharing the same space. You also share space with things that are nonliving. What's in your space, besides you?

In Chapter 11 you will find and use different ways to represent information. You can use arrows, labels, and pictures.

SCIENCE WORDS

ecosystem all the living and nonliving things in an environment

community all the living things in an ecosystem

population all the members of a certain type of living thing in an area

habitat the place where a plant or animal naturally lives and grows

Places to Live

What might happen if a giraffe found itself in a desert? How well do you think it would survive?

Organisms live in special places. A frog lives in a pond. A cactus lives in a desert. A giraffe lives on a kind of grassland called a savanna. Each place has special things that the organisms need. The pond has water to keep the frog wet. The desert has sunshine to help the cactus grow. What does the savanna provide for the giraffe?

EXPLORE

HYPOTHESIZE **Why do organisms live where they do? Write a hypothesis in your *Science Journal*. How might you test your ideas?**

Investigate Where Plants and Animals Live

Explore why plants and animals live where they do.

PROCEDURES

1. Using the magazines and scissors, cut out pictures of 4 different environments. Look for pictures of deserts, forests, ponds, and grasslands. Spread the pictures on a table.

2. **OBSERVE** Cut out 8 pictures of different plants and animals and trade them for the plant and animal pictures cut out by another group. Look at the pictures carefully. To which environment do you think each plant or animal is best suited for survival? Give reasons for your choices.

3. **MAKE DECISIONS** Place the plant and animal pictures under the environment you have chosen for them.

CONCLUDE AND APPLY

1. **IDENTIFY** What are the characteristics of the organisms that live in each environment? Make a list.

GOING FURTHER: Apply

2. **INFER** What determines where organisms live?

MATERIALS

- magazines
- scissors
- *Science Journal*

Where Do Plants and Animals Live?

The Explore Activity shows that different plants and animals live in different places. However, all plants and animals live in **ecosystems** (ek'ō sis'temz). An ecosystem is made up of all the living and nonliving things in a certain area. What living things might you find in one area? What nonliving things might you find?

An ecosystem can be as small as the space underneath a rock.

An ecosystem can be as large as one of the Great Lakes.

The living and nonliving parts of an ecosystem affect each other in different ways. For example, a tree grows in soil. When dead leaves fall from the tree, small organisms in the soil break down the leaves. The leaves now become part of the soil.

What might you see if you looked under a rock? A **community** (kə mū'ni tē) of insects, worms, and fungi! A community is all the living things in an ecosystem.

Each community can be divided into **populations** (pop'yə lā'shənz). A population is all the members of a single type of organism. For example, you might find a population of pill bugs under a rock.

Each living thing has a **habitat** (hab'i tat'). A habitat is a living thing's home. A frog's habitat is in or near a pond. A centipede's habitat is in the soil under a rock.

A FOREST ECOSYSTEM

1 Leaves fall from the tree.

2 Small organisms in the soil break down the leaves.

3 Leaves become part of the soil.

4 The tree grows in the soil.

READING ⚡ DIAGRAMS

1. DISCUSS How do the living and nonliving parts of this ecosystem affect each other?

2. DISCUSS What might happen to the tree if all the organisms in the soil died? Why?

What Habitats Are Found in a Pond?

A pond ecosystem has many different habitats. Each habitat meets the needs of the organisms that live there. Living things need food, water, and a place to live. They also need space to grow and reproduce.

In an ecosystem such as a pond or wetland, all living things depend on other living things. Wetlands are low areas of land with a lot of water in the soil. The living part of the ecosystem also depends on the non-living part of the ecosystem.

A POND ECOSYSTEM

1 The Banks
Plants like ferns and moss live along pond banks. Animals include insects, mice, snakes, raccoons, and birds.

2 The Water's Edge
Plants on the water's edge live partly underwater. Animals include salamanders, snails, and water bugs.

3 Shallow Water
Floating plants live in the shallow water. Frogs sit on top of lily pads and hunt insects. Turtles come up on rocks or logs to lie in the Sun.

4 Algae
Algae are single-celled or many-celled organisms. A pond may contain billions of algae. You can see algae on rocks and logs in a pond.

In a pond or wetland, algae depend on sunlight and water to survive. Insects and small animals depend on the algae for food. Frogs depend on these insects and other animals for food. Fish depend on frogs and tadpoles for food. The heron depends on both frogs and fish for food. Each organism depends on others. All of the organisms depend on the pond.

5 Deep Water
Floating plants live here too. Fish also live in deep water.

6 Great Blue Heron
The heron flies to different habitats. It comes to the pond to get its favorite foods — frogs, fish, and tadpoles.

7 Dragonfly
Adult dragonflies live out of the water. Young dragonflies are like fish. They live in the water and breathe through gills.

8 Bladderwort
Bladderwort is a floating plant. The stems and leaves of the plant have air sacs. When a small organism touches an air sac, it is sucked into the air sac and eaten!

Skill: Defining Terms Based on Observations

A FOREST COMMUNITY

You have learned that a community is all the living things in an ecosystem. Different ecosystems have different communities. For example, the pond community on pages 326 and 327 included bladderwort, frogs, algae, and dragonflies. What makes up a forest community? Look at the picture on this page. Use your observations to define a forest community.

PROCEDURES

1. OBSERVE Look at the illustration of a forest. What do you see? Make a list in your *Science Journal*.

2. CLASSIFY Which of the things on your list are living? Which are nonliving?

CONCLUDE AND APPLY

DEFINE Using your lists, define a forest community.

Ecosystems, communities, habitats, and populations are part of your own life. You live in an ecosystem. It has living and nonliving parts. You also occupy a habitat in your ecosystem.

REVIEW

1. What is an ecosystem?

2. What is a community? List some members of a community in a pond ecosystem.

3. How is a community different from a population?

4. **DEFINE** Think about the habitat of a pet dog. List some of its characteristics. Use your list to write your own definition of *habitat*.

5. **CRITICAL THINKING** *Apply* How would a pond ecosystem change if the water in the pond dried up?

WHY IT MATTERS THINK ABOUT IT Describe the kinds of living things that share your habitat.

WHY IT MATTERS WRITE ABOUT IT Of all the living things that share your habitat, which is your favorite? Which is your least favorite? Why?

Homes
on Land and Sea

Caribou are a kind of deer. They live in cold northern regions.

Where do animals and plants live? Everywhere! Some strange creatures live at the bottom of the sea . . . by underwater volcanoes!

Giant tube worms live at the bottom of the sea.

Most life on Earth depends in some way on the Sun, but no sunlight reaches the bottom of the sea. However, boiling water flows out of volcanoes on the ocean floor. The water contains chemicals from deep within the Earth.

Unusual bacteria use these chemicals instead of sunlight to make their own food. Many other living things depend on the bacteria, including giant tube worms. The worms are about 4 meters (12 feet) long. One end of each worm is attached to the ocean floor. The other end gathers material from the seawater.

Rather live where it's not so hot? Try the tundra. It's a cold, dry region where no trees grow. The ground just below the surface is frozen all the time!

Very few animals make their homes on the tundra. Caribou spend half of the year here. They have broad feet that help them walk in snow and dig through snow to find food. Caribou travel in large herds and are always on the move. That way they don't run out of food.

Discussion Starter

1 Could tube worms live near the ocean surface? Why or why not?

2 A pipeline was built across the tundra to move oil. Would that have hurt the caribou? What could be done to protect the tundra and the animals?

*inter*NET CONNECTION To learn more about different environments, visit www.mhschool.com/science and enter the keyword **SETTINGS.**

WHY IT MATTERS

You depend on other living things for food.

SCIENCE WORDS

producer an organism that makes its own food

consumer an organism that eats producers or other consumers

food chain a series of organisms that depend on one another for food

decomposer an organism that breaks down dead plant and animal material

food web several food chains that are connected

energy pyramid a diagram that shows how energy is used in an ecosystem

Food

Can three different animals eat one plant? Yes! Thomson's gazelle, the zebra, and the wildebeest all eat the same grass for food. Each animal eats a different part of the grass.

Thomson's gazelle likes the bottom part of the grass. The zebra eats the top part of the grass and the wildebeest eats the middle. Which animal do you think eats the grass first?

EXPLORE

HYPOTHESIZE People eat many different kinds of foods. Does more of the food you eat come from plants or animals? Write a hypothesis in your *Science Journal*. How might you investigate your ideas?

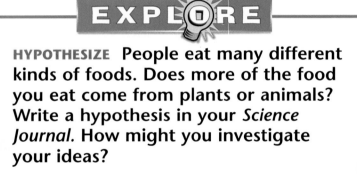

Investigate Where Food Comes From

Analyze a pizza to infer where food comes from.

MATERIALS
• *Science Journal*

PROCEDURES

1. OBSERVE Look carefully at the picture of the pizza. What types of foods do you see? Make a list in your *Science Journal*.

2. CLASSIFY Divide your list of foods into groups. Which foods come from plants? Which foods come from animals?

3. Plants can make their own food. Animals cannot. Look at your list of foods that come from animals. What animal does each of the foods come from? What food does that animal eat?

CONCLUDE AND APPLY

1. CAUSE AND EFFECT If there were no plants, which foods would be left to make pizza? (Hint: Think about what animals eat in order to survive.)

2. INFER Do all foods come from plants? Write down another type of food that you like to eat. See if you can trace the ingredients back to plants.

GOING FURTHER: Apply

3. COMMUNICATE Create a chart that shows where the ingredients in question 2 come from.

Where Does Food Come From?

The Explore Activity demonstrates that all food comes from producers. Plants are **producers** (prə dü′sərz). Producers are organisms that make their own food. For example, the plants on page 332 are producers. The three grazing animals are **consumers** (kən sü′mər). Consumers are organisms that eat producers or other consumers.

What is food? Food is material that organisms use to get energy. To make food, producers need water, sunlight, air, and minerals. Organisms that are producers include plants and algae. The cells of producers contain a special chemical. Organisms with this chemical can make food.

Producers and consumers make up a **food chain** (füd chān). A food chain is a series of organisms that depend on one another for food. Food chains start with producers. Consumers eat those producers. Other consumers eat the first consumers.

This plant is a producer. The caterpillars are consumers.

334

DESERT FOOD CHAIN

OCEAN FOOD CHAIN

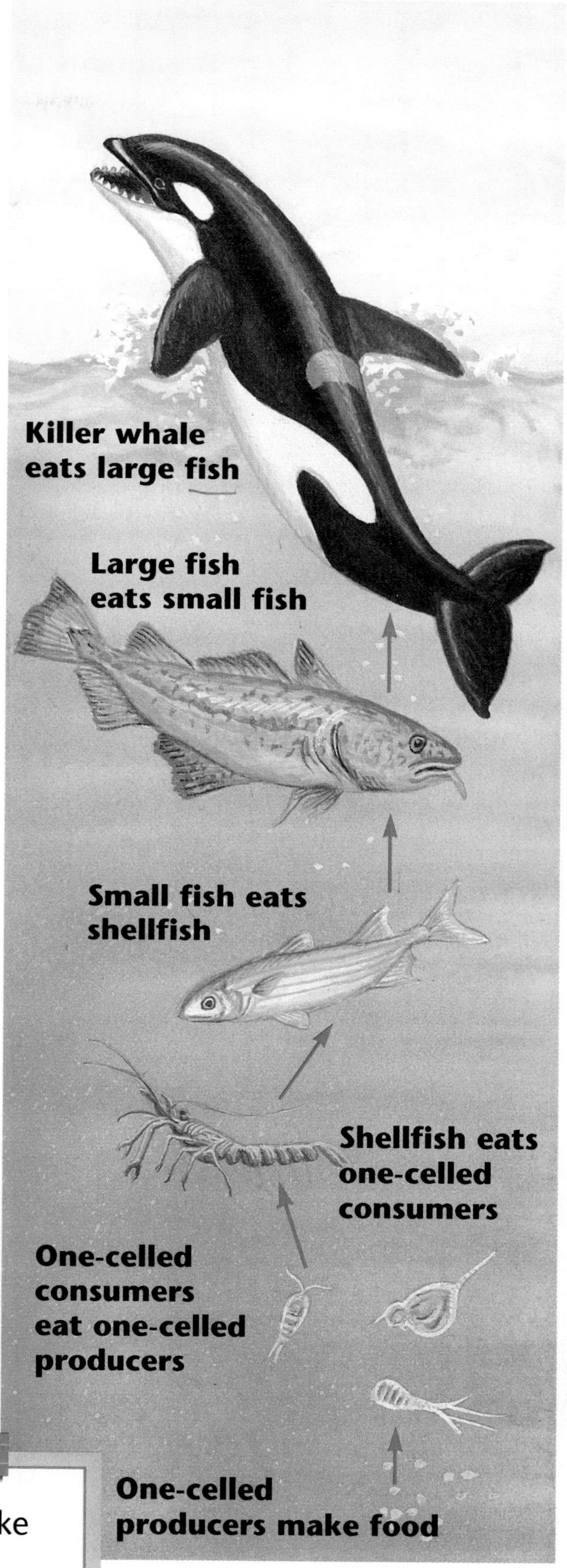

Hawk eats snake

Snake eats mouse

Mouse eats insect

Insect eats plant

Plant makes food

Killer whale eats large fish

Large fish eats small fish

Small fish eats shellfish

Shellfish eats one-celled consumers

One-celled consumers eat one-celled producers

One-celled producers make food

READING 📐 DIAGRAMS

1. **WRITE** List the organisms that make up each food chain.
2. **DISCUSS** How are these two food chains different? How are they alike?

How Are Materials Recycled?

As living things go through their life cycles, new organisms are produced. Old organisms die. What happens to all the dead plant and animal material in an ecosystem? It must be cleaned up. **Decomposers** (dē'kəm pō'zərz) are the organisms that do the cleaning. A decomposer breaks down dead plant and animal material. It recycles chemicals so they can be used again.

Decomposers include *bacteria*. Bacteria are one-celled organisms. Some bacteria cause infections and disease. However, without bacteria, Earth would be covered by dead plant and animal material. Decomposers also include *fungi* (fun'jī). Fungi are organisms that take in chemicals from dead material. You might see fungi growing on a dead log.

When you see decomposing material, you are seeing an energy transformation. Some of the energy in the material goes to the decomposer. Some of the energy changes to heat.

Producers, consumers, and decomposers work together to recycle materials through an ecosystem. Producers use the recycled material to make new food. Consumers eat that food. When producers and consumers die, decomposers recycle the dead material. Then the cycle is repeated.

QUICK LAB

Decomposers

HYPOTHESIZE What will happen to bread and apples if they are left out for one week? Write a hypothesis in your *Science Journal*.

SAFETY: Don't open the sealed bags.

PROCEDURES

1. Put the bread in one plastic bag. Put the apple pieces in the other bag. Seal the bags.

2. **OBSERVE** Leave the materials in the bags for one week. What happens to each material?

MATERIALS
- 2 self-sealing plastic bags
- apple pieces
- slice of bread
- *Science Journal*

CONCLUDE AND APPLY

1. **IDENTIFY** What evidence of decomposers do you see? Is there more than one decomposer? How do you know?

2. **INFER** Do different types of decomposers break down different types of material? Explain.

What Is a Food Web?

Ecosystems contain more than one food chain. They contain **food webs** (füd webz). Food webs are made up of several food chains that are connected. Take a look at the desert ecosystem food web. Can you recognize the original desert food chain from page 335?

There are many food chains in this food web. The original desert food chain is just one of the chains. Which animals does it link together?

Notice how other food chains connect to the original chain. For example, try to find the cactus-jackrabbit-hawk chain.

DESERT FOOD WEB

Brain Power

How many different food chains can you find in the diagram? Make a list.

An ecosystem has different kinds of organisms. Each type of organism forms its own level on an **energy pyramid** (en'ər jē pir'ə mid'). An energy pyramid is a diagram that shows how energy is used in an ecosystem.

Each level in an energy pyramid has more members in it than the level above it. There are more producers than plant-eaters. There are more plant-eaters than meat-eaters. This means that for every frog in a pond, there might be hundreds of bugs and thousands of producers.

WHY IT MATTERS

You are a consumer. You are part of a food web. You probably depend on many different producers and other consumers for food. You also depend on decomposers to recycle plant and animal materials in your ecosystem.

ENERGY PYRAMID

Meat eaters

Plant eaters

Producers

REVIEW

1. Where does food come from?

2. What is a producer? A consumer? A decomposer?

3. How is a food web different from a food chain?

4. **INFER** What does an energy pyramid tell you about a community?

5. **CRITICAL THINKING** *Evaluate* What would happen if an ecosystem had more consumers than producers? Could this ecosystem last?

WHY IT MATTERS THINK ABOUT IT
Like other organisms, you belong to a food web. Describe the food web that you are part of.

WHY IT MATTERS WRITE ABOUT IT
Draw a diagram of your food web. How do you fit into your food web?

READING SKILL All foods come from producers. Use pictures and arrows to show the events that must take place for you to have a glass of milk.

FOODS
Around the World

Why do people in different countries eat different foods? Different foods grow in different places. Even though foods are shipped all around the world, people often eat the foods that grow near them naturally.

Europe and the Near East

Your body uses foods that contain starch and fat for energy. For thousands of years, people in Europe and the Near East have used wheat as their main starch. People near the Mediterranean grow olives that provide fat through oil. Farther north, there are not as many plants with oil. People there have traditionally used animal fat in their diet.

The Americas

Potatoes are an important starch in the Americas. Corn, or maize, was once the main starch in North America. Today most corn is fed to animals or made into sugars, oils, or chemicals. However, corn is still the main starch in Mexico.

340

Social Studies Link

Asia

Rice is the main starch of Southeast Asia. In northern Asia, it's too cold to grow rice. People in northern China use wheat. The Chinese may have invented pasta using wheat. The Chinese also use oil from soybeans or peanuts. In India, people use rice and wheat. Food is cooked in butter from milk or oil from sesame seeds.

The Tropics

Grasses such as wheat are difficult to grow in the tropics. So are potatoes. In South and Central America, people grow a different starchy underground tuber called a yuca, manioc, or cassava. In West Africa, people get oil from palm trees. Palm oil and coconut oil are also popular in the American tropics.

DISCUSSION STARTER

1. If fats from plants are better for us than fats from animals, why have people in colder regions traditionally used animal fat?

2. Most basic foods—wheat, rice, potatoes, yuca—have very little flavor. Is this an advantage or a disadvantage? Explain.

To learn more about basic, or staple, foods, visit **www.mhschool.com/science** and enter the keyword BASIC.

*inter*NET
CONNECTION

WHY IT MATTERS

All living things depend on other living things to meet their needs for survival.

SCIENCE WORDS

carbon dioxide and oxygen cycle the exchange of gases between producers and consumers

parasite an organism that lives in or on another organism

host the organism a parasite lives in or on

Roles for Living Things

What do these fish need to survive? What do you think the plants need?

You probably know that taking care of a pet takes a lot of work. Even a plant needs some care. What would you do to take care of the living things in this aquarium?

EXPLORE

HYPOTHESIZE Pets and houseplants have people to take care of them. How do plants and animals in nature get what they need to live and grow? Write a hypothesis in your *Science Journal.* How might you test your ideas?

Investigate How Living Things Meet Their Needs

Observe an aquarium to infer how plants and animals meet their needs.

PROCEDURES

1. MAKE A MODEL Put a 3 cm layer of gravel into the plastic drink bottle. Fill the bottle about half full of water. Anchor the plants by gently pushing their roots into the gravel. Cover the bottle with the bottom of another bottle. Put the container in a place where it receives plenty of light, but do not place it directly in the Sun.

2. After 2 days, use the fish net to gently place the fish into the bottle. Add a few flakes of fish food to the bottle through one of the holes in the top. Later in the week, add some more.

3. OBSERVE Observe your ecosystem every few days for 4 weeks. Feed the fish twice each week. Record your observations in your *Science Journal.*

CONCLUDE AND APPLY

1. COMPARE How has your ecosystem changed over the 4 weeks?

2. IDENTIFY What did the fish need to survive? What did the plant need to survive?

3. INFER You probably observed bubbles in your ecosystem. What do you think those bubbles were? Where did they come from?

GOING FURTHER: **Apply**

4. INFER Did the living things in this ecosystem meet their needs? How do you know?

MATERIALS

- fish food
- gravel
- small guppy or goldfish
- fish net
- 2 small elodea or other water plants
- 2 L plastic drink bottle
- bottom of another drink bottle with holes
- water
- meter tape
- *Science Journal*

How Do Living Things Meet Their Needs?

The ecosystem in the Explore Activity shows how organisms depend on one another to meet their needs. The ecosystem had two populations. Each population used some of what the other put into the water. The bubbles in the water were a clue that a gas was in the water. Where did the gas come from? The plant gave off oxygen for the fish to use. The fish gave off carbon dioxide for the plant to use.

The fish and the plant take part in the **carbon dioxide and oxygen cycle** (kär′bən dī ok′sīd and ok′sə jən sī kəl). The carbon dioxide and oxygen cycle is the process of trading oxygen and carbon dioxide. This cycle is based on needs of producers and consumers. These gases are passed from one population to another in both water and land habitats. If gases were used up instead of exchanged in this cycle, living things would die. You can follow the carbon dioxide and oxygen cycle in the steps below.

Step 1
Producers give off oxygen as they make their own food.

Step 2
Consumers take in the oxygen that producers make.

oxygen

carbon dioxide

Step 3
Consumers give off carbon dioxide.

Step 4
Producers take in carbon dioxide from consumers.

Gases are recycled in the carbon dioxide and oxygen cycle. Animals breathe in oxygen and breathe out carbon dioxide. Plants take in carbon dioxide and give off oxygen. Plants need some oxygen, too. Plants need oxygen to get energy from food. During the day, plants make oxygen and release it into the air. They also take in some oxygen. At night, plants don't make food or oxygen. They take in oxygen from the air, just like animals do.

Where does the world's oxygen supply come from? Green plants and algae give off oxygen. Forests are big suppliers of oxygen. Trees are the world's largest oxygen-producing organisms. However, the most important source of oxygen is in the oceans. Algae make more oxygen than all the land plants in the world.

How are you a part of the carbon dioxide and oxygen cycle? You are a consumer. You breathe oxygen in and carbon dioxide out.

Pitcher plants eat insects. However, sometimes ants live inside pitcher plants. The ants "fish" for insect victims in the pitcher plant. The ants also protect the plant from other insects. What other plants "work" with animals in this way?

How Else Do Populations Depend on Each Other?

You know that plants and animals depend on each other for oxygen and carbon dioxide. Organisms depend on one another in other ways, too.

Sometimes two populations help each other to survive. Each type of organism depends on the other. For example, the clownfish and the sea anemone help each other.

Sea anemones are dangerous organisms. Their poison tentacles can be deadly to many kinds of fish. However, the clownfish swims near to the anemone without being harmed. Its body is coated with special slime that protects it from the anemone's stingers.

The clownfish uses the anemone for protection. When it is threatened, the clownfish swims to the anemone's tentacles for safety. The anemone uses the clownfish to get food. The anemone feeds on scraps that fall out of the clownfish's mouth.

Sometimes only one of the populations depends on the other to survive. The second population isn't helped by the first.

The clownfish and the sea anemone help each other survive.

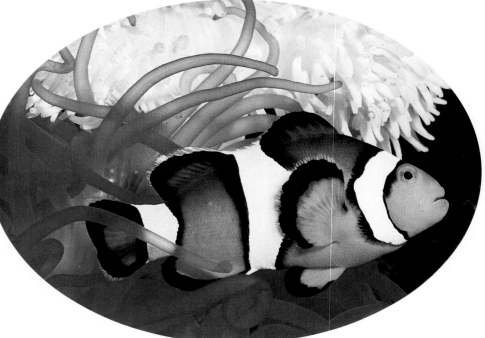

Cattle egrets are birds that could find food in many places. However, they spend their time following cattle. Wherever the cattle go, the egrets follow. What does the cattle egret get from the cattle? The cattle are so big that they stir up insects and other small animals wherever they feed. The egrets follow behind the cattle to get food. The cattle aren't always helped by the egrets. They aren't harmed, either.

Sometimes one population does harm another population. A tapeworm like the one shown cannot live on its own. It lives inside the body of other organisms. Tapeworms are **parasites** (par'ə sīt'z). A parasite is an organism that lives in or on a **host** (hōst). A host is the organism that a parasite lives with.

The host of a tapeworm can be an animal or a human. The tapeworm gets food by attaching itself to the host. Then it takes in food that the host has digested. Parasites like the tapeworm harm their hosts. A tapeworm can make its host sick. In some cases it can even kill its host.

Parasites are more common than you may think. Fleas are parasites to dogs. They eat the blood of dogs as food. The dogs are harmed by the parasites, but rarely killed.

A tapeworm is a parasite.

Cattle egrets are helped by cattle.

Squirrels bury acorns to store them for winter.

How Do Animals Help Plants Reproduce?

An oak tree makes seeds called acorns. Acorns will develop into new oak trees if they fall in the right place to grow. Most acorns fall right under the tree. Is this a good place for the acorns? No. There is not enough light to grow. Somehow the acorns must be moved to a better location.

How do the acorns move to another place? Animals help. Squirrels find the acorns. They bury the acorns in the ground to store them for winter. Most of the acorns get eaten by the squirrels, but a few of them are forgotten. They stay buried in the ground, far from the tree. They will grow into new trees.

Traveling Seeds

HYPOTHESIZE Animals with fur often help plants spread their seeds. How might they do this? Write a hypothesis in your *Science Journal.*

PROCEDURES

1. PREDICT What will happen when you toss the seeds onto the fur? Record your prediction in your *Science Journal.*

2. EXPERIMENT Test your prediction. Have your partner hold up the fur. Toss different seeds at it. Record the results.

MATERIALS
- seeds
- fake fur
- *Science Journal*

CONCLUDE AND APPLY

1. IDENTIFY Which of the seeds stuck to the fur?

2. INFER How might animals with fur help plants spread their seeds?

Brain Power

Some seeds can travel for miles without being helped by any animals. How do these seeds move from place to place? (Hint: Think of a dandelion seed.)

WHY IT MATTERS

You have seen how organisms depend on one another. You also depend on other organisms. You depend on plants and animals for food. You also depend on them for other things. You depend on trees for wood to make houses and furniture. You depend on plants and animals to make fabric for clothes. Do you have a pet? If you do, you depend on an animal for companionship.

REVIEW

1. How do living things meet their needs?

2. What gases are exchanged in the carbon dioxide and oxygen cycle? Who uses the gases?

3. Give an example of two organisms that depend on each other for survival.

4. **HYPOTHESIZE** What might happen to a population of oak trees if the squirrels that live nearby disappear? Why?

5. **CRITICAL THINKING** *Apply* What is the disadvantage of a parasite killing its host?

WHY IT MATTERS THINK ABOUT IT Describe an organism that depends on you or a person you know for its survival. How are its needs met?

WHY IT MATTERS WRITE ABOUT IT In what ways do you depend on this organism? Who else depends on this organism?

349

People Who

Everyone needs help sometime. Like plants and other animals, people depend on one another. That's why communities have special people to lend a hand.

What if a house catches on fire? What would people do without the community fire department? The home might be destroyed. A family might be hurt, too. Instead, the firefighters put out the fire . . . safely.

People provide other services for citizens—the people who live in a community. Some people are police officers. Others collect the garbage or fix holes in the streets. Still others drive buses or run recycling centers.

People have other helpful jobs in their communities. They may teach or help homeless people find somewhere to live. They may be doctors, nurses, or counselors who work at the community clinic.

Community services are expensive. To pay for them, citizens pay taxes. The money they pay buys the services they need.

Need People

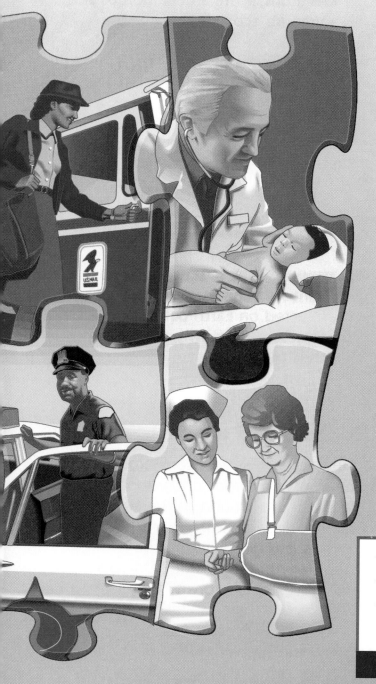

People in a community also buy individual services and goods. They buy gas, electricity, telephone, and cable services from local companies. They buy food, clothing, and other goods from local stores. The money they pay helps the community grow.

Which job would you like to do in your community? Why?

DISCUSSION STARTER

1. Why do people pay taxes?

2. What would happen if many people in the community wanted to be police officers, but no one wanted to collect the garbage?

To learn more about jobs, visit *www.mhschool.com/science* and enter the keyword WORKERS.

*inter*NET
CONNECTION

SCIENCE WORDS

community p.324
consumers p.334
decomposers p.336
ecosystem p.324
food chain p.334
food web p.338
habitat p.324
host p.347

carbon dioxide
  and oxygen
  cycle p.344
parasite p.347
population p.324
producers p.334

USING SCIENCE WORDS

Number a paper from 1 to 10. Fill in 1 to 5 with words from the list above.

1. A series of organisms that rely on each other for food is called a ___?___.

2. Oxygen is traded for carbon dioxide in the ___?___.

3. A parasite lives in or on a ___?___.

4. A group of food chains that are connected together make a ___?___.

5. Dead plant and animal material is broken down by ___?___.

6–10. Pick five words from the list above that were not used in 1 to 5 and use each in a sentence.

UNDERSTANDING SCIENCE IDEAS

11. How is it possible to grow a plant from the rain forest inside of a house in the desert?

12. Producers can get along without consumers. Why can't consumers get along without producers?

USING IDEAS AND SKILLS

13. **READING SKILL: REPRESENT TEXT IN DIFFERENT WAYS** Read the second paragraph on page 348. Use pictures and arrows to represent the ideas in the text.

14. **DEFINE** Using your observations, write a definition of an aquarium ecosystem.

15. **THINKING LIKE A SCIENTIST** Most scientists think that plants appeared on Earth before animals. Suggest reasons why they think this is true.

PROBLEMS and PUZZLES

Habitat Hideouts Look around outdoors for a rock or cardboard lying on the ground. Is there a habitat underneath? Wear a pair of gloves and gently lift up the rock. Is anything growing? Do you see any life forms? Why is this their habitat? Write down your observations.

CHAPTER 12
KEEPING IN BALANCE

Earth is carefully balanced. It has many parts that must work together. A change in one part of the system affects other parts. What kinds of changes might take place? How do living things survive these changes?

In Chapter 12 you will compare and contrast different environments. When you compare two things, you tell how they are alike. When you contrast two things, you tell how they are not alike.

353

WHY IT MATTERS

Living things compete against each other to meet their needs.

SCIENCE WORDS

competition when one organism works against another to get what it needs to live

predator an animal that hunts other animals for food

prey the animal a predator hunts

niche the job or role an organism has in an ecosystem

Competition

Who gets the worm? All of the young birds want it. Which one will get it? The loudest bird? The bird that looks hungriest? Birds compete to get worms. In what ways do you compete in your own life? What do you think is the best way to get something you need? If you were a baby bird, what would you do?

EXPLORE

HYPOTHESIZE You know that space is one of the needs of living things. When there are too many people in one place it gets uncomfortable! What happens when there are too many plants in one place? Does the amount of space available affect the way plants grow? Write a hypothesis in your *Science Journal.*

EXPLORE ACTIVITY

Investigate How Much Room Plants Need

Explore how crowding affects how plants grow.

MATERIALS

- soil
- bean seeds
- 4 milk cartons
- measuring cup
- water
- marker
- masking tape
- scissors
- *Science Journal*

PROCEDURES

1. Cut the tops from the milk cartons. Use the masking tape and the marker to label the cartons A to D. Carefully punch 3 drainage holes in the bottom of each carton. Use the measuring cup to fill each carton with the same amount of soil.

2. **USE VARIABLES** Plant 3 bean seeds in carton A. Plant 6 bean seeds in carton B. Plant 12 bean seeds in carton C and 24 bean seeds in carton D.

3. **PREDICT** What do you think each carton will look like in 14 days? Draw a picture in your *Science Journal* that shows your predictions.

4. **EXPERIMENT** Place the cartons in a well-lighted area. Water the plants every 2 days. Use the same amount of water for each carton.

CONCLUDE AND APPLY

1. **COMPARE** How many plants are there in each carton? How do the plants in carton D compare to the plants in the other cartons?

2. **IDENTIFY** For what things are the plants in each container competing?

3. **EXPLAIN** How did the number of plants in carton D affect the ability of each plant to get what it needs?

GOING FURTHER: Problem Solving

4. **EXPERIMENT** How could you test how much space pet gerbils need? Write a plan.

How Much Room Do Plants Need?

The Explore Activity shows that **competition** (kom′pi tish′ən) for space affects how plants grow. Competition occurs when one organism works against another to get what it needs to live. Organisms may compete for space, water, food, or some other need.

Desert plants compete for water. A cactus soaks up all of the moisture in a single area. No other plants can grow in this area. Rabbits compete for food. If there are too many rabbits, all of the grass will be eaten. Some of the rabbits won't survive.

Predators (pred′ə tərz) also compete. Predators are animals that hunt for food. Predators compete for **prey** (prā). Prey are the animals that predators hunt. Prey try to escape from predators. Predators compete with each other. Hawks, owls, and snakes all compete to catch lizards for food.

The owl is a predator. The lizard is its prey.

356

Different ecosystems support different numbers of organisms. The chart below compares the number of different types of trees and birds in a rain forest to those in a *temperate* (tem'pər it) forest. Temperate forests are the most common type of forest in the United States. Rain forests support many more types of trees and birds than temperate forests.

The same pattern is true for other living things. Why are there so many more types of organisms in the rain forest? Rain forests are much wetter and warmer than temperate forests. More plants can grow in this environment. More plants mean more animals, too.

MATH LINK — COMPARE TWO FORESTS

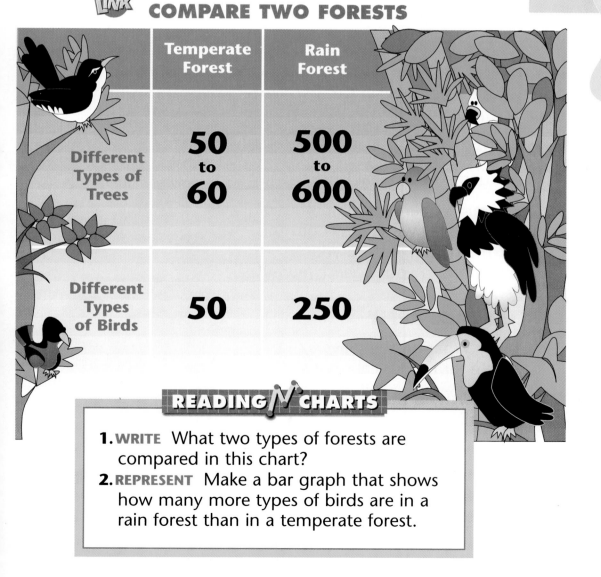

	Temperate Forest	Rain Forest
Different Types of Trees	50 to 60	500 to 600
Different Types of Birds	50	250

READING N' CHARTS

1. **WRITE** What two types of forests are compared in this chart?
2. **REPRESENT** Make a bar graph that shows how many more types of birds are in a rain forest than in a temperate forest.

How Can Competition Be Avoided?

Competition is a struggle for survival. In order to survive, organisms find ways to avoid competing. Many different types of organisms share the same ecosystem. Each type of organism has its own **niche** (nich). A niche is the job or role an organism has in an ecosystem. An organism's niche includes what an organism does, what it eats, and how it interacts with other organisms.

QUICK LAB

Musical Chairs

HYPOTHESIZE How does changing the number of chairs affect the game Musical Chairs? Write a hypothesis in your *Science Journal*.

MATERIALS
- chairs
- *Science Journal*

PROCEDURES

1. Play a game of Musical Chairs.

2. **EXPERIMENT** Change the number of chairs you play with. How does this affect the game? Record your observations in your *Science Journal*.

CONCLUDE AND APPLY

1. **EXPLAIN** What do the players compete for in Musical Chairs?

2. **IDENTIFY** Why is there a competition?

3. **COMPARE AND CONTRAST** How is the competition in the game like competition in a real ecosystem? How is it different?

For example, there are many types of pigeons in the forests of New Guinea. Each type of pigeon has a different niche in the forest ecosystem. They avoid competition by living in different places and eating different foods.

The Victoria crowned pigeon is one type of pigeon found in New Guinea. The niche of Victoria crowned pigeons includes eating fruits, berries, and large seeds. They nest in trees, and search for food on the ground of the forest.

WHY IT MATTERS

As a living thing, you have a niche in your ecosystem. Your niche includes the roles you have at home and at school. How is your niche different from the niches of other animals and people in the ecosystem?

Victoria crowned pigeon

REVIEW

1. What is competition?

2. What things do organisms compete for?

3. What is a niche?

4. **INFER** Why do some ecosystems have more types of organisms than others?

5. **CRITICAL THINKING** *Apply* Does a desert have more types of organisms than a rain forest? How do you know?

WHY IT MATTERS THINK ABOUT IT
Describe the niche you fill in your ecosystem.

WHY IT MATTERS WRITE ABOUT IT
How might your niche change as you grow?

ENOUGH to Go Around

Life's a contest! Who will win? A bluebird and sparrow both compete for space to build their nests. A fast-growing maple tree and slower-growing dogwood compete for the sunlight they both need to make food.

There's a problem. There's a limited amount of space for birds, sunlight for trees, and energy for people! If we don't cut back on our uses of some of our resources, someday they'll be gone!

How can we use energy today and know we'll have enough to go around in the future? We can choose alternate, or replacement, energy resources. It takes Earth millions of years to create coal, oil, and gas. They are nonrenewable resources.

"Let the sunshine in! Let the Sun... shine in!"

Solar energy is renewable. It comes from the Sun! The Sun's heat can boil water and provide steam energy. Solar power is already used to run small calculators and watches. It can be used to run many more things.

Wind energy is another renewable resource. The wind can be used to turn windmills. They in turn run big machines that produce electricity!

Water is a renewable resource. The power of fast-running rivers can be used to run machines and create electricity.

What other ways can we conserve our resources? How can we make sure there's always enough to go around?

DISCUSSION STARTER

1. Name as many ways as you can that people, plants, and animals use energy from the Sun.

2. For what other kinds of things do people, plants, and animals compete?

To learn more about competition, visit *www.mhschool.com/science* and enter the keyword COMPETE.

*inter*NET
CONNECTION

Fit for Surviving

Could a goose perch on a tree branch? Why or why not? What kind of feet would be best for perching on a tree branch? Parts of animals are like tools. Each part has a job to do. The job of goose feet is to paddle through water. Compare the feet of a goose to the feet of an eagle. How are they different? What jobs do you think the eagle's feet have?

WHY IT MATTERS

Certain characteristics allow living things to survive in their environment.

SCIENCE WORDS

adaptation a characteristic that helps an organism survive in its environment

camouflage an adaptation that allows animals to blend into their surroundings

EXPLORE

HYPOTHESIZE You know that animals are made up of different parts. All birds have beaks, but different kinds of birds have different kinds of beaks. How does a bird's beak help it eat the foods it needs? Write a hypothesis in your *Science Journal*. How might you test your ideas?

362

Design Your Own Experiment

HOW DOES THE SHAPE OF A BIRD'S BEAK AFFECT WHAT IT EATS?

MATERIALS
- chopsticks
- spoon
- tweezers
- clothespin
- drinking straw
- rubber worm
- peanut in shell
- rice
- water in paper cup
- *Science Journal*

PROCEDURES

1. PLAN How can you model how a bird's beak helps it to eat? Look at the materials given to you. How will you use them? Record your plan in your *Science Journal.*

2. COLLECT DATA Follow your plan. Be sure to record all your observations in your *Science Journal.* You might want to create a chart in which to record your data.

CONCLUDE AND APPLY

1. COMPARE Share your chart with other groups. How are your results similar? How are they different?

2. DRAW CONCLUSIONS Are some tools better suited to different jobs? How do you know?

GOING FURTHER: Apply

3. INFER How might the shape of a bird's beak help it to eat the foods it needs?

How Does the Shape of a Bird's Beak Affect What It Eats?

The Explore Activity shows that tools work in different ways. Some tools are good for picking up small things. Other tools are better for picking up large things. Parts of organisms also work like tools. A bird uses its beak as a tool for eating. Different beak shapes are suited to different kinds of food.

The honeycreeper is a kind of bird. There are different types of honeycreepers. Each type has a beak that is shaped differently. Each beak shape is an **adaptation** (ad′əp tā′shən). An adaptation is a special characteristic that helps an organism survive. How do different kinds of beaks help honeycreepers survive?

THE HONEYCREEPER BIRD

Each type of honeycreeper has one of these three basic beak shapes.

A long, curved beak is good for eating nectar from flowers.

A beak that is short, thick, and strong is just right for eating seeds and nuts.

A straight beak is good for eating insects.

Hawaiian honeycreepers live only on the islands of Hawaii.

READING /\/ CHARTS

1. **DISCUSS** How are honeycreepers alike? How are they different?
2. **WRITE** Compare the beak of a honeycreeper that eats seeds to the beak of a honeycreeper that eats insects.

Honeycreeper beaks are just one type of adaptation. There are many other types. In fact, most organisms have a variety of adaptations. Each adaptation helps the organism survive.

How is the wool of a lamb an adaptation? It keeps the lamb warm. A warm coat helps the lamb survive cold winter days. A giraffe's long neck is an adaptation, too. It helps the giraffe find food in high places. Finding food that others can't reach increases the giraffe's chances of survival. A frog has a long, sticky tongue. It helps the frog catch insects. Catching insects helps the frog get the food energy it needs to survive. The bright coloring of a flower is an adaptation. It attracts insects that help the flower reproduce. By reproducing this type of plant survives.

A frog's long, sticky tongue is an adaptation.

What Adaptations Help Protect Living Things?

Adaptations help organisms survive in different ways. Some of the most important adaptations are for protection. Organisms need protection from the weather and from their predators.

The shell of a turtle is an example of an adaptation that protects a living thing. When a turtle needs protection, it curls up inside of its shell. A rabbit may use its speed for protection. If a predator comes too close, the rabbit can run to safety. Rabbits also use **camouflage** (kam'ə fläzh) for protection. Camouflage is an adaptation that allows an organism to blend in with its environment. White rabbits blend in with the snow. Brown rabbits match their forest habitat.

This Indian leaf butterfly uses camouflage to protect itself. With its wings folded up, it looks like a dead leaf. Can you find the butterfly?

Brain Power

What purpose do you think the eyespots of this butterfly have?

Skill: Observing

IDENTIFYING PROPERTIES OF AN ENVIRONMENT

You know that camouflage is one way animals keep safe. In this activity you will observe an area of your classroom. When you observe something, you use one or more of your senses to learn about the properties of objects. You will use your observations of your classroom to help you design an animal that could hide in that environment.

MATERIALS
- construction paper
- crayons
- cotton balls
- yarn
- scissors
- tape
- *Science Journal*

PROCEDURES

1. OBSERVE Your teacher will help you select an area to observe. This area is the environment for the organism that you will design. What do you notice about the area? Record your observations in your *Science Journal.*

2. PLAN Discuss your observations with your group members. Make a list of features that would help an organism hide in this environment.

3. Use the materials given to you to create a plant or animal that will blend into its surroundings. Put your plant or animal into its environment.

CONCLUDE AND APPLY

1. OBSERVE Look for the organisms that your classmates designed. What are the features of each environment? Can you find the camouflaged organism? What characteristics help it to blend in?

2. COMMUNICATE Describe the characteristics of the organism that you made. Explain why you included each one.

3. INFER Some animals can change the color of their body covering. When might they do this? Why?

How Do Organisms in Different Environments Adapt?

Organisms in different environments have different types of adaptations. For example, a wolf that lives in a cold forest has a thick coat. A wolf that lives in a hot desert has a much thinner coat.

ADAPTATIONS IN DIFFERENT ENVIRONMENTS

	Desert	Arctic Tundra	River
Trees	A mesquite tree has deep roots.	No trees grow in the cold tundra.	A cottonwood tree has shallow roots.
Bears	No bears live in the desert.	A polar bear has thick white fur.	A black bear has black fur.
Birds	A roadrunner has brown feathers.	A snowy owl has white feathers.	A duck has waterproof feathers.

READING IN CHARTS

1. **DISCUSS** Why does the cottonwood tree have shallow roots? Why does the mesquite tree have deep roots?
2. **WRITE** Which environment has the greatest number of different organisms? Why do you think this is so?

People also have special adaptations that suit their environment. Your hands are a special adaptation. You can use your hands to do things that no other organism can do. For example, you can paint a picture, throw a ball, or play the piano. What other things can you do with your hands?

REVIEW

1. What is an adaptation?

2. What is camouflage? Give an example of camouflage.

3. Describe some adaptations that protect organisms.

4. **OBSERVE** Look at the picture of the frog on page 365. Write a description of the frog. What adaptations help it survive?

5. **CRITICAL THINKING** *Analyze* Compare reptiles that live in the desert and the rainforest. In what ways would you expect them to be different? How might they be the same?

WHY IT MATTERS **THINK ABOUT IT** Describe your favorite animal. What environment does it live in?

WHY IT MATTERS **WRITE ABOUT IT** What are some of your favorite animal's adaptations?

READING SKILL Compare and contrast the adaptations of your favorite animal with the adaptations of a giraffe. How are they alike? How are they different?

LEAPIN' LIZARDS!

Lizards are the favorite food of snakes, hawks, and other animals. Even so, lizards are pretty good at staying alive.

Some Lizards Disappear

The leaf-tailed gecko looks like a bump on a tree. It uses camouflage to blend in with the tree bark and moss found in its forest habitat. The gecko sits quietly all day, hiding in plain sight. At night it searches for food.

Some Lizards Scare Predators

When the frilled lizard of Australia is attacked, it raises the stiff skin around its neck. It hisses and lashes its tail. Even large snakes back off... wouldn't you?

What does the Texas horned lizard do when grabbed by an attacker? This lizard squirts blood out of its eyes! Most attackers let go . . . very quickly!

A Closer Look

Some Lizards Hide Out

The chuckwalla lives in Mexico and the southwestern United States. When it sees a predator, this lizard slips into a crack between two rocks. Then it puffs itself full of air. Even if the predator does find the chuckwalla, it can't pull the lizard out!

Some Lizards Run

Most lizards run fast, but the basilisk of Central and South America even runs on water! How? It has special scales on the bottoms of its rear feet. If the basilisk slows down, it sinks into the water and must swim to safety!

DISCUSSION STARTER

1. Why did lizards develop these ways to escape from their predators?

2. What would happen if hawks learned how to spot geckos sitting on branches?

To learn more about lizards, visit *www.mhschool.com/science* and enter the keyword LIZARDS.

*inter*NET
CONNECTION

Things Change

Before the spring of 1980, Mt. St. Helens was a sleeping volcano. Bears and elk roamed its deep green forests. Fish swam in its cool, clear streams. Wildflowers bloomed on its slopes.

Then, on May 18, 1980, Mt. St. Helens erupted. A huge eruption changed local habitats forever. How do you think these changes affected wildlife in the area?

WHY IT MATTERS

A change in an ecosystem affects the organisms that live there.

SCIENCE WORDS

perish to not survive

relocate to find a new home

endangered in danger of becoming extinct

extinct when there are no more of a certain plant or animal

EXPLORE

HYPOTHESIZE A big storm or volcanic eruption can cause a lot of change in a short amount of time. How do changes like these affect the living things in a particular area? Write a hypothesis in your *Science Journal*. How might you use a model to investigate your ideas?

Investigate What Happens When Ecosystems Change

Model what may happen when an ecosystem changes.

PROCEDURES

1. Make the 3 predator and 12 prey cards listed in the Materials. Give 1 predator card to each player. Stack the prey cards in the deck.

2. The object of the game is to get all 4 prey cards. To play:

- Predators take turns drawing a prey card from the deck. Keep prey cards that match the color of your predator card. Return all other prey cards to the pile. Play until one predator gets all 4 matching prey cards.

3. EXPERIMENT Add a card that says "fire" to the deck of prey cards. Play the game again. Any predator who draws the fire card must go out of the game. Return the fire card to the deck. The other two players continue to play until a predator gets all 4 prey cards or all players are out.

CONCLUDE AND APPLY

1. COMPARE AND CONTRAST What happened when you played the game the first time? What happened the second time?

2. CAUSE AND EFFECT The fire card represented a change to the ecosystem. What effect did the change have?

3. INFER What may happen when an ecosystem changes?

GOING FURTHER: Problem Solving

4. PREDICT What might happen if you changed the number of prey cards?

MATERIALS

- 3 Predator cards:
  Red hawk
  Blue owl
  Green snake
- 12 Prey cards:
  4 red
  4 blue
  4 green
- *Science Journal*

What Happens When Ecosystems Change?

The Explore Activity demonstrates that ecosystems can change. When change occurs, the organisms that live in that ecosystem are affected. Some have trouble surviving.

How did habitats near Spirit Lake change? After the eruption the forest was buried in ash. When it rained the ash turned muddy. Then the ash hardened into a tough crust. Plants were killed under the thick ash crust. Other living things that lived near the ground had their habitats destroyed. A wind of hot steam and rock blasted the area. The wind lifted trees right out of the ground. Organisms that lived on or near trees had their habitats destroyed.

Animals that roam the forest also lost their habitats. Some moved on to find new habitats far from Mt. St. Helens. Others could not find new habitats. Most of these organisms lost their lives.

These photographs show Spirit Lake on Mt. Saint Helens before and after the volcanic eruption.

As the years pass, the green forests may return to Mt. St. Helens. The wildflowers and animals may return, too. How long might it take?

Over time, some organisms found new habitats. The fireweed plant began to grow right through the cracks in the crust. As one organism moved back in, others followed. Seeds from different plants traveled through the air. They found places to grow under uprooted tree stumps. Squirrels that were hiding underground came out. Other organisms hiding underground also appeared. After a few years, a new ecosystem began to form on the crust of ash. It is different from the ecosystem that was there before.

A volcanic eruption is one event that can change an ecosystem. A flood or drought can change an ecosystem, too. Floods are caused by heavy rains or snow. Rivers rise up over their banks, and the rising water covers dry land. A drought is the opposite of a flood. During a drought it doesn't rain for weeks or months. Rivers and lakes dry up. Wet places become dry. Other natural disasters, such as fires, earthquakes, and storms, can also change an ecosystem.

How Do Ecosystems Come Back?

After a big change, ecosystems usually come back. A fire can destroy almost all the habitats in a forest. How does a forest come back after all its habitats are destroyed? There are several stages the forest must go through.

Stage 1 Habitat destruction
Bulbs and seeds may survive the fire. They begin to grow in the ash.

Stage 2 Grasses
Over time, grasses cover the bare ground. The grasses add nutrients to the soil. They also provide a home for insects. The insects attract larger animals.

Stage 3 Larger plants
Small trees begin to grow. The trees block the Sun. Without light the grasses begin to die.

Stage 4 Forest
Small trees are replaced by different, larger trees. The forest is the final stage.

READING ✳ DIAGRAMS

1. **DISCUSS** What happens to a forest right after it is destroyed?
2. **DISCUSS** Why do animals return after the grasses and insects instead of before them?

How Do Organisms Respond to Change?

Organisms may respond to change in one of three ways. Some organisms respond to a change in their habitat by adapting. Adapting means adjusting to the new habitat. The fireweed on Mt. St. Helens was covered by crust. It adapted to its new habitat by growing through the crust.

Some organisms **perish** (per'ish). Organisms that perish do not survive. A turtle may survive a fire. Where will it find food after the fire? If it cannot meet its needs, it may not survive. Some organisms **relocate** (rē lō'kāt). An organism that relocates finds a new home. Trees were destroyed on Mt. Saint Helens. Birds that lived in the trees could fly to new trees.

This box turtle survived a forest fire.

Dodo birds once covered the island of Mauritius near Africa. They became extinct in 1680.

Habitat destruction and overcrowding are not the only threats to organisms. Other threats include hunting and pollution. In some cases, organisms become **endangered** (en dān′jərd). An endangered organism is one that has very few of its kind still alive. Endangered organisms may become **extinct** (ek stingkt′). Extinct means that there are no more of that type of organism alive. Extinct animals include the dodo bird and the saber-toothed tiger.

QUICK LAB

MATH LINK

Crowd Control

HYPOTHESIZE What happens when the same number of organisms move into a smaller habitat? Write a hypothesis in your *Science Journal*.

MATERIALS
- 20 paper clips
- small box
- small book
- *Science Journal*

PROCEDURES

1. Toss the paper clips into the box. Remove any two paper clips that touch each other.

2. Gather the paper clips that remain from step 1 and toss them a second time. Again, remove all paper clips that touch. Repeat the process until all the paper clips are gone. Record the number of tosses you made in your *Science Journal*.

3. **EXPERIMENT** Play the game again. This time put a book into the box to make the box smaller.

CONCLUDE AND APPLY

INFER What happens when you crowd organisms together? How do their chances of survival change?

How do endangered organisms affect your life? When an organism becomes extinct, it is gone forever. Everyone would notice if a large animal like the Bengal tiger were to disappear. Small organisms are important, too. Many medicines are made from plants. If plants become extinct, they can't be used to make medicines.

The saber-toothed tiger above looks similar to tigers alive on Earth today, but it is extinct. Bengal tigers are endangered. Today these tigers live in protected parks.

REVIEW

1. What causes ecosystems to change? What happens when an ecosystem changes?

2. How does a forest recover from destruction?

3. How do organisms respond to habitat changes?

4. **COMMUNICATE** What is the difference between endangered organisms and extinct organisms?

5. **CRITICAL THINKING** *Evaluate* A forest is cut down to build a parking lot. Why is this habitat destruction more serious than if there had been a forest fire?

WHY IT MATTERS THINK ABOUT IT
Describe an endangered organism that you would want to save.

WHY IT MATTERS WRITE ABOUT IT
Write an article for the newspaper. Tell why it is important to save this endangered organism.

TOO MANY RABBITS!

Rabbits are cute and cuddly. There could never be too many, right? Wrong! Ask people in Australia. In the late 1800s, people first took rabbits there, and let them go free.

Before too long, the country had 600 million rabbits! They ate grass until the fields were bare, causing erosion. Sheep and other grass-eating animals starved.

In the 1950s, scientists used a virus to kill nearly all the rabbits. The few that lived had more babies, so ferrets were brought in to kill the rabbits.

The ferrets spread a disease to cattle and deer. Scientists used a different virus to kill the ferrets.

Since 1995, a new virus has killed most of the rabbits. Some people worry that a few rabbits will survive, reproduce, and take over Australia again.

DISCUSSION STARTER

1. Why do you think the rabbits became such a big problem in Australia?

2. What should scientists know before they bring in one kind of organism to get rid of another kind of organism?

To learn more about rabbits, visit **www.mhschool.com/science** and enter the keyword BUNNY.

*inter*NET
CONNECTION

SCIENCE WORDS

adaptation p.364
camouflage p.366
competition p.356
endangered p.378

extinct p.378
niche p.358
predator p.356
prey p.356

USING SCIENCE WORDS

Number a paper from 1 to 10. Fill in 1 to 5 with words from the list above.

1. The white fur of the polar bear is an example of ___?___.

2. A special characteristic that helps an organism survive is a(n) ___?___.

3. An organism that could become extinct is ___?___.

4. An animal that hunts is a ___?___.

5. Organisms that all want the same thing are in ___?___.

6–10. Pick five words from the list above. Include all words that were not used in 1 to 5. Use each word in a sentence.

UNDERSTANDING SCIENCE IDEAS

11. One group of rabbits lives on an island without predators. A second group on a different island lives with predators. Which group is more likely to be faster runners? Explain.

12. The walking stick insect looks just like a twig. What does this adaptation tell you about the insect's habitat?

USING IDEAS AND SKILLS

13. **READING SKILL: COMPARE AND CONTRAST** Look at page 374. Compare and contrast the two pictures of Spirit Lake on this page.

14. **OBSERVE** Draw a picture of your favorite animal. How many adaptations can you count on the animal? What purpose does each adaptation serve?

15. **THINKING LIKE A SCIENTIST** How can people build roads to cause as little habitat destruction as possible? Think of some ways to do this.

PROBLEMS and PUZZLES

Color Blind How does color help protect animals? Find a grassy area. Bring 24 plain toothpicks, 24 green toothpicks, and 24 red toothpicks. Have a friend throw the toothpicks on the grass. How many toothpicks can you pick up in one minute? Which colors did you pick the most of? Which color was hardest to see?

USING SCIENCE WORDS

adaptation p.364
camouflage p.366
decomposer p.336
endangered p.378
extinct p.378
food web p.338
habitat p.324

host p.347
niche p.358
parasite p.347
population p.324
predator p.356
prey p.356
producers p.334

Number a paper from 1 to 10. Beside each number write the word or words that best completes the sentence.

1. The place where a plant or an animal lives is its ___?___.

2. Organisms that make their own food are ___?___.

3. Dead plant and animal material may be broken down by ___?___.

4. A flea on a dog is an example of a ___?___.

5. A parasite lives in or on a ___?___.

6. An animal that hunts other animals is called a ___?___.

7. The shell of a turtle is an example of an ___?___ that protects a living thing.

8. A rabbit's white fur provides ___?___ in the snow.

9. If there are only a few of one kind of plant, then that plant is ___?___.

10. If there were no more blue whales, they would be ___?___.

UNDERSTANDING SCIENCE IDEAS

Write 11 to 15. For each number write the letter for the best answer. You may wish to use the hints provided.

11. What is probably NOT found in a pond ecosystem?
    a. cactus
    b. frog
    c. heron
    d. algae
    (Hint: Read pages 326-327.)

12. Which of the following is a consumer?
    a. an ant
    b. a mushroom
    c. a lettuce plant
    d. an apple tree
    (Hint: Read page 334.)

13. Producers and consumers exchange carbon dioxide and
    a. food
    b. water
    c. habitats
    d. oxygen
    (Hint: Read page 344.)

14. Which of the following might survive best in the Arctic tundra?
    a. a cottonwood tree
    b. a mesquite tree
    c. a polar bear
    d. a road runner
    (Hint: Read page 368.)

15. Which of the following animals is now extinct?
    a. dodo bird
    b. pigeon
    c. blue whale
    d. elephant
    (Hint: Read page 379.)

USING IDEAS AND SKILLS

16. What are three plants and three animals that share your habitat?

17.  DEFINE Make a list of different adaptations you have learned about in this unit. Using your list, write your own definition of adaptation.

18. Give an example of how animals help plants to reproduce.

THINKING LIKE A SCIENTIST

19. OBSERVE Jungle birds often have bright colors. What colors do city birds usually have? Explain why.

20. How can fire change an ecosystem?

WRITING IN YOUR JOURNAL

SCIENCE IN YOUR LIFE
Make a list of some insect members of your ecosystem's community. How are these insects important to your ecosystem?

PRODUCT ADS
Sometimes insects, such as ants, can become pests. Ads for products that kill pests often say that the products are very strong and will get rid of all pests. Is this always a good thing? How might destroying a pest affect other living things in an ecosystem?

HOW SCIENTISTS WORK
Scientists observe living things to learn how they affect each other. Scientists also study how living things are affected by the nonliving parts of their ecosystems. Why do you think it is important for scientists to learn about these things?

Design your own Experiment

What animals (not pets) in your neighborhood use camouflage? Plan to make a survey of animals in your neighborhood to find out. Tell what characteristics allow each animal to blend in with its surroundings.

interNET CONNECTION

For help in reviewing this unit, visit *www.mhschool.com/science*

PROBLEMS and PUZZLES

Competing Birds

Study competition between different kinds of birds. With the help of a parent or teacher, build a bird feeder from a plastic milk jug or aluminum pie pan. Place bird seed, sunflower seeds, and cracker crumbs in the feeder. Observe the different birds that visit the feeder. Use a tape recorder and a camera to get more data. Use the sounds you recorded to help you identify the different birds. What kind of food does each bird eat? Do all the birds compete for the same food? Do some birds avoid competition by eating different foods? Write a report that tells what you learn from your observations.

Active Algae

Place some green pond water in a clear jar. Add some tap water that has sat out overnight. Cover the jar with foil. Cut a small hole in the foil and place the jar in a window. Make sure the hole in the foil faces the sunlight. After a few hours, carefully lift the cover off the jar. What happened? Why?

Seeds and Soil

HYPOTHESIZE

Do bean seeds grow better in sandy soil or potting soil? Write a hypothesis.

EXPERIMENT

Plan an experiment that will test your hypothesis. What materials will you need? What variables do you need to control? What variable do you need to change? Once you have a plan approved by your teacher, try your experiment.

ANALYZE THE RESULTS

Write a report that summarizes your observations. What conclusions can you draw? List three questions you would like to answer next.

UNIT 7

HUMAN BODY: KEEPING HEALTHY

CHAPTER 13
PROTECTION AGAINST DISEASE

The news report says the flu is spreading. You had the flu once. You wonder whether or not you will get it again.

So far you still feel fine. Could parts of your body be protecting you? If you do get sick, do you know which parts of your body will help you get better?

In Chapter 13 you will read to find important ideas. Finding important ideas helps you remember the information you've read.

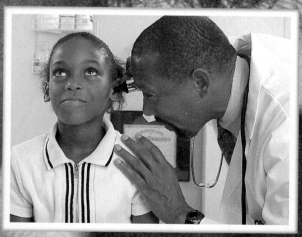

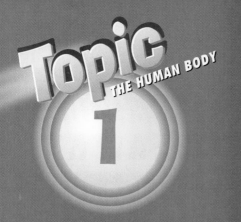

WHY IT MATTERS

Taking care of your skin will help keep your whole body healthy.

SCIENCE WORDS

epidermis the outer layer of skin

melanin a substance that gives skin its color

gland a part of the body that makes substances the body needs

dermis the layer of skin just below the epidermis

nerve cells cells that carry messages to and from all parts of the body

pore a tiny opening in the skin

You Are Covered

Do you ever wonder what is inside your computer? It is full of parts you cannot see or touch. The parts are sealed in a hard case. Hard cases make good sense. Without them, machine parts could fall out or get damaged.

You, too, are full of parts you cannot see or touch. Yet no hard case protects them. It is up to your skin to keep your insides safe inside you.

EXPLORE

HYPOTHESIZE **Your skin does more than cover your body. What other jobs do you think it does? Write a hypothesis in your *Science Journal*. How might you examine your skin to investigate what its jobs are?**

Design Your Own Experiment

WHAT DOES SKIN DO?

PROCEDURES

1. OBSERVE How can you use your senses to find out more about your skin? You might record how your skin feels when you touch it, breathe on it, or blow on it.

2. OBSERVE How can you use the hand lens to observe your skin? What do you see? Record your observations.

3. OBSERVE How does water affect your skin?

CONCLUDE AND APPLY

1. COMPARE AND CONTRAST How does your skin feel when you touch it? When you blow on it? When you breathe on it?

2. HYPOTHESIZE How does water affect your skin? What does this tell you about what skin can keep in or keep out of your body?

GOING FURTHER: Apply

3. DRAW CONCLUSIONS What do you think some of the jobs of skin are? How do you know?

MATERIALS
- water
- hand lens
- *Science Journal*

FUNtastic Facts

What organ grows to be 22 square feet in size, the size of a blanket? Your skin—the body's largest organ! The palm of your hand is one of the thickest parts of your skin. One square inch of skin contains hundreds of sweat glands and up to 15 feet of blood vessels. What's the smallest human organ?

MATH LINK

What Does Skin Do?

The Explore Activity demonstrates that skin has many jobs. One job is to cover your body. Another job is protection. Your skin is a barrier that protects your body by keeping harmful germs out. Another important job of skin is helping you sense the world around you. Your skin helps you feel whether something is hot or cold, hard or soft.

Some of your skin's jobs are done by the **epidermis** (ep'i dür' mis). The epidermis is the outer layer of skin. Your epidermis is soft, smooth, and tough. It is a shield that keeps out dust, dirt, and germs. Water cannot soak into it. The water inside you can't leak out of it either. Water makes up about two-thirds of your body. If it leaked out of your skin, there would not be much left of you!

THE EPIDERMIS

1 The epidermis protects the inside of your body by keeping out dust, dirt, and germs.

Drop of water

2 New living skin cells are being made here. The new cells contain **melanin** (mel' ə nin). Melanin is a substance that colors the skin. The more melanin a cell contains, the darker the skin is.

You touch the world around you with your epidermis. Your hair and nails grow out of it. Next to each of your hairs there is an oil **gland** (gland). A gland is a part of the body that makes substances that the body needs. Oil glands make waxy oil that covers the surface of your skin and hair. The oil keeps them soft, smooth, and bendable. It also makes your skin waterproof.

Your skin does a lot more than just cover you!

3 These living cells are being pushed up by the cells growing under them.

4 The surface of your skin is made up of dead cells. They flake off from morning to night. Replacing the top layer of protective dead cells is one of the jobs of the epidermis!

READING *N'* DIAGRAMS

1. **DISCUSS** If you have more melanin in your skin, is your skin darker or lighter?
2. **REPRESENT** Where do dead skin cells come from? Draw a diagram.

What's Beneath the Epidermis?

No matter how hard you look at your epidermis, you won't be able to see your oil glands or the roots of your hairs. That's because the glands and the roots are deep in pits that reach down into the **dermis** (dûr′ mis). The dermis is the layer of skin just below the epidermis.

The dermis is the thickest layer of your skin. It is made up of living cells. The dermis contains **nerve cells** (nûrv selz). Nerve cells are cells that carry messages to and from all parts of the body.

Nerve cells in your skin help your brain to understand what is happening in your environment.

THE DERMIS

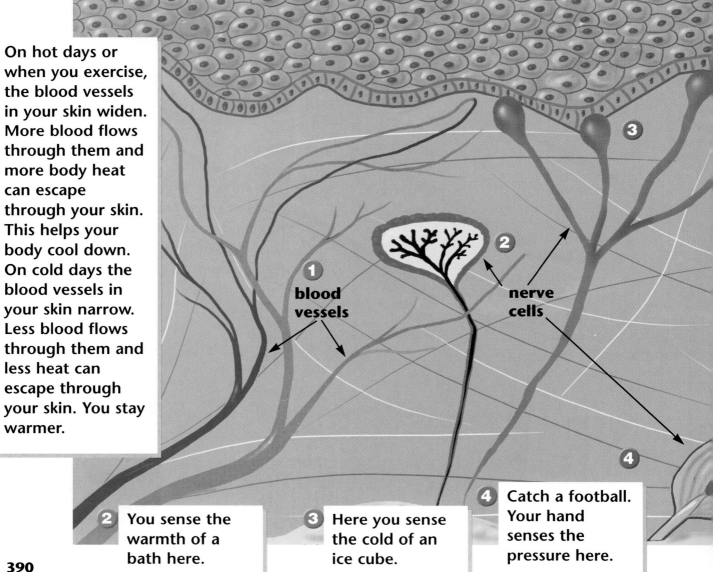

1 On hot days or when you exercise, the blood vessels in your skin widen. More blood flows through them and more body heat can escape through your skin. This helps your body cool down. On cold days the blood vessels in your skin narrow. Less blood flows through them and less heat can escape through your skin. You stay warmer.

1 blood vessels

2 nerve cells

2 You sense the warmth of a bath here.

3 Here you sense the cold of an ice cube.

4 Catch a football. Your hand senses the pressure here.

390

The different nerve cells in your dermis get different messages. Numbers 2 to 4 in the diagram below describe what different nerve cells can sense.

There are many blood vessels in your dermis. Blood delivers food and oxygen to living cells so they can do their jobs. Blood picks up wastes and carries them away. Blood also helps keep your body at the right temperature all day long. Your body will not work right if it gets too hot or too cold. Numbers 1, 5, and 6 in the diagram below describe some ways skin and blood vessels keep your body at the right temperature.

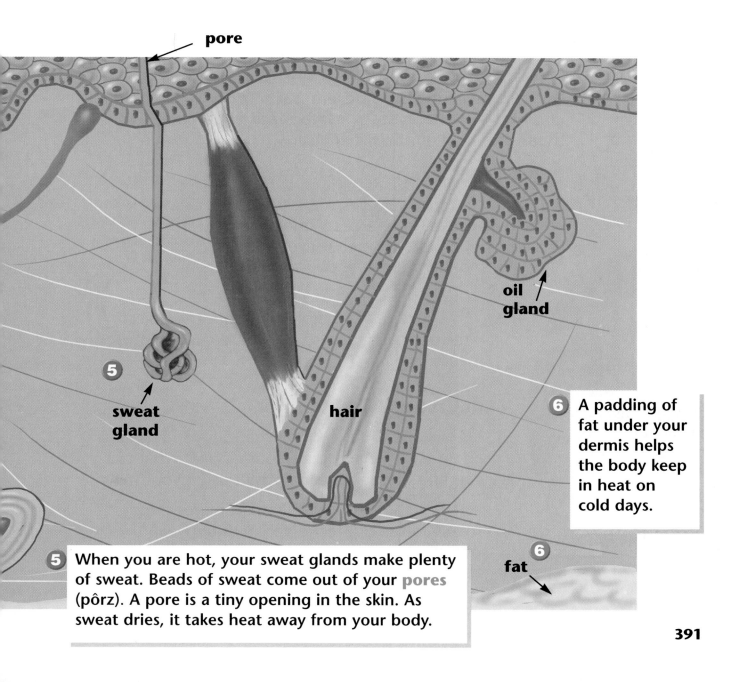

pore

oil gland

5

sweat gland

hair

6 A padding of fat under your dermis helps the body keep in heat on cold days.

6

fat

5 When you are hot, your sweat glands make plenty of sweat. Beads of sweat come out of your pores (pôrz). A pore is a tiny opening in the skin. As sweat dries, it takes heat away from your body.

How Can You Take Care of Your Skin?

Your skin does many important jobs. It's important to keep your skin healthy. To keep your skin healthy, shower or bathe often. Otherwise dirt, sweat, oil, and germs will build up on your skin. You won't look good or smell good.

QUICK LAB

Skin Sense

HYPOTHESIZE **How do different parts of your skin help you find out about the world around you? Write a hypothesis in your** *Science Journal.*

PROCEDURES

1. OBSERVE Close your eyes. Have your partner place 3 or 4 objects on your desk. Roll up one of your sleeves and try to find out about the objects with your elbow.

MATERIALS
- 3 or 4 classroom objects
- *Science Journal*

2. OBSERVE Now try to find out about the objects with your hand. Record your observations in your *Science Journal.*

CONCLUDE AND APPLY

1. COMPARE AND CONTRAST What did you find out about each object using your elbow? What did you find out about each object using your hand?

2. DRAW CONCLUSIONS Which part of your body made it easier to feel differences between the objects? Which part of your body made it harder? Why?

Wash your hands often, and always wash them before you eat. If you get a cut, wash and bandage it at once. That way your skin won't get infected and will be able to heal itself quickly.

You can help keep your skin healthy by getting plenty of rest and exercise and eating healthful foods. Protect your skin from too much sun. Use a sunscreen whenever you spend time outdoors.

Brain Power

Why should you wash your hands before you eat? What are some other occasions when you should wash your hands? Why?

WHY IT MATTERS

Your skin is about as thick as a piece of cardboard. Yet think of all it does for you every day! Your skin protects you. It keeps you warm or cools you down. It helps your brain sense what is happening in your environment.

A sunscreen can help protect you from sunburn.

REVIEW

1. What are the two layers of the skin called?

2. What are the jobs of each layer of skin?

3. How does your dermis help you control the temperature of your body?

4. **COMMUNICATE** How can you take care of your skin?

5. **CRITICAL THINKING** *Evaluate* Why is it important to care for your skin? What might happen if you don't?

WHY IT MATTERS THINK ABOUT IT
How does your skin keep itself healthy? How can you help protect your skin?

WHY IT MATTERS WRITE ABOUT IT
Describe the kinds of things that skin helps keep out of your body. Why is it important that these things stay out of your body?

World of SCIENCE

Good Sun, Bad Sun

The ultraviolet rays in sunlight can burn your skin.

Health Link

Do you have fun in the sun? Did you know that too much sun is no fun for your skin?

Sunlight is made of different kinds of rays. Many of these rays are helpful. Some let you see things. Some make you feel warm and toasty. The ultraviolet rays, however, can be dangerous.

Your skin uses some ultraviolet rays to make vitamin D. This vitamin helps you build strong bones and teeth. However, too many ultraviolet rays can burn your skin and damage your skin cells. Your skin could become tough and dry. You might even get skin cancer!

How can you enjoy the Sun without harming your skin? Limit your time outdoors in sunlight. Wear a hat with a wide brim to shade your face. Rub on sunscreen to keep most ultraviolet rays from touching your skin.

There are many kinds of sunscreens. Choose one with a sun-protection factor, or SPF, of 15 or more. Don't forget to read the directions carefully before using sunscreen or any other skin cream.

Enjoy the Sun, but be Sun smart. Protect your skin. It's covered you for a long time. Now it's your turn to cover it!

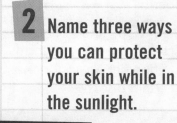

With an umbrella, a hat, and sunscreen, this boy is well protected!

Discussion Starter

1 Which rays from the Sun can harm your skin?

2 Name three ways you can protect your skin while in the sunlight.

inter **CONNECTION** To learn more about solar rays, visit **www.mhschool.com/science** and enter the keyword **SUNSMART.**

WHY IT MATTERS

When you are healthy you have the energy to do all the things you need to do.

Fighting Disease

Do you remember the last time you were sick? How did you feel? Germs are around you every hour of every day. They are trying to get inside you so that they can live and make more germs. Yet you aren't sick every day. How does your body defend itself against germs?

SCIENCE WORDS

bacteria one-celled living things

virus a tiny particle that can reproduce only inside a living cell

white blood cells cells in the blood that fight bacteria and viruses

antibody a chemical made by the immune system to fight a particular disease

immunity the body's ability to fight diseases caused by germs

vaccine a medicine that causes the body to form antibodies against a certain disease

EXPLORE

HYPOTHESIZE Which parts of your body help protect you from invading germs? Write a hypothesis in your *Science Journal*. How might you use a model to test your ideas?

Investigate How the Body Protects Itself

Use a model to investigate how your body protects itself from invading germs.

MATERIALS

- sugar
- water
- clay
- a sheet of paper
- a comb
- sticky tape
- 3 cups
- *Science Journal*

PROCEDURES

1. MAKE A MODEL Write the words *EAR, SKIN, STOMACH, EYE,* and *NOSE* on the paper as shown. Press the clay above the word EAR. The clay stands for earwax. Draw bricks over the word *SKIN.* The bricks stand for dead cells in the epidermis. Wad up a piece of the sticky tape and drop the wad inside one of the cups. It stands for mucus. Place the cup above the word *NOSE* and lay the comb on top of the cup. The comb stands for nose hairs.

2. OBSERVE The sugar stands for germs. Drop some sugar on the clay, comb, and bricks. What happens? Write your observations in your *Science Journal.*

3. MAKE A MODEL Turn a cup over and place it above the word *EYE.* Place a cup over the word *STOMACH.*

4. OBSERVE Drop some sugar on the upside-down cup. Add a few drops of water. The water stands for tears. What happens? Drop some sugar into the cup that stands for the stomach. Add water. This time the water stands for stomach juices.

CONCLUDE AND APPLY

1. INFER Name some ways the body protects itself from invading germs?

GOING FURTHER: Problem Solving

2. MAKE A MODEL What happens to germs when you have a cut in your skin? How might you use a model to find out?

397

How Does the Body Protect Itself?

Germs can make you sick, and no one likes that! The Explore Activity shows that certain parts of your body work to keep germs from entering. These body parts are the body's first line of defense against germs. How do they do it? The diagram explains what each of these body parts do.

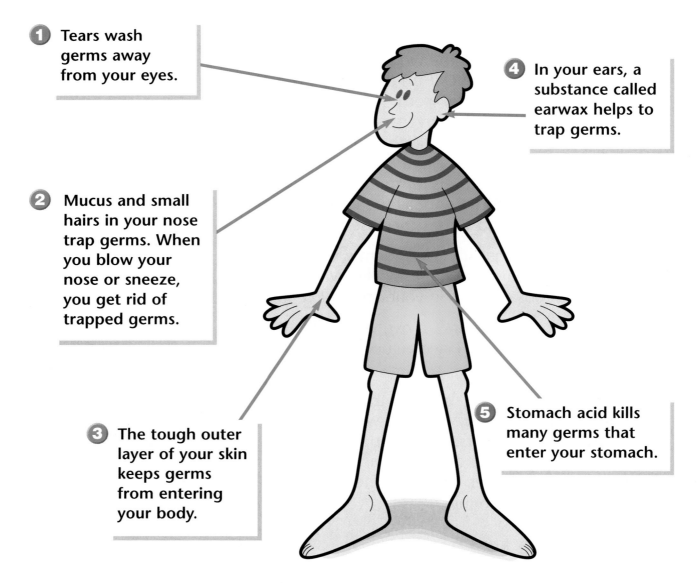

1 Tears wash germs away from your eyes.

2 Mucus and small hairs in your nose trap germs. When you blow your nose or sneeze, you get rid of trapped germs.

3 The tough outer layer of your skin keeps germs from entering your body.

4 In your ears, a substance called earwax helps to trap germs.

5 Stomach acid kills many germs that enter your stomach.

Most of the time, your body does a great job keeping germs out. So how do germs get inside you? Sometimes they can slip past your earwax and your nose hairs. They can also slip in through a cut in your skin. That's why you should clean and bandage cuts.

What's Making You Sick?

Did someone near you sneeze or cough? That's one way germs go from one person to another. If you touch something with germs on it and then touch your nose, mouth, or food, the germs may get inside you. There are many ways that germs can infect your body.

You know that germs can make you sick. Did you know that there are different kinds of germs? Some types of **bacteria** (bak tîr′ ē ə) are germs. Bacteria are one-celled living things that can be helpful or harmful. Some helpful bacteria are decomposers that break down dead plant and animal matter. Other helpful bacteria produce yogurt and cheese from milk. However, some harmful bacteria cause disease. Different kinds of harmful bacteria cause different diseases.

Another kind of germ is a **virus** (vī′ rəs). A virus is a tiny particle that can only reproduce inside a living cell. Viruses are very, very small. One million lined up in a row would not measure 3 cm (about 1 inch). When a virus enters one of your cells it makes that cell make hundreds of copies of itself. When the copies burst out of the cell, the cell dies. The copies of the virus are now free to enter other cells. Soon there are thousands of copies of the virus in your body.

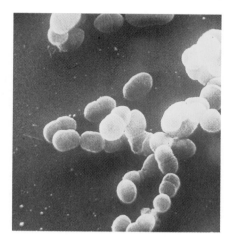

These bacteria cause strep throat.

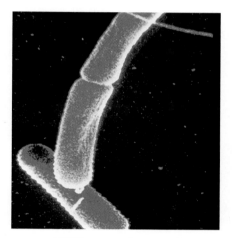

Different bacteria have different shapes.

A virus uses your cells to make copies of itself.

What Does Your Body Do When Germs Attack?

Once germs get into your body, your body's **white blood cells** (hwît blud selz) fight back. White blood cells are cells in the blood that fight bacteria and viruses. You have millions of these germ fighters inside you. When germs invade, white blood cells travel to where they are needed. Different kinds of white blood cells do different jobs. The diagram tells you what those jobs are.

GETTING RID OF GERMS

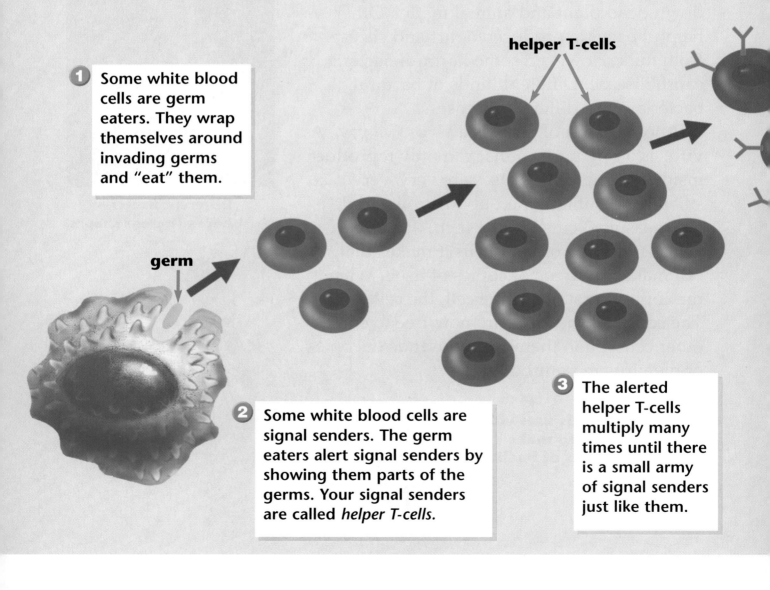

helper T-cells

1 Some white blood cells are germ eaters. They wrap themselves around invading germs and "eat" them.

germ

2 Some white blood cells are signal senders. The germ eaters alert signal senders by showing them parts of the germs. Your signal senders are called *helper T-cells.*

3 The alerted helper T-cells multiply many times until there is a small army of signal senders just like them.

white blood cell

Special white blood cells "eat" and destroy bacteria.

bacteria

6 The antibodies attach themselves to the invading germs and make them harmless. Your body keeps making antibodies until all the germs are destroyed.

B cells

4 Signals sent by helper T-cells alert another kind of white blood cell. These cells are called *B cells*.

5 The B cells make Y-shaped **antibodies** (an' ti bod' ēz). An antibody is a chemical made by the body to fight a particular disease.

READING ∕ DIAGRAMS

1. **WRITE** Discuss What is the job of the helper T-cells?
2. **WRITE** What is an antibody?

Skill: Making a Model

GERMS AND ANTIBODIES

A key must fit a lock or the lock won't open. Just like a key in a lock, an antibody has to fit a germ for the antibody to work correctly. You can make a model to show this. Making a model means constructing a representation of something. The model can be used to explain how something works.

MATERIALS

- construction paper
- scissors
- *Science Journal*

PROCEDURES

1. Cut the construction paper into several squares. Then cut the squares into two pieces, like a puzzle. Label one half of each cutout with the letter G. The G stands for germ. Label the other part of the cutout with the letter A. The A stands for antibody.

2. **MAKE A MODEL** Swap your G and A pieces with pieces from another group. Try to match each G piece to an A piece. How many pairs fit together? Record the number in your *Science Journal*. Return the G and A pieces to the group that made them.

3. Change some of your shapes. You might tear or fold a small section of the paper.

4. **MAKE A MODEL** Repeat Step 2. How many pairs fit together now?

CONCLUDE AND APPLY

1. **COMPARE AND CONTRAST** What happened the first time you matched shapes together? What happened the second time?

GOING FURTHER: *Apply*

2. **COMMUNICATE** Use your model to explain why it is important for an antibody to fit a germ.

Why Do You Get Colds Over and Over Again?

Some diseases, like chicken pox, you get only once. Other diseases, like a cold, you may get over and over again. Why does this happen?

Once your body has won the battle against a certain type of invading germ, your white blood cells will "remember" the germs they destroyed. If that same germ ever invades again, they will recognize it. Your white blood cells will attack and destroy that germ before it can make you sick.

You probably have had many colds.

When your body kills a germ before it can make you sick, you have **immunity** (imū′ ni tē) to that germ. Immunity is the body's ability to protect itself or fight diseases caused by germs. Your *immune system* is all the body parts and activities that fight diseases.

There is only one kind of germ that causes chicken pox. Once you've had chicken pox, you won't get it again. However, there are many different kinds of germs that cause colds. Each time you get a cold, your body must fight a new germ.

Brain Power

Suppose you've had chicken pox once. What might your white blood cells do if a chicken pox virus enters your body again?

How Can You Keep Healthy?

Your immune system is at work 24 hours a day. It is your best defense against germs. Without it you could not stay alive. Germs would take over your body and kill your cells.

That's why it is important to keep your immune system working at its best. It will be at its best if you eat healthfully, get plenty of rest, and make sure that you get all your **vaccines** (vak' sēnz).

A vaccine is a medicine that causes the body to form antibodies against a certain disease. You've learned that your body makes antibodies to develop immunity to diseases. A vaccine helps your body develop immunity to a certain disease without actually having had the disease. A vaccine contains weak or dead germs that cannot make you sick. Before you started school, you probably had to have several vaccines.

Gertrude Elion won the Nobel Prize in 1988. She helped develop medicines used to treat diseases caused by viruses.

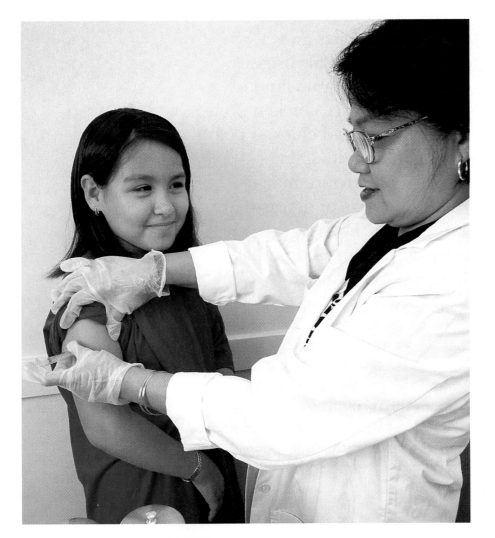

Vaccines help protect people from diseases like polio, measles, and whooping cough.

You probably know when your body is working at its best. You have energy to work and play. Being sick makes you tired. You may miss out on fun things you want to do. Your immune system works to keep you healthy. Taking care of yourself will help your immune system take care of you.

REVIEW

1. What are some of the ways the body protects itself from invading germs?

2. What kinds of cells help you to fight germs?

3. What does it mean to be immune to a germ?

4. **MAKE A MODEL** Draw a picture that shows what might happen if your white blood cells can't do their jobs.

5. **CRITICAL THINKING** *Apply* A friend you often play with at school has a cold. Now she is home sick. You feel fine. Why didn't you get sick?

WHY IT MATTERS THINK ABOUT IT
Describe how you felt the last time you were sick. How did you help yourself feel better?

WHY IT MATTERS WRITE ABOUT IT
What healthy habits will help your immune system do its job? If you do get sick, how can you take care of yourself until you get better?

READING SKILL What is the most important idea of the paragraph on page 400?

Smog Alert!

"A smog alert has been issued today for the city and all surrounding counties. Doctors urge people with asthma or other breathing problems to stay indoors."

What is smog? It's a cloud of fog and smoke. Most clouds float high in the sky, but, some form in damp air close to the ground as fog. The fog in smog is part of the water cycle.

Fog becomes smog when it forms around both dust and smoke particles. Smoke comes from the chimneys of houses and factories. It also comes from the exhausts of cars, trucks, and buses. Smog pollutes the air people need to breathe!

Even though the particles in smog aren't germs, our immune system treats them just like any other invaders. However, our immune system can't always handle all the particles in smog. Many people have trouble breathing. People who already have breathing problems may get very sick. Some may die.

All living things need clean air to breathe, so we must help keep our air clean. How? Walk or ride bikes for short trips instead of using cars that pollute the air. Look for ways to save electricity. Many power plants burn fossil fuels to make the electricity you use!

The smog in the city makes it hard for people to breathe.

Earth Science Link

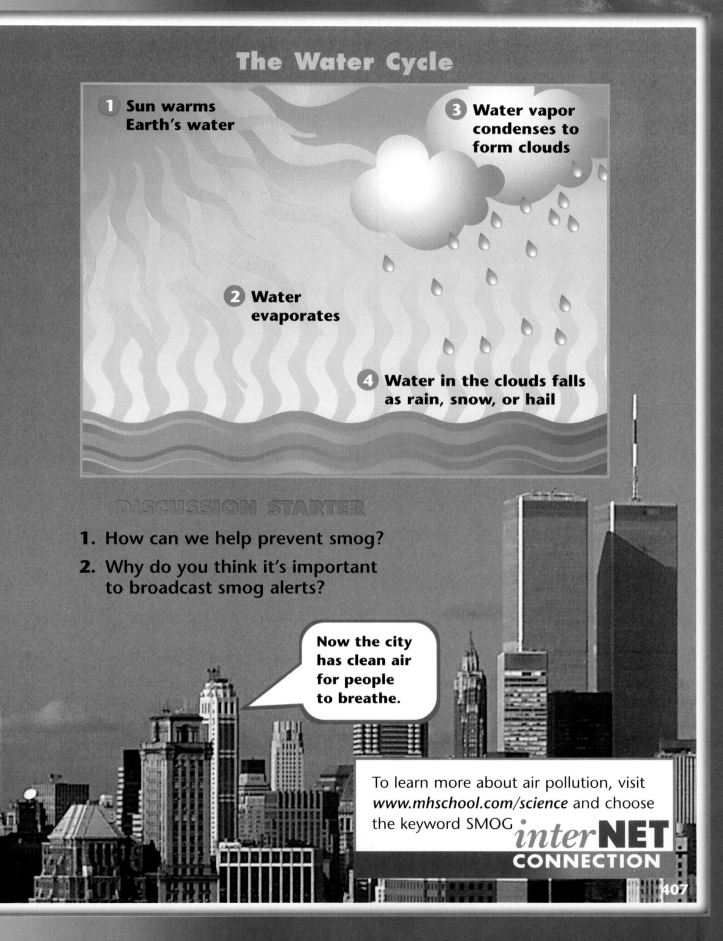

The Water Cycle

1. Sun warms Earth's water
2. Water evaporates
3. Water vapor condenses to form clouds
4. Water in the clouds falls as rain, snow, or hail

DISCUSSION STARTER

1. How can we help prevent smog?
2. Why do you think it's important to broadcast smog alerts?

Now the city has clean air for people to breathe.

To learn more about air pollution, visit **www.mhschool.com/science** and choose the keyword SMOG

*inter*NET CONNECTION

SCIENCE WORDS

antibody p.401
bacteria p.399
dermis p.390
epidermis p.388
gland p.389
immunity p.403
melanin p.388

nerve cells p.390
pore p.391
white blood
  cells p.400
vaccine p.404
virus p.399

USING SCIENCE WORDS

Number a paper from 1 to 10. Fill in 1 to 5 with words from the list above.

1. The layer of skin just below the epidermis is the __?__.

2. A part of the body that makes substances the body needs is a __?__.

3. The substance that gives skin its color is __?__.

4. The cells in the blood that fight bacteria and viruses are __?__.

5. A medicine that causes the body to form antibodies against a certain disease is a __?__.

6–10. **Pick five words from the list above that were not used in 1 to 5 and use each in a sentence.**

UNDERSTANDING SCIENCE IDEAS

11. Why is taking care of your skin so important?

12. Explain the different ways your body protects itself from disease.

USING IDEAS AND SKILLS

13. **READING SKILL: FIND IMPORTANT IDEAS** What are some of the important ideas of this chapter?

14. **MAKE A MODEL** Model what happens when a virus gets inside a cell. Make a drawing that shows what the virus does and how the body works to protect itself.

15. **THINKING LIKE A SCIENTIST** Do you think a cut covered with a bandage will heal faster than one without a bandage? Write a hypothesis. Explain how you would test your ideas.

PROBLEMS and PUZZLES

Thick and Thin Use a toothpick to find where on your foot the skin is thicker and where it is thinner. Draw an outline of your foot. Mark on it where your skin is thicker and where it is thinner. Why is there a difference? Does your skin change?

CHAPTER 14
NUTRITION AND DIGESTION

Why does your body need food? You probably know that food gives you energy. Food also provides you with the materials you need to grow healthy and strong. Do you know what foods are best to eat?

In Chapter 14 you will summarize information about how your body uses food. Summarizing helps you remember the most important ideas.

WHY IT MATTERS

Eating healthful foods is an important step in helping your body grow healthy and strong.

SCIENCE WORDS

nutrients substances that your body needs for energy and growth

carbohydrates substances used by the body as its main source of energy

fats substances that are used by the body as long-lasting sources of energy

protein substances that the body uses for growth and the repair of cells

fiber material that helps move wastes through the body

vitamins substances used by the body for growth

Food for Health

What is your favorite food? Are there some foods that you dislike? Eating your favorite foods is fun. Eating is important, too. Eating the right foods helps to keep your body healthy. Different foods contain different things that your body needs. Do you know what kinds of foods your body needs to stay healthy?

EXPLORE

HYPOTHESIZE How can you tell what is in different foods? Write a hypothesis in your *Science Journal*. How might you test your ideas?

Investigate What's in Food

Look for clues of whether these foods contain substances called fats.

MATERIALS

- samples of different foods
- scissors
- brown paper bags
- *Science Journal*

PROCEDURES

1. Your teacher will give you samples of different foods. Predict which ones you think contain fat. Write your predictions in your *Science Journal*.

2. EXPERIMENT Cut the paper bag into squares. Write the name of each food on a square. Rub a little of each food on the square that has its name. Let the squares dry for an hour.

3. OBSERVE What has happened to the paper squares?

CONCLUDE AND APPLY

1. IDENTIFY Foods that contain a lot of fats often leave a greasy mark on surfaces they touch. Can you identify which of the foods contain fats?

2. INFER What can you say about the foods that left no greasy mark on the paper?

GOING FURTHER: Apply

3. CLASSIFY Divide the foods into two groups. In one group place the foods that contain fats. In the second group place the foods that do not. What can you say about these two groups of foods?

What's in Food?

The Explore Activity shows that some foods contain substances called fats. Fats are a type of **nutrient** (nü′ trē ənt). A nutrient is a substance that your body needs for energy and growth. There are different kinds of nutrients. Over the next four pages you will find out what these different nutrients are and why they are so important.

Carbohydrates

One type of nutrient is **carbohydrates** (kär′ bō hi′ drātz). Carbohydrates are nutrients used by the body as its main source of energy.

Carbohydrates are in foods that contain sugar, such as fruits. When you run and play you need quick energy. Most of this energy comes from sugar in the food you eat. Plants make sugar using the energy in sunlight. When you eat fruits and other plant foods you get sugar from them. Carbohydrates are also in foods such as breads, cereals, and pasta.

Fats

The Explore Activity shows some foods that have **fats** (fatz) in them. Fats are substances used by the body as long-lasting sources of energy. Eating too many fats can add unhealthy weight to your body, but that doesn't mean that fats are bad. You don't need a lot of fat each day, but you do need some. Nuts, meats, and oils are foods that contain fat.

Some foods that contain fat have few other nutrients. Many people eat more fat than they need. Eating too many fatty foods can lead to heart disease. Be heart smart now and limit how many fatty foods you eat.

Proteins

A third nutrient that your body needs is **proteins** (prō′ tēnz). Proteins are nutrients that the body uses for growth and the repair of cells. You can get proteins from meat, milk, cheese, nuts, and beans.

Brain Power

Snack foods like potato chips contain a lot of fat and few other nutrients. What healthful foods could you snack on instead?

What Else Does Your Body Need?

Why should you drink water while you are exercising?

Fiber

Another substance your body needs is **fiber** (fī'bər). Fiber is a substance that helps move wastes through the body. Fiber is found in fruits and vegetables. Beans and whole wheat breads are also good sources of fiber.

Vitamins and Minerals

Vitamins (vī' tə minz) and minerals are nutrients needed for the body to work properly. Vitamins are nutrients used by the body for growth. Some vitamins help prevent diseases. Each kind of vitamin does a different job. Vitamins have a letter of the alphabet as their names, and sometimes a number, too. Vitamins and minerals help you use other nutrients. Since no single food contains all the vitamins and minerals you need, you should eat a variety of foods.

Water

Water is inside of every cell of your body. Water is outside of every cell, too. It is in your blood, sweat, tears, and saliva. Water is important for almost every process in your body. You should drink six to eight glasses of water every day. How important is water? No one can live more than a few days without it.

Interpreting Data

READING A NUTRITION LABEL

Most foods have a nutrition label on them. A nutrition label lists the amounts of different nutrients in the food. The information in the label can help you identify which foods are good for you to eat. Look at the label pictured. Each line gives you information, or data. For example, look at the line labeled Serving Size. It says 1 container. This is the amount of food that is recommended you eat at one time. Now look at the line labeled Protein. How many grams of protein are there in one serving of this food? By answering this question, you are interpreting data. Interpret the data on the nutrition labels given to you to answer the questions below.

PROCEDURES

1. Look at the nutrition labels given to you. List the names of the foods in the table in your *Science Journal*.

2. INTERPRET DATA Look at the food labels. How much fat is in one serving of each food? How much protein? Carbohydrates?

3. INTERPRET DATA What other nutrients are in each of the foods? Are there vitamins and minerals? Does the food contain fiber?

CONCLUDE AND APPLY

1. COMPARE AND CONTRAST Which food has the most fat? Which has the least? Which food has the most carbohydrates? Which has the least? Which has the most protein? Which has the least?

2. EVALUATE Which of these foods should you try to avoid? Which foods should you eat more often? Why?

MATERIALS

- food nutrition labels
- *Science Journal*

Yogurt

Nutrition Facts

Serving Size	1 container	220 g

Amount per serving

Calories	195	
Calories from Fat	27	

% Daily value *

Total Fat	3 g	5%
Cholesterol	12 mg	6%
Sodium	155 mg	7%
Potassium	510 mg	15%
Total Carbohydrate	33 g	12%
Fiber	0 g	0%
Sugars	32 g	
Protein	12 g	
Vitamin A	4%	
Vitamin C	4%	
Calcium	40%	
Iron	0%	

Ingredients: Grade A milk, skim milk, sugar, natural vanilla flavor, pectin, active yogurt cultures

* *Percent Daily Values are based on a 2,000 calorie diet.*

What Is the Food Guide Pyramid?

The Food Guide Pyramid shows the five basic food groups. The larger the section of the food group in the pyramid, the more servings you should have from it each day.

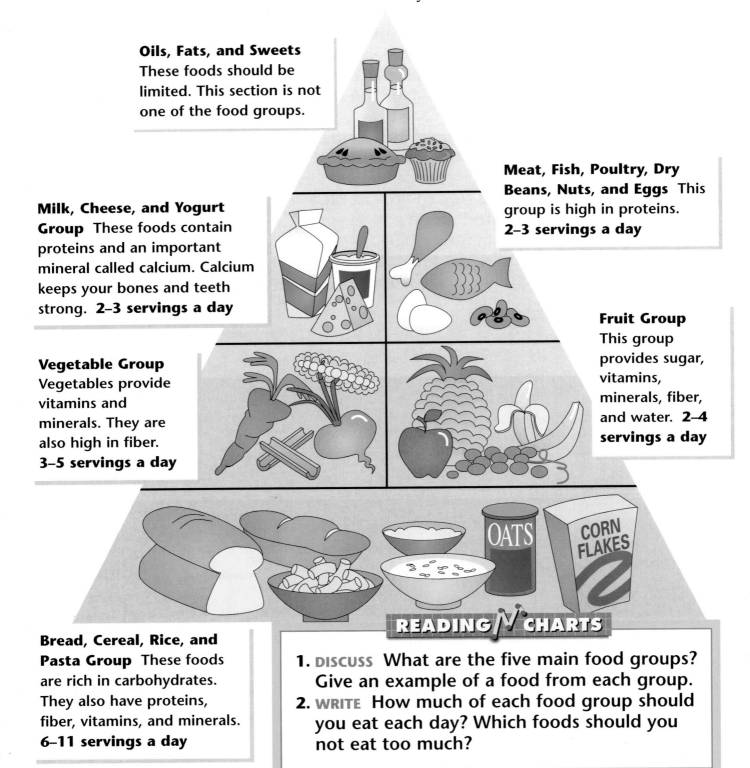

Oils, Fats, and Sweets These foods should be limited. This section is not one of the food groups.

Meat, Fish, Poultry, Dry Beans, Nuts, and Eggs This group is high in proteins. **2–3 servings a day**

Milk, Cheese, and Yogurt Group These foods contain proteins and an important mineral called calcium. Calcium keeps your bones and teeth strong. **2–3 servings a day**

Fruit Group This group provides sugar, vitamins, minerals, fiber, and water. **2–4 servings a day**

Vegetable Group Vegetables provide vitamins and minerals. They are also high in fiber. **3–5 servings a day**

Bread, Cereal, Rice, and Pasta Group These foods are rich in carbohydrates. They also have proteins, fiber, vitamins, and minerals. **6–11 servings a day**

READING / CHARTS

1. **DISCUSS** What are the five main food groups? Give an example of a food from each group.
2. **WRITE** How much of each food group should you eat each day? Which foods should you not eat too much?

416

Food does more than keep you alive. It is the key to how your body grows and how well it works. When you eat vegetables and drink milk, you take in the vitamins, minerals, and other nutrients that your body needs. When you begin the day with a healthy breakfast, you have the energy to do work and play. Eating the right foods is a big step towards having good health.

REVIEW

1. What are the main groups of nutrients?

2. How does the body use carbohydrates, fats, and proteins?

3. Why are water, fiber, vitamins, and minerals important to your body?

4. **INTERPRET DATA** Look at the nutrition label on page 415. How many carbohydrates are in one serving of this food?

5. **CRITICAL THINKING** *Apply* Draw a food pyramid. Be sure to include the five basic food groups and give examples of foods that belong in each group.

WHY IT MATTERS THINK ABOUT IT
What are three of your favorite foods? Why are they your favorites?

WHY IT MATTERS WRITE ABOUT IT
Are your three favorite foods healthful foods? Why or why not? In which of the five basic food groups do your favorite foods go?

READING SKILL Write a summary of the information on page 416.

SCIENCE MAGAZINE

Way Out Food

What would you have for lunch if you were traveling in space? Probably not a bowl of soup. The liquid would float around inside your spacecraft!

The first spacecraft were small, with little room for movement. New foods were developed for astronauts to eat in flight. Nutritious meals were prepared in pastes that could be squeezed from tubes. Powdered orange juice was mixed with water.

Today's spacecraft are roomier. Still, preparing and eating food is different than on Earth. In space, all the foods and drinks are in single-serving packets. Drinks are still powders—water is added to make them liquids.

Most of today's space foods are dried or freeze-dried. They also need water added. An astronaut sticks one end of a needle into a water tube and the other end through the top of the food packet. A switch on the tube releases the water needed. Then, the astronaut shakes the packet to mix the food. Some foods are heated on an electric burner.

The meal is stuck to a tray with material. Each astronaut has a straw, knife, fork, and two spoons. They also stick to the tray when not in use.

A Closer Look

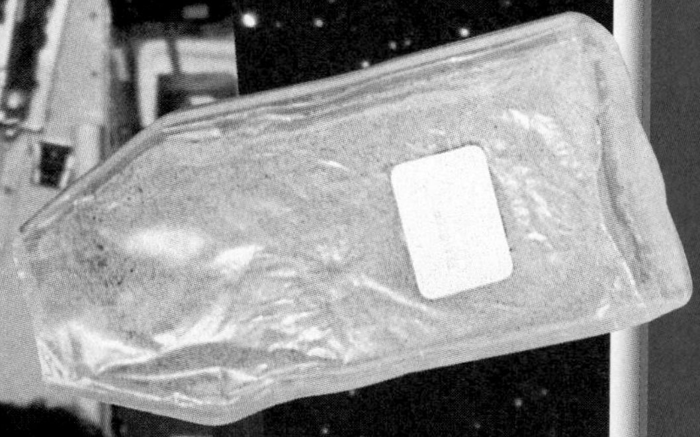

DISCUSSION STARTER

1. What would happen to foods or eating utensils that were not stuck to the tray? Why?

2. Why do astronauts have to stick a needle into their food to add water instead of just pouring it?

To learn more about, visit *www.mhschool.com/science* and enter the keyword SPACEFOOD.

*inter*NET
CONNECTION

BREAD SUBSTITUTE
READY TO EAT.

419

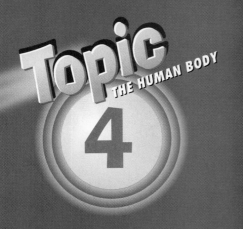
WHY IT MATTERS

Special parts of your body help you use food as fuel for energy.

SCIENCE WORDS

digestion the process of breaking down food

taste buds thousands of cells on your tongue that send the signals for sweet, sour, bitter, and salty to your brain

saliva a liquid in your mouth that helps soften and break down food

stomach part of your body with walls made of strong muscles that squeeze and mash food

small intestine a tube-like part of your body where most digestion takes place

large intestine the part of the body that removes water from undigested food

Food, a Fuel

Does your stomach sometimes growl? Your body is telling you something. It needs food! You know that food provides your body with the nutrients you need to live and grow. Before your body can use the nutrients in food, the food must be broken down. There are many parts of your body that help to do that job. Do you know what those parts are?

EXPLORE

HYPOTHESIZE How is food broken down? Write a hypothesis in your *Science Journal.* Remember that foods may be broken down in more than one way. How would you test your ideas?

Investigate How Food Is Broken Down

Model how the body breaks down food.

PROCEDURES

1. Place the paper towel on top of the foil. Place the potato on top of the paper towel.

2. **EXPERIMENT** How can you use the fork to divide the potato into smaller pieces? Record your ideas in your *Science Journal*. Test your ideas.

3. **EXPERIMENT** How can you use the fork to crush the potato into even smaller pieces?

4. **OBSERVE** What happens if you squeeze the pieces of potato in the paper towel? Throw the towel and the pieces of potato in a wastebasket.

MATERIALS

- a small baked potato
- a fork
- a paper towel
- a piece of aluminum foil
- *Science Journal*

CONCLUDE AND APPLY

1. **COMPARE AND CONTRAST** How did the potato change from the beginning of the activity to the end?

2. **COMMUNICATE** How were you able to break apart the potato?

3. **INFER** What do you think came out of the potato when you squeezed it?

GOING FURTHER: Apply

4. **INFER** Which part of your body do you think cuts and crushes food? How do you know?

421

How Is Food Broken Down?

The Explore Activity shows that food can be broken down into smaller pieces by being crushed and cut. Crushing and cutting food is part of **digestion** (di jes′ chən). Digestion is the process of breaking down food.

Eating a Cracker

HYPOTHESIZE Does digestion begin in the mouth? Write a hypothesis in your *Science Journal*.

PROCEDURES

OBSERVE Slowly chew the cracker for 1 minute. Observe all the ways the cracker changes inside your mouth. Swallow the cracker.

MATERIALS
- 1 unsalted cracker
- *Science Journal*

CONCLUDE AND APPLY

1. **IDENTIFY** How did the shape of the cracker change inside your mouth?

2. **COMPARE AND CONTRAST** How did the cracker taste when you put it in your mouth? How did it taste right before you swallowed it?

3. **DRAW CONCLUSIONS** Does digestion begin in the mouth? How do you know?

Digestion begins in your mouth. When you put food in your mouth, you taste it with your **taste buds** (tāst budz). Taste buds are thousands of cells on your tongue that send the signals for sweet, sour, bitter, and salty to your brain. Your taste buds taste food by sensing the chemicals in it. Most foods contain a mixture of chemicals and of tastes.

When you put food into your mouth, **saliva** (sə lī′ və) pours onto it. Saliva is a liquid in your mouth that helps soften and break down food. Saliva is released by salivary (sal′ə ver′ē) glands.

Your teeth bite, slice, and tear solid food to pieces. They crush, grind, and chew it. The longer your teeth chew your food, the smaller the pieces get. Smaller pieces are easier to swallow and to digest. How was the fork in the Explore Activity like your teeth?

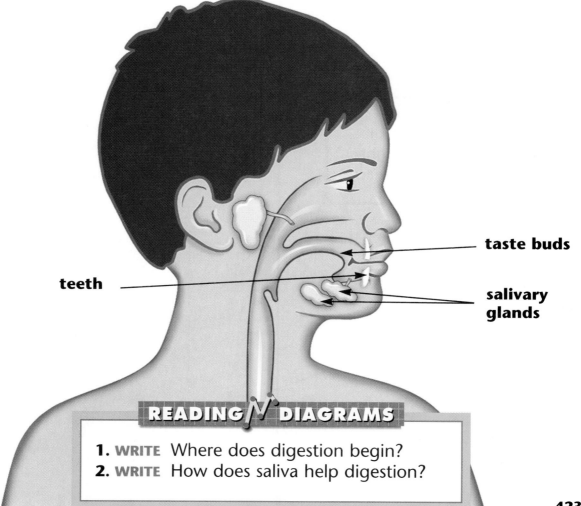

teeth

taste buds

salivary glands

READING ⋀ DIAGRAMS

1. **WRITE** Where does digestion begin?
2. **WRITE** How does saliva help digestion?

Where Does Your Food Go Next?

When you swallow, food moves down the *esophagus* (i säf'ə gəs). The esophagus is a muscular tube that carries food to your **stomach** (stum' ək). The stomach is a part of your body with walls made of strong muscles that squeeze and mash food. It takes five to ten seconds for swallowed food to reach your stomach.

Your stomach is like an elastic bag. It stretches to hold all the food you swallow. Stomach muscles mix and mash the food you have swallowed. After two to four hours, the food has changed into a thick, soupy mixture.

There are tiny glands in your stomach. These glands make stomach juices. Some of the juices are chemicals that start to break down proteins in your foods. Other juices kill harmful germs.

Brain Power

Why do you think your stomach has juices that kill harmful germs? How might germs get into your stomach?

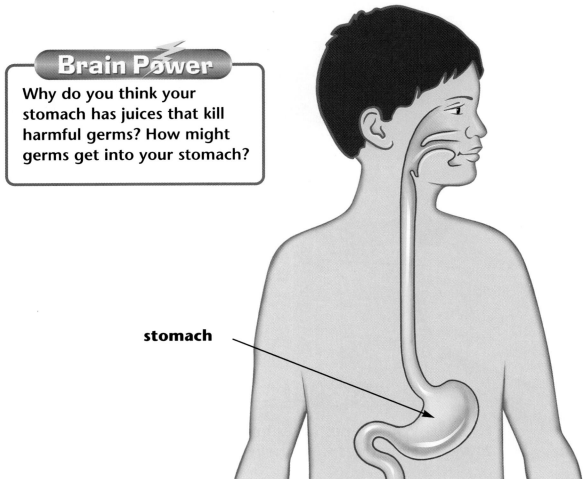

stomach

424

Little by little, your stomach muscles squeeze the paste out of your stomach and into your **small intestine** (smôl in tes' tin). Your small intestine is a tube-like part of your body where most digestion takes place.

The job of the small intestine is to finish breaking down food. The digested nutrients are now small enough to go out of your small intestine and into your blood. Your blood carries the nutrients to cells all over your body.

Not all food is broken down during digestion. Undigested parts of food, such as fiber, are moved from your small intestine into your **large intestine** (lärj in tes' tin). Your large intestine is the part of the body that removes water from undigested food. What's left is solid waste. The waste is pushed along by muscles in the walls of the intestine until it leaves the body.

large intestine

small intestine

425

How Can You Take Care of Your Digestive System?

How can you take care of your digestive system? First, eat fresh fruits and vegetables every day. They contain fiber that helps your large intestine get rid of food wastes.

Second, limit how many sweets you eat. Sugar helps mouth bacteria grow. Those bacteria can cause tooth decay.

Third, chew your food thoroughly to make it easier to digest. Help your digestion stay on schedule by having regular mealtimes each day.

Finally, never eat spoiled food. Germs that cause food to spoil can make you sick and send you to the hospital. Watch out for your digestive system. It is the only one you have.

Spoiled milk smells bad! Milk must be refrigerated to keep it fresh.

The next time you eat, think of how many parts of your body work to digest food. Every one of those parts affects how you feel, how you grow, and how healthy you stay. You can't live without the nutrients you get from food. You can't live if your digestive system stops doing its job.

REVIEW

1. What is digestion?

2. What happens to food in your mouth?

3. What are the jobs of the stomach and intestines in digestion?

4. **PREDICT** You are in a rush to get somewhere after dinner. You want to eat quickly so you can go. Is eating quickly a good idea? How might eating quickly affect digestion?

5. **CRITICAL THINKING** *Apply* Why do you think a young baby eats only liquid or mashed foods?

WHY IT MATTERS THINK ABOUT IT
Describe the role of teeth in digestion. Why are teeth important?

WHY IT MATTERS WRITE ABOUT IT
Have you ever had loose or missing teeth? How did it affect what you ate? Were there any foods you ate more of? Less of?

A Trapdoor in Your Throat

What goes down your throat besides what you eat and drink? Air does! It flows through your mouth or nose, down your throat, and into your windpipe.

Your windpipe's right in front of your food tube. If food or liquid get into your windpipe, you choke. It's the job of your epiglottis to keep the windpipe clear. Like a trapdoor, the epiglottis quickly covers your windpipe when you swallow food. When you breathe, the trapdoor stays open.

Help keep food and liquids from "going down the wrong pipe." Carefully chew and swallow food, and don't talk while you're eating!

Epiglottis

Food tube

Windpipe

DISCUSSION STARTER

1. What happens if food goes into your windpipe?

2. What stops food from going into your windpipe?

To learn more about your epiglottis, visit **www.mhschool.com/science** and enter the keyword EPIGLOTTIS.

*inter***NET** CONNECTION

SCIENCE WORDS

carbohydrates p.412

digestion p.422

fats p.413

fiber p.414

large intestine p.425

nutrients p.412

protein p.413

saliva p.423

small intestine p.425

stomach p.424

taste buds p.423

vitamins p.414

USING SCIENCE WORDS

Number a paper from 1 to 10. Fill in 1 to 5 with words from the list above.

1. The process of breaking down food is ___?___.

2. A part of the body with walls made of strong muscles that mix and mash food is the ___?___.

3. Substances that your body needs for energy and growth are ___?___.

4. The liquid in your mouth that helps soften and break down food is ___?___.

5. The tube-like part of the body where most digestion takes place is the ___?___.

6–10. Pick 5 words from the list above that were not used in 1 to 5 and use each in a sentence.

UNDERSTANDING SCIENCE IDEAS

11. How do taste buds help with digestion?

12. Why is it important to eat a wide variety of foods?

USING IDEAS AND SKILLS

13. **READING SKILL: SUMMARIZE** Write a summary of the main ideas in this chapter.

14. **INTERPRET DATA** Look at the nutrition label below. How many grams of protein are in one serving?

Nutrition Facts (15 g)

Serving Size 5 crackers

Calories 70

Calories from Fat 20

Amount per serving	% Daily Value*
Total Fat 2 g	3%
Cholesterol 0mg	0%
Sodium 90 mg	4%
Total Carbohydrate 10 g	3%
Dietary Fiber less than 1g	2%
Sugars 0 g	
Protein 1 g	

* Percent Daily Values are based on a 2,000 calorie diet.

15. **THINKING LIKE A SCIENTIST** Which do you think is a more healthful snack: Peanut butter and crackers or yogurt with fruit? How might you find out?

PROBLEMS and PUZZLES

Food for Thought Make a list of what you ate yesterday. Draw a Food Guide Pyramid and fill it in with each type of food you ate. Did you eat something from every food group? What do you need to eat more of? What do you need less of?

USING SCIENCE WORDS

bacteria p.399

carbohydrates p.412

digestion p.422

epidermis p.388

fiber p.414

gland p.389

melanin p.388

pore p.391

protein p.413

stomach p.424

taste buds p.423

virus p.399

vitamins p.414

white blood cells p.400

Number a paper from 1 to 10. Beside each number write the word or words that best completes the sentence.

1. A tiny opening in your skin is called a(n) __?__.

2. The outer layer of skin is the __?__.

3. A part of the body that makes substances the body needs is called a(n) __?__.

4. One-celled living things are __?__.

5. Cells that fight viruses are __?__.

6. A body's main source of energy comes from __?__.

7. Substances used by a body for growth are __?__.

8. The material that helps move wastes through the body is __?__.

9. Cells on the tongue that can detect sweet, sour, bitter, and salty tastes are __?__.

10. Food is squeezed and mashed by the walls of the __?__.

UNDERSTANDING SCIENCE IDEAS

Write 11 to 15. For each number write the letter for the best answer. You may wish to use the hints provided.

11. The skin cells just below the outer layer of skin make up the
    a. taste buds
    b. nerves
    c. dermis
    d. glands
    (Hint: Read page 391.)

12. People can protect themselves from measles by getting a
    a. vaccine
    b. virus
    c. cold
    d. bath
    (Hint: Read page 404.)

13. Potato chips leave greasy spots on paper because they contain
    a. salt
    b. fats
    c. water
    d. vitamins
    (Hint: Read page 411.)

14. It is easier for you to digest food if
    a. it tastes good
    b. you chew it well
    c. your stomach is growling
    d. you get exercise
    (Hint: Read page 423.)

15. One good way to take care of your digestive system is to
    a. eat food with fiber
    b. eat quickly
    c. eat lots of candy
    d. use a lot of salt
    (Hint: Read page 426.)

USING IDEAS AND SKILLS

16. What does the padding of fat under your dermis do?

17.  **MAKE A MODEL** How are a germ and an antibody like pieces in a jigsaw puzzle?

18. Having some fat in your diet is important, but having too much can cause what kinds of problems?

THINKING LIKE A SCIENTIST

19. **INTERPRET DATA** Look at the label on page 415. How many calories come from fat? How many calories DON'T come from fat?

20. What might be wrong with bad-smelling milk?

WRITING IN YOUR JOURNAL

SCIENCE IN YOUR LIFE
Make a list of some things that help you digest your food well. Why are they important?

PRODUCT ADS
Think of some ads you have seen for soft drinks. What do the ads tell you about why you should drink them? Do you think the soft drinks are good for you?

HOW SCIENTISTS WORK
Scientists make models to help them explain how things work. How did you use a model in this unit?

Design your own Experiment

How can you find out how healthy your school lunches are? Think of a way to evaluate which nutrients (such as carbohydrates, fats, proteins, and vitamins and minerals) are in the lunches. Check your experiment with your teacher before you perform it.

For help in reviewing this unit, visit *www.mhschool.com/science*

PROBLEMS and PUZZLES

Telling by Touch

Find out whether people differ in their ability to identify materials by touch. Blindfold a partner. Have your partner feel different surfaces. Can your partner identify the material that he or she is feeling? Using the same materials, test someone else's sense of touch.

Eating Eggs

Vinegar has some of the same properties as stomach juices.
SAFETY: Wear goggles. Place a few pieces of boiled egg white in a container of vinegar. Place the same number of egg white pieces in a container of water. Observe the sealed containers. What happens? In which container does the egg white protein break down faster? Why?

A Very Long Way

How long is your digestive system? Food that you eat has a long journey through your body. In fact, the journey may take several days!

You can make a model that shows how long your digestive system is. Cut 10 cm of blue yarn, 30 cm of red yarn, 15 cm of yellow yarn, 5 meters of green yarn, and $1\frac{1}{2}$ meters of orange yarn. Make a label for each of the parts of the digestive system.

mouth	blue
esophagus	red
stomach	yellow
small intestine	green
large intestine	orange

Lay the labels on the floor in order. Match the strings to the label by color. Use the string to connect each of the labels together.

How long is your digestive system? Using your model and the information you have learned in this unit, draw a diagram of the digestive system. Write a description to go with the diagram.

mouth

REFERENCE SECTION

DIAGRAM BUILDERS

Building a Food Web

All living things need food. Plants get energy from the Sun's light. They use it to make food. Most other living things get energy by taking in food. One living thing becomes the food for another. **In the diagram on the next page, which living things are food for others?**

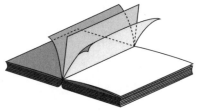

BASE

To answer the question, lift up all the plastic overlays (1, 2, 3). The page beneath them is the base. The base shows a food chain. It is made up of many organisms that depend on each other for food.
What happens to each living thing in this chain?

OVERLAY 1

1 Now drop overlay 1 onto the base. You see a second food chain. Describe it.
What do the two food chains have in common?

OVERLAY 2

2 Now drop overlay 2 onto overlay 1. You see a third food chain. Describe it.
What do the three food chains have in common?

OVERLAY 3

3 Now drop overlay 3 onto overlay 2. You see a food web. It shows how all the food chains are connected.
How are all the food chains connected?

SUMMARIZE

How many different food chains can you find in this web? List them.

BASE: Start with a food chain.

DIAGRAM BUILDERS
Activities

1 Make a Model

You need: spool of yarn, scissors, paper

In a group of ten or more, write the name of each organism from the food web on a sheet of paper. Write one name on a sheet. Hand out the sheets to ten group members. The students with papers should arrange themselves to show food chains. Other students help by tying a length of yarn from person to person to form the chain. (Tie a loop and knot around each person's wrist.) Decide how to connect the chains into a web.

2 Cause and Effect

Take out one of the organisms from the model above. What happens to the rest of the food web? Put the organism back and take out another. What happens this time? Repeat several times. What happens if a second hawk joins the food web?

3 Write an Explanation

What if there was no rain for a long time? The grass would dry up and much of it may die. What would happen to the food web? Write your ideas.

REFERENCE SECTION

HANDBOOK

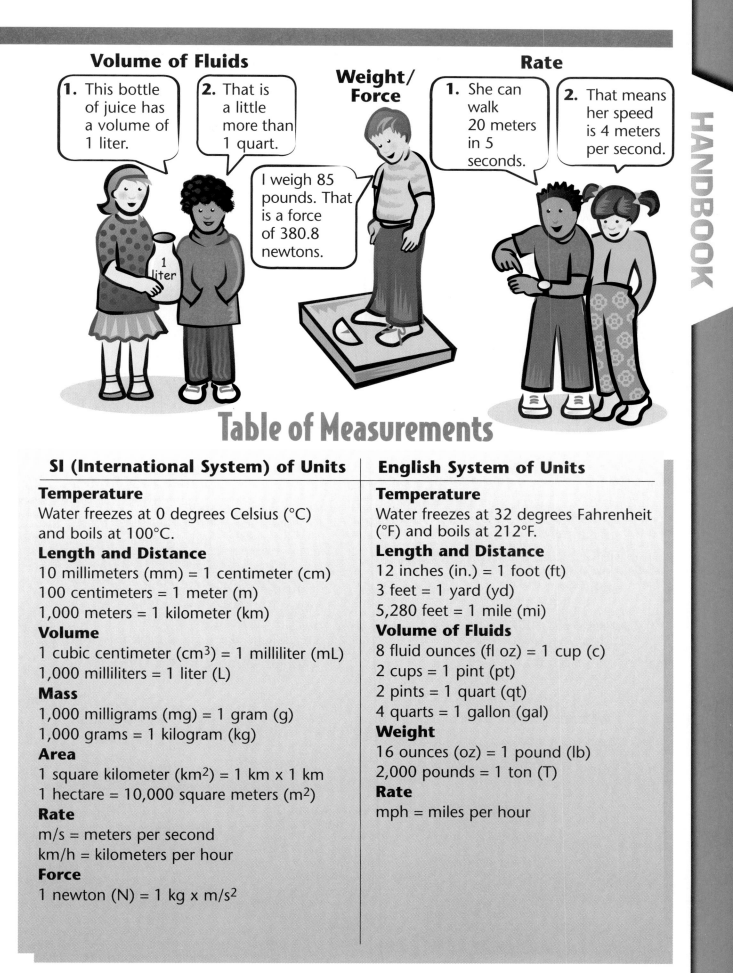

Volume of Fluids

1. This bottle of juice has a volume of 1 liter.

2. That is a little more than 1 quart.

I weigh 85 pounds. That is a force of 380.8 newtons.

Weight/Force

Rate

1. She can walk 20 meters in 5 seconds.

2. That means her speed is 4 meters per second.

Table of Measurements

SI (International System) of Units	English System of Units
Temperature Water freezes at 0 degrees Celsius (°C) and boils at 100°C.	**Temperature** Water freezes at 32 degrees Fahrenheit (°F) and boils at 212°F.
Length and Distance 10 millimeters (mm) = 1 centimeter (cm) 100 centimeters = 1 meter (m) 1,000 meters = 1 kilometer (km)	**Length and Distance** 12 inches (in.) = 1 foot (ft) 3 feet = 1 yard (yd) 5,280 feet = 1 mile (mi)
Volume 1 cubic centimeter (cm^3) = 1 milliliter (mL) 1,000 milliliters = 1 liter (L)	**Volume of Fluids** 8 fluid ounces (fl oz) = 1 cup (c) 2 cups = 1 pint (pt) 2 pints = 1 quart (qt) 4 quarts = 1 gallon (gal)
Mass 1,000 milligrams (mg) = 1 gram (g) 1,000 grams = 1 kilogram (kg)	**Weight** 16 ounces (oz) = 1 pound (lb) 2,000 pounds = 1 ton (T)
Area 1 square kilometer (km^2) = 1 km x 1 km 1 hectare = 10,000 square meters (m^2)	**Rate** mph = miles per hour
Rate m/s = meters per second km/h = kilometers per hour	
Force 1 newton (N) = 1 kg x m/s^2	

In the Classroom

The most important part of doing any experiment is doing it safely. You can be safe by paying attention to your teacher and doing your work carefully. Here are some other ways to stay safe while you do experiments.

Before the Experiment

- Read all of the directions. Make sure you understand them. When you see

  ◤◤◤, be sure to follow the safety rule.
- Listen to your teacher for special safety directions. If you don't understand something, ask for help.
- Wash your hands with soap and water before an activity.

During the Experiment

- Wear safety goggles when your teacher tells you to wear them and whenever you see 🥽. Wear goggles when working with something that can fly into your eyes
- Wear splash-proof goggles when working with liquids.
- Wear a safety apron if you work with anything messy or anything that might spill.

- If you spill something, wipe it up right away or ask your teacher for help.
- Tell your teacher if something breaks. If glass breaks do not clean it up yourself.
- Keep your hair and clothes away from open flames. Tie back long hair and roll up long sleeves.

- Be careful around a hot plate. Know when it is on and when it is off. Remember that the plate stays hot for a few minutes after you turn it off.
- Keep your hands dry around electrical equipment.
- Don't eat or drink anything during the experiment.

After the Experiment

- Put equipment back the way your teacher tells you.
- Dispose of things the way your teacher tells you.
- Clean up your work area and wash your hands with soap and water.

In the Field

- Always be accompanied by a trusted adult—like your teacher or a parent or guardian.
- Never touch animals or plants without the adult's approval. The animal might bite. The plant might be poison ivy or another dangerous plant.

Responsibility

Acting safely is one way to be responsible. You can also be responsible by treating animals, the environment, and each other with respect in the class and in the field.

Treat Living Things with Respect

- If you have animals in the classroom, keep their homes clean. Change the water in fish tanks and clean out cages.
- Feed classroom animals the right amounts of food.

- Give your classroom animals enough space.
- When you observe animals, don't hurt them or disturb their homes.
- Find a way to care for animals while school is on vacation.

Treat the Environment with Respect

- Do not pick flowers.
- Do not litter, including gum and food.
- If you see litter, ask your teacher if you can pick it up.

- Recycle materials used in experiments. Ask your teacher what materials can be recycled instead of thrown away. These might include plastics, aluminum, and newspapers.

Treat Each Other with Respect

- Use materials carefully around others so that people don't get hurt or get stains on their clothes.
- Be careful not to bump people when they are doing experiments. Do not disturb or damage their experiments.
- If you see that people are having trouble with an experiment, help them.

Use a Hand Lens

You use a hand lens to magnify an object, or make the object look larger. With a hand lens, you can see details that would be hard to see without the hand lens.

Magnify a Piece of Cereal

1. Place a piece of your favorite cereal on a flat surface. Look at the cereal carefully. Draw a picture of it.

2. Hold the hand lens so that it is just above the cereal. Look through the lens, and slowly move it away from the cereal. The cereal will look larger.

3. Keep moving the hand lens until the cereal begins to look blurry. Then move the lens a little closer to the cereal until you can see it clearly.

4. Draw a picture of the cereal as you see it through the hand lens. Fill in details that you did not see before.

5. Repeat this activity using objects you are studying in science. It might be a rock, some soil, a flower, a seed, or something else.

Use a Microscope

Hand lenses make objects look several times larger. A microscope, however, can magnify an object to look hundreds of times larger.

Examine Salt Grains

1. Place the microscope on a flat surface. Always carry a microscope with both hands. Hold the arm with one hand, and put your other hand beneath the base.

2. Look at the drawing to learn the different parts of the microscope.

3. Move the mirror so that it reflects light up toward the stage. Never point the mirror directly at the Sun or a bright light. Bright light can cause permanent eye damage.

4. Place a few grains of salt on the slide. Put the slide under the stage clips on the stage. Be sure that the salt grains are over the hole in the stage.

5. Look through the eyepiece. Turn the focusing knob slowly until the salt grains come into focus.

6. Draw what the grains look like through the microscope.

7. Look at other objects through the microscope. Try a piece of leaf, a strand of human hair, or a pencil mark.

8. Draw what each object looks like through the microscope. Do any of the objects look alike? If so, how? Are any of the objects alive? How do you know?

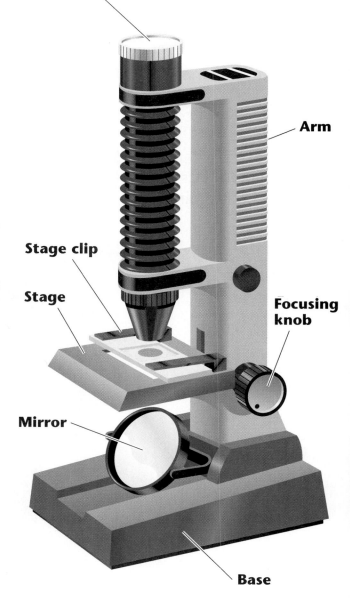

Eyepiece

Arm

Stage clip

Stage

Focusing knob

Mirror

Base

Use a Compass

You use a compass to find directions. A compass is a small, thin magnet that swings freely, like a spinner in a board game. One end of the magnet always points north. This end is the magnet's north pole. How does a compass work?

1. Place the compass on a surface that is not made of magnetic material. A wooden table or a sidewalk works well.
2. Find the magnet's north pole. The north pole is marked in some way, usually with a color or an arrowhead.
3. Notice the letters *N, E, S,* and *W* on the compass. These letters stand for the directions north, east, south, and west. When the magnet stops swinging, turn the compass so that the *N* lines up with the north pole of the magnet.
4. Face to the north. Then face to the east, to the south, and to the west.
5. Repeat this activity by holding the compass in your hand and then at different places indoors and outdoors.

Use a Telescope

A telescope makes faraway objects, like the Moon, look larger. A telescope also lets you see stars that are too faint to see with just your eyes.

Look at the Moon

1. Look at the Moon in the night sky. Draw a picture of what you see. Draw as many details as you can.

2. Point a telescope toward the Moon. Look through the eyepiece of the telescope. Move the telescope until you see the Moon. Turn the knob until the Moon comes into focus.

3. Draw a picture of what you see. Include details. Compare your two pictures.

Look at the Stars

1. Find the brightest star in the sky. Notice if there are any other stars near it.

2. Point a telescope toward the brightest star. Look through the eyepiece and turn the knob until the stars come into focus. Move the telescope until you find the brightest star.

3. Can you see stars through the telescope that you cannot see with just your eyes?

Use a Camera, Tape Recorder, Map, and Compass

Camera

You can use a camera to record what you observe in nature. Keep these tips in mind.

1. Hold the camera steady. Gently press the button so that you do not jerk the camera.
2. Try to take pictures with the Sun at your back. Then your pictures will be bright and clear.
3. Don't get too close to the subject. Without a special lens, the picture could turn out blurry.
4. Be patient. If you are taking a picture of an animal, you may have to wait for the animal to appear.

Tape Recorder

You can record observations on a tape recorder. This is sometimes better than writing notes because a tape recorder can record your observations at the exact time you are making them. Later you can listen to the tape and write down your observations.

Map and Compass

When you are busy observing nature, it might be easy to get lost. You can use a map of the area and a compass to find your way. Here are some tips.

1. Lightly mark on the map your starting place. It might be the place where the bus parked.
2. Always know where you are on the map compared to your starting place. Watch for landmarks on the map, such as a river, a pond, trails, or buildings.
3. Use the map and compass to find special places to observe, such as a pond. Look at the map to see which direction the place is from you. Hold the compass to see where that direction is.
4. Use your map and compass with a friend.

Length

Find Length with a Ruler

1. Look at this section of a ruler. Each centimeter is divided into 10 millimeters. How long is the paper clip?
2. The length of the paper clip is 3 centimeters plus 2 millimeters. You can write this length as 3.2 centimeters.
3. Place the ruler on your desk. Lay a pencil against the ruler so that one end of the pencil lines up with the left edge of the ruler. Record the length of the pencil.
4. Trade your pencil with a classmate. Measure and record the length of each other's pencils. Compare your answers.

Measuring Area

Area is the amount of surface something covers. To find the area of a rectangle, multiply the rectangle's length by its width. For example, the rectangle here is 3 centimeters long and 2 centimeters wide. Its area is 3 cm x 2 cm = 6 square centimeters. You write the area as 6 cm².

1. Find the area of your science book. Measure the book's length to the nearest centimeter. Measure its width.
2. Multiply the book's length by its width. Remember to put the answer in cm².

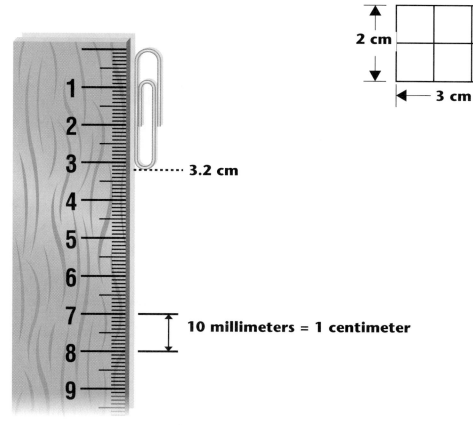

3.2 cm

10 millimeters = 1 centimeter

2 cm

3 cm

HANDBOOK

Time

You use timing devices to measure how long something takes to happen. Some timing devices you use in science are a clock with a second hand and a stopwatch. Which one is more accurate?

Comparing a Clock and a Stopwatch

1. Look at a clock with a second hand. The second hand is the hand that you can see moving. It measures seconds.
2. Get an egg timer with falling sand or some device like a windup toy that runs down after a certain length of time. When the second hand of the clock points to 12, tell your partner to start the egg timer. Watch the clock while the sand in the egg timer is falling.
3. When the sand stops falling, count how many seconds it took. Record this measurement. Repeat the activity, and compare the two measurements.
4. Switch roles with your partner.
5. Look at a stopwatch. Click the button on the top right. This starts the time. Click the button again. This stops the time. Click the button on the top left. This sets the stopwatch back to zero. Notice that the stopwatch tells time in hours, minutes, seconds, and hundredths of a second.
6. Repeat the activity in steps 1–3, but use the stopwatch instead of a clock. Make sure the stopwatch is set to zero. Click the top right button to start timing.

Click the button again when the sand stops falling. Make sure you and your partner time the sand twice.

0 minutes   25 seconds

72 hundredths of a second

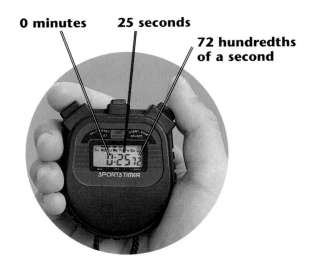

More About Time

1. Use the stopwatch to time how long it takes an ice cube to melt under cold running water. How long does an ice cube take to melt under warm running water?
2. Match each of these times with the action you think took that amount of time.

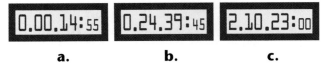

a.   b.   c.

1. A Little League baseball game
2. Saying the Pledge of Allegiance
3. Recess

Volume

Have you ever used a measuring cup? Measuring cups measure the volume of liquids. Volume is the amount of space something takes up. To bake a cake, you might measure the volume of water, vegetable oil, or melted butter. In science you use special measuring cups called beakers and graduated cylinders. These containers are marked in milliliters (mL).

Measure the Volume of a Liquid

1. Look at the beaker and at the graduated cylinder. The beaker has marks for each 25 mL up to 200 mL. The graduated cylinder has marks for each 1 mL up to 100 mL.

2. The surface of the water in the graduated cylinder curves up at the sides. You measure the volume by reading the height of the water at the flat part. What is the volume of water in the graduated cylinder? How much water is in the beaker? They both contain 75 mL of water.

3. Pour 50 mL of water from a pitcher into a graduated cylinder. The water should be at the 50-mL mark on the graduated cylinder. If you go over the mark, pour a little water back into the pitcher.

4. Pour the 50 mL of water into a beaker.

5. Repeat steps 3 and 4 using 30 mL, 45 mL, and 25 mL of water.

6. Measure the volume of water you have in the beaker. Do you have about the same amount of water as your classmates?

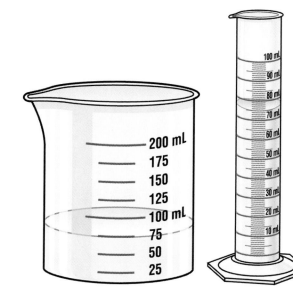

MATH
LiNK

HANDBOOK

Mass

Mass is the amount of matter an object has. You use a balance to measure mass. To find the mass of an object, you balance it with objects whose masses you know. Let's find the mass of a box of crayons.

Measure the Mass of a Box of Crayons

1. Place the balance on a flat, level surface. Check that the two pans are empty and clean.
2. Make sure the empty pans are balanced with each other. The pointer should point to the middle mark. If it does not, move the slider a little to the right or left to balance the pans.

3. Gently place a box of crayons on the left pan. The pan will drop lower.
4. Add masses to the right pan until the pans are balanced. You can use paper clips.
5. Count the number of paper clips that are in the right pan. Two paper clips equal about one gram. What is the mass of the box of crayons? Record the number. After the number, write a *g* for "grams."

Predict the Mass of More Crayons

1. Leave the box of crayons and the masses on the balance.
2. Get two more crayons. If you put them in the pan with the box of crayons, what do you think the mass of all the crayons will be? Write down what you predict the total mass will be.
3. Check your prediction. Gently place the two crayons in the left pan. Add masses, such as paper clips, to the right pan until the pans are balanced.
4. Calculate the mass as you did before. Record this number. How close is it to your prediction?

More About Mass

What was the mass of all your crayons? It was probably less than 100 grams. What would happen if you replaced the crayons with a pineapple? You may not have enough masses to balance the pineapple. It has a mass of about 1,000 grams. That's the same as 1 kilogram because *kilo* means "1,000."

MAKE MEASUREMENTS

Weight/Force

You use a spring scale to measure weight. An object has weight because the force of gravity pulls down on the object. Therefore, weight is a force. Like all forces weight is measured in newtons (N).

Measure the Weight of an Object

1. Look at your spring scale to see how many newtons it measures. See how the measurements are divided. The spring scale shown here measures up to 10 N. It has a mark for every 1 N.

2. Hold the spring scale by the top loop. Put the object to be measured on the bottom hook. If the object will not stay on the hook, place it in a net bag. Then hang the bag from the hook.

3. Let go of the object slowly. It will pull down on a spring inside the scale. The spring is connected to a pointer. The pointer on the spring scale shown here is a small arrow.

4. Wait for the pointer to stop moving. Read the number of newtons next to the pointer. This is the object's weight. The mug in the picture weighs 3 N.

More About Spring Scales

You probably weigh yourself by standing on a bathroom scale. This is a spring scale. The force of your body stretches or presses a spring inside the scale. The dial on the scale is probably marked in pounds—the English unit of weight. One pound is equal to about 4.5 newtons.

Here are some spring scales you may have seen.

Temperature

Temperature is how hot or cold something is. You use a thermometer to measure temperature. A thermometer is made of a thin tube with colored liquid inside. When the liquid gets warmer, it expands and moves up the tube. When the liquid gets cooler, it contracts and moves down the tube. You may have seen most temperatures measured in degrees Fahrenheit (°F). Scientists measure temperature in degrees Celsius (°C).

Read a Thermometer

1. Look at the thermometer shown here. It has two scales—a Fahrenheit scale and a Celsius scale. Every 20 degrees on each scale has a number.

2. What is the temperature shown on the thermometer? At what temperature does water freeze? Give your answers in °F and in °C.

How Is Temperature Measured?

1. Fill a large beaker about one-half full of cool water. Find the temperature of the water by holding a thermometer in the water. Do not let the bulb at the bottom of the thermometer touch the sides or bottom of the beaker.

2. Keep the thermometer in the water until the liquid in the tube stops moving—about a minute. Read and record the temperature on the Celsius scale.

3. Fill another large beaker one-half full of warm water from a faucet. Be careful not to burn yourself by using hot water.

4. Find and record the temperature of the warm water just as you did in steps 1 and 2.

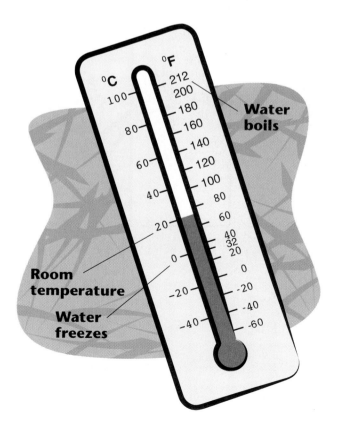

Weather

What was the weather like yesterday? What is it like today? The weather changes from day to day. You can observe different parts of the weather to find out how it changes.

Measure Temperature

1. Use a thermometer to find the air temperature outside. Look at page R17 to review thermometers.
2. Hold a thermometer outside for two minutes. Then read and record the temperature.
3. Take the temperature at the same time each day for a week. Record it in a chart.

Clear skies; no clouds   **Partly cloudy**   **Cloudy**

2. Record in your chart if it is raining or snowing.
3. At the end of the week, how has the weather changed from day to day?

Observe Wind Speed and Direction

1. Observe how the wind is affecting things around you. Look at a flag or the branches of a tree. How hard is the wind blowing the flag or branches? Observe for about five minutes. Write down your observations.
2. Hold a compass to see which direction the wind is coming from. Write down this direction.
3. Observe the wind each day for a week. Record your observations in your chart.

Observe Clouds, Rain, and Snow

1. Observe how much of the sky is covered by clouds. Use these symbols to record the cloud cover in your chart each day.

Systems

What do a toy car, a tomato plant, and a yo-yo have in common? They are all systems. A system is a set of parts that work together to form a whole. Look at the three systems below. Think of how each part helps the system work.

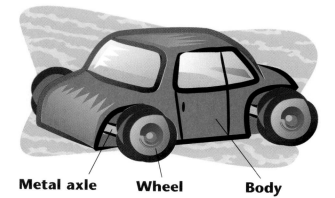

Metal axle   **Wheel**   **Body**

This system has three main parts— the body, the axles, and the wheels. Would the system work well if the axles could not turn?

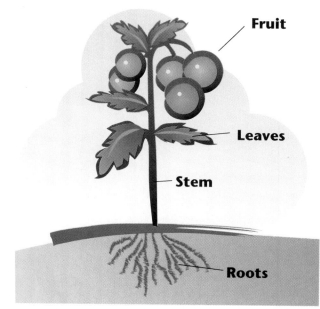

Fruit

Leaves

Stem

Roots

In this system roots take in water, and leaves make food. The stem carries water and food to different parts of the plant. What would happen if you cut off all the leaves?

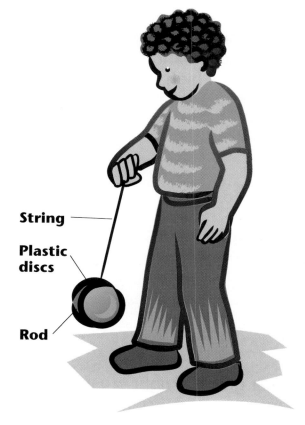

String

Plastic discs

Rod

Even simple things can be systems. How do all the parts of the yo-yo work together to make the toy go up and down?

Look for some other systems at school, at home, and outside. Remember to look for things that are made of parts. List the parts. Then describe how you think each part helps the system work.

Make Graphs to Organize Data

When you do an experiment in science, you collect information. To find out what your information means, you can organize it into graphs. There are many kinds of graphs.

Bar Graphs

A bar graph uses bars to show information. For example, suppose you are growing a plant. Every week you measure how high the plant has grown. Here is what you find.

Week	Height (cm)
1	1
2	3
3	6
4	10
5	17
6	20
7	22
8	23

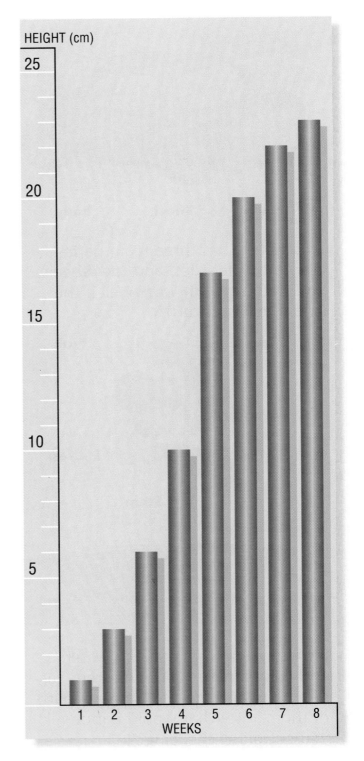

The bar graph at right organizes the measurements you collected so that you can easily compare them.

1. Look at the bar for week 2. Put your finger at the top of the bar. Move your finger straight over to the left to find how many centimeters the plant grew by the end of week 2.

2. Between which two weeks did the plant grow most?

3. When did plant growth begin to level off?

Pictographs

A pictograph uses symbols, or pictures, to show information. Suppose you collect information about how much water your family uses each day. Here is what you find.

Activity	Water Used Each Day (L)
Drinking	10
Showering	180
Bathing	240
Brushing teeth	80
Washing dishes	140
Washing hands	30
Washing clothes	280
Flushing toilet	90

You can organize this information into the pictograph shown here. The pictograph has to explain what the symbol on the graph means. In this case, each bottle means 20 liters of water. A half bottle means half of 20, or 10 liters of water.

1. Which activity uses the most water?
2. Which activity uses the least water?

Make a Graph

Suppose you do an experiment to find out how far a toy car rolls on different surfaces. The results of your experiment are shown below.

Surface	Distance Car Rolled (cm)
Wood Floor	525
Sidewalk	325
Carpet Floor	150
Tile Floor	560
Grass	55

1. Decide what kind of graph would best show these results.
2. Make your graph.

A Family's Daily Use of Water

Drinking
Showering
Bathing
Brushing teeth
Washing dishes
Washing hands
Washing clothes
Flushing toilet

= 20 liters of water

Make Maps to Show Information

Locate Places

A map is a drawing that shows an area from above. Most maps have numbers and letters along the top and side. They help you find places easily. For example, what if you wanted to find the library on the map below. It is located at D7. Place a finger on the letter D along the side of the map and another finger on the number 7 at the top. Then move your fingers straight across and down the map until they meet. The library is located where D and 7 meet, or very nearby.

1. What building is located at G3?
2. The hospital is located three blocks south and three blocks east of the library. What is its number and letter?
3. Make a map of an area in your community. It might be a park or the area between your home and school. Include numbers and letters along the top and side. Use a compass to find north, and mark north on your map. Exchange maps with classmates.

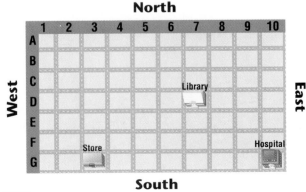

Idea Maps

The map below left shows how places are connected to each other. Idea maps, on the other hand, show how ideas are connected to each other. Idea maps help you organize information about a topic.

Look at the idea map below. It connects ideas about water. This map shows that Earth's water is either fresh water or salt water. The map also shows four sources of fresh water. You can see that there is no connection between "rivers" and "salt water" on the map. This reminds you that salt water does not flow in rivers.

Make an idea map about a topic you are learning in science. Your map can include words, phrases, or even sentences. Arrange your map in a way that makes sense to you and helps you understand the ideas.

Make Tables and Charts to Organize Data

Tables help you organize data during experiments. Most tables have columns that run up and down, and rows that run across. The columns and rows have headings that tell you what kind of data goes in each part of the table.

A Sample Table

What if you are going to do an experiment to find out how long different kinds of seeds take to sprout? Before you begin the experiment, you should set up your table. Follow these steps.

1. In this experiment you will plant 20 radish seeds, 20 bean seeds, and 20 corn seeds. Your table must show how many of each kind of seed sprouted on days 1, 2, 3, 4, and 5.

2. Make your table with columns, rows, and headings. You might use a computer. Some computer programs let you build a table with just the click of a mouse. You can delete or add columns and rows if you need to.

3. Give your table a title. Your table could look like the one here.

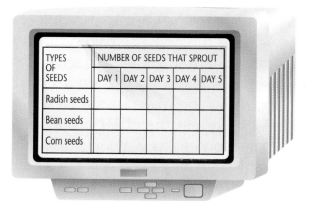

TYPES OF SEEDS	NUMBER OF SEEDS THAT SPROUT				
	DAY 1	DAY 2	DAY 3	DAY 4	DAY 5
Radish seeds					
Bean seeds					
Corn seeds					

Make a Table

Now what if you are going to do an experiment to find out how temperature affects the sprouting of seeds? You will plant 20 bean seeds in each of two trays. You will keep each tray at a different temperature, as shown below, and observe the trays for seven days. Make a table that you can use for this experiment. You can use the table to record, examine, and evaluate the information of this experiment

Make a Chart

A chart is simply a table with pictures as well as words to label the rows or columns. Make a chart that shows the information of the experiment above.

R23

Computer

A computer has many uses. The Internet connects your computer to many other computers around the world, so you can collect all kinds of information. You can use a computer to show this information and write reports. Best of all you can use a computer to explore, discover, and learn.

You can also get information from CD-ROMs. They are computer disks that can hold large amounts of information. You can fit a whole encyclopedia on one CD-ROM.

Use Computers for a Project

Here is how one group of students uses computers as they work on a weather project.

1. The students use instruments to measure temperature, wind speed, wind direction, and other parts of the weather. They input this information, or data, into the computer. The students keep the data in a table. This helps them compare the data from one day to the next.

2. The teacher finds out that another group of students in a town 200 kilometers to the west is also doing a weather project. The two groups use the Internet to talk to each other and share data. When a storm happens in the town to the west, that group tells the other group that it's coming its way.

email: It's going to storm here. The sky is turning dark gray. The winds are sometimes 65 km per hour from the northwest.

3. The students want to find out more. They decide to stay on the Internet and send questions to a local TV weather forecaster. She has a Web site and answers questions from students every day.

4. Meanwhile some students go to the library to gather more information from a CD-ROM disk. The CD-ROM has an encyclopedia that includes movie clips with sound. The clips give examples of different kinds of storms.

5. The students have kept all their information in a folder called Weather Project. Now they use that information to write a report about the weather. On the computer they can move paragraphs, add words, take out words, put in diagrams, and draw their own weather maps. Then they print the report in color.

6. Use the information on these two pages to plan your own investigation. You can study the weather, use a computer, Internet, CD-ROM, or any technological device.

MATH LINK

Calculator

Sometimes after you make measurements, you have to add or subtract your numbers. A calculator helps you do this.

HANDBOOK

Add and Subtract Rainfall Amounts

The table shows the amount of rain that fell in a town each week during the summer. The amounts are given in centimeters (cm). Use a calculator to find the total amount of rain that fell during the summer.

Week	Rain (cm)
1	3
2	5
3	2
4	0
5	1
6	6
7	4
8	0
9	2
10	2
11	6
12	5

1. Make sure the calculator is on. Press the **ON** key.
2. To add the numbers, enter a number and press ➕ . Repeat until you enter the last number. Then press ➖ . You do not have to enter the zeroes. Your total should be 36.

3. Suppose you found out that you made a mistake in your measurements. Week 1 should be 2 cm less, Week 6 should be 3 cm less, Week 11 should be 1 cm less, and Week 12 should be 2 cm less. Subtract these numbers from your total. You should have 36 displayed on the calculator. Press ➖ and enter the first number you want to subtract. Repeat until you enter the last number. Then press ➖ . Compare your new total to your classmates' new totals.

GLOSSARY

This Glossary will help you to pronounce and understand the meanings of the Science Words introduced in this book. The page number at the end of the definition tells where the word appears.

A

adaptation (ad′əp tā′shən) A characteristic that helps an organism survive in its environment. (p. 364)

antibody (an′ti bod′ē) A chemical made by the immune system to fight a particular disease. (p. 401)

asteroid (as′tə roid′) A small chunk of rock or metal that orbits the Sun. (p. 250)

atom (at′əm) The smallest particle of matter. (p. 157)

atmosphere (at′məs fîr′) A layer of gases surrounding a planet. (p. 238)

axis (ak′sis) A real or imaginary line through the center of a spinning object. (p. 197)

B

bacteria (bak tîr′ē ə) One-celled living things. (p. 399)

PRONUNCIATION KEY

a	at	e	end	o	hot	u	up	hw	white	ə	about
ā	ape	ē	me	ō	old	ū	use	ng	song		taken
ä	far	i	it	ô	fork	ü	rule	th	thin		pencil
âr	care	ī	ice	oi	oil	u̇	pull	<u>th</u>	this		lemon
		îr	pierce	ou	out	ûr	turn	zh	measure		circus

′ = primary accent; shows which syllable takes the main stress, such as **kil** in **kilogram** (kil′ə gram′)

′ = secondary accent; shows which syllables take lighter stresses, such as **gram** in **kilogram**

C

camouflage (kam'ə fläzh') An adaptation that allows organisms to blend into their surroundings. (p. 366)

carbohydrate (kär'bō hī'drāt) A substance used by the body as its main source of energy. (p. 412)

carbon dioxide and oxygen cycle (kär'bən dī ok'sīd and ok'sə jən sī'kəl) The exchange of gases between producers and consumers. (p. 344)

cell (sel) **1.** Tiny box-like part that is the basic building block of living things. (p. 56) **2.** A source of electricity. (p. 184)

cell membrane (sel mem'brān) A thin outer covering of plant and animal cells. (p. 57)

circuit (sûr'kit) The path electricity flows through. (p. 184)

comet (kom'it) A body of ice and rock that orbits the Sun. (p. 250)

communicate (kə mū'ni kāt') To share information by sending, receiving, and responding to signals. (p. 8)

community (kə mū'ni tē) All the living things in an ecosystem. (p. 324)

competition (kom'pi tish'ən) When one organism works against another to get what it needs to live. (p. 356)

compound (kom'pound) Two or more elements put together. (p. 158)

compound machine (kom'pound mə shēn') Two or more simple machines put together. (p. 122)

conifer (kon'ə fər) A tree that produces seeds inside of cones. (p. 35)

GLOSSARY

consumer (kən sü′mər) An organism that eats producers or other consumers. (p. 334)

corona (kə rō′nə) The outermost layer of gases surrounding the Sun. (p. 229)

crater (krā′tər) A hollow area in the ground. (p. 208)

cytoplasm (sī′tə plaz′əm) A clear, jelly-like material that fills plant and animal cells. (p. 57)

D

data (dā′tə) Information. (p. 82)

decomposer (dē′kəm pō′zər) An organism that breaks down dead plant and animal material. (p. 336)

degree (di grē′) The unit of measurement for temperature. (p. 166)

dermis (dûr′mis) The layer of skin just below the epidermis. (p. 390)

development (di vel′əp mənt) The way a living thing changes during its life. (p. 4)

digestion (di jes′chən) The process of breaking down food. (p. 422)

E

earthquake (ûrth′kwāk′) A sudden movement in the rocks that make up Earth's crust. (p. 282)

eclipse (i klips′) When one object passes into the shadow of another object. (p. 218)

ecosystem (ek′ō sis′təm) All the living and nonliving things in an environment. (p. 324)

element (el′ə mənt) A building block of matter. (p. 157)

PRONUNCIATION KEY

a **at**; ā **ape**; ä **far**; âr **care**; e **end**; ē **me**; i **it**; ī **ice**; îr **pierce**; o **hot**; ō **old**; ô **fork**; oi **oil**; ou **out**; u **up**; ū **use**; ü **rule**; ù **pull**; ûr **turn**; hw **white**; ng **song**; th **thin**; <u>th</u> **this**; zh **measure**; ə **about, taken, pencil, lemon, circus**

electric current (i lek′trik kûr′ənt) Electricity that flows through a circuit. (p. 184)

embryo (em′brē ō) A young organism that is just beginning to grow. (p. 34)

endangered (en dān′jərd) In danger of becoming extinct. (p. 378)

energy (en′ər jē) The ability to do work. (p. 14, 101)

energy pyramid (en′ər jē pir′ə mid′) A diagram that shows how energy is used in an ecosystem. (p. 339)

environment (en vī′rən mənt) The things that make up an area, such as the land, water, and air. (p. 6)

epidermis (ep′ə dûr′mis) The outer layer of skin. (p. 388)

erosion (i rō′zhən) The process that occurs when weathered materials are carried away. (p. 272)

extinct (ek stingkt′) When there are no more of a certain plant or animal. (p. 378)

F

fats (fatz) Substances used by the body as long-lasting sources of energy. (p. 413)

fertilizer (fûr′tə lī′zər) A substance used to keep plants healthy. (p. 311)

fiber (fī′bər) Material that helps move wastes through the body. (p. 414)

flowering plant (flou′ər ing plant) A plant that produces seeds inside of flowers. (p. 35)

food chain (füd chān) A series of organisms that depend on one another for food. (p. 334)

food web (füd web) Several food chains that are connected. (p. 338)

force (fôrs) A push or pull. (p. 78)

friction (frik'shən) A force that occurs when one object rubs against another. (p. 90)

fuel (fū'əl) Something burned to provide heat or power. (p. 230)

G

gas (gas) Matter that has no definite shape or volume. (p. 142)

germinate (jûr'mə nāt) To begin growing. (p. 34)

glacier (glā'shər) A large mass of ice in motion. (p. 272)

gland (gland) A part of the body that makes substances the body needs. (p. 389)

gravity (grav'i tē) The pulling force between two objects. (p. 80)

H

habitat (hab'i tat') The place where a plant or animal naturally lives and grows. (p. 324)

heat (hēt) A form of energy that makes things warmer. (p. 166)

helper T-cells (hel'pər tē selz) White blood cells that send signals to warn that germs have invaded the body. (p. 401)

hibernate (hī'bər nāt') To rest or sleep through the cold winter. (p. 18)

host (hōst) The organism a parasite lives in or on. (p. 347)

hurricane (hûr'i kān') A violent storm with strong winds and heavy rains. (p. 280)

PRONUNCIATION KEY

a at; ā ape; ä far; âr care; e end; ē me; i it; ī ice; îr pierce; o hot; ō old; ô fork; oi oil; ou out; u up; ū use; ü rule; ù pull; ûr turn; hw white; ng song; th thin; <u>th</u> this; zh measure; ə about, taken, pencil, lemon, circus

I

immune system (i mūn' sis'təm) All the body parts and activities that fight diseases. (p. 403)

immunity (i mū'ni tē) The body's ability to fight diseases caused by germs. (p. 403)

inclined plane (in klīnd' plān) A flat surface that is raised at one end. (p. 118)

inherited trait (in her'i təd trāt) A characteristic that comes from your parents. (p. 28)

insulator (in'sə lā'tər) A material that heat doesn't travel through easily. (p. 170)

L

landform (land'fôrm') A feature on the surface of Earth. (p. 264)

large intestine (lärj in tes'tin) Part of the body that removes water from undigested food. (p. 425)

learned trait (lûrnd trāt) Something that you are taught or learn from experience. (p. 28)

lens (lenz) A curved piece of glass. (p. 240)

lever (lev'ər) A straight bar that moves on a fixed point. (p. 109)

life cycle (līf sī'kəl) All the stages in an organism's life. (p. 24)

liquid (lik'wid) Matter that has a definite volume, but not a definite shape. (p. 142)

lunar eclipse (lü'nər i klips') When Earth's shadow blocks the Moon. (p. 219)

M

machine (mə shēn′) A tool that makes work easier to do. (p. 108)

magnetism (mag′ni tiz′əm) The property of an object that makes it attract iron. (p. 154)

mass (mas) How much matter is in an object. (p. 133)

matter (mat′ər) What makes up an object. (p. 80)

melanin (mel′ə nin) A substance that gives skin its color. (p. 388)

metal (met′əl) A shiny material found in the ground. (p. 154)

metamorphosis (met′ə môr′fə sis) A change in the body form of an organism. (p. 25)

migrate (mī′grāt) To move to another place. (p. 18)

mineral (min′ə rəl) A substance found in nature that is not a plant or an animal. (pp. 49, 260)

mixture (miks′chər) Different types of matter mixed together. (p. 147)

motion (mō′shən) A change of position. (p. 70)

N

natural resource (nach′ər əl rē′sôrs′) A material on Earth that is necessary or useful to people. (p. 292)

nerve cells (nûrv selz) Cells that carry messages to and from all parts of the body. (p. 390)

newton (nü′tən) The unit used to measure pushes and pulls. (p. 78)

niche (nich) The job or role an organism has in an ecosystem. (p. 358)

PRONUNCIATION KEY

a **at**; ā **ape**; ä **far**; âr **care**; e **end**; ē **me**; i **it**; ī **ice**; îr **pierce**; o **hot**; ō **old**; ô **fork**; oi **oil**; ou **out**; u **up**; ū **use**; ü **rule**; u̇ **pull**; ûr **turn**; hw **white**; ng **song**; th **thin**; <u>th</u> **this**; zh **measure**; ə **about, taken, pencil, lemon, circus**

GLOSSARY

nonrenewable resource
(non′ri nü′ə bəl rē′sôrs′) A resource that cannot be reused or replaced in a useful amount of time. (p. 302)

nucleus (nü′klē əs) A main control center found in plant and animal cells. (p. 57)

nutrient (nüt′rē ənt) A substance that your body needs for energy and growth. (p. 412)

O

opaque (ō pāk′) Does not allow light to pass through. (p. 176)

orbit (ôr′bit) The path an object follows as it revolves. (p. 198)

organ (ôr′gən) A group of tissues that work together. (p. 58)

organism (ôr′gə niz′əm) A living thing. (p. 4)

oxygen (ok′sə jən) A gas that is in air and water. (p. 16)

P

parasite (par′ə sīt) An organism that lives in or on another organism. (p. 347)

perish (per′ish) To not survive. (p. 377)

phase (fāz) Apparent change in the Moon's shape. (p. 207)

plain (plān) A large area of land with few hills. (p. 264)

planet (plan′it) A satellite of the Sun. (p. 228)

plateau (pla tō′) A flat area of land that rises above the land that surrounds it. (p. 265)

pollution (pə lü'shən) What happens when harmful substances get into water, air, or land. (p. 310)

population (pop'yə lā'shən) All the members of a certain type of living thing in an area. (p. 324)

pore (pôr) A tiny opening in the skin. (p. 391)

position (pə zish'ən) The location of an object. (p. 68)

pound (pound) The unit used to measure force and weight in the English system of measurement. (p. 81)

predator (pred'ə tər) An animal that hunts other animals for food. (p. 356)

prey (prā) The animal a predator hunts. (p. 356)

producer (prə dü'sər) An organism that makes its own food. (p. 334)

property (prop'ər tē) A characteristic of something. (p. 135)

protein (prō'tēn) A substance that the body uses for growth and the repair of cells. (p. 413)

pulley (pu̇l'ē) A simple machine that uses a wheel and a rope. (p. 112)

R

recycle (rē sī'kəl) To treat something so it can be used again. (p. 314)

reduce (ri düs') To make less of something. (p. 312)

reflect (ri flekt') To bounce off a surface. (p. 177)

relocate (ri lō'kāt) To find a new home. (p. 377)

PRONUNCIATION KEY

a at; ā ape; ä far; âr care; e end; ē me; i it; ī ice; îr pierce; o hot; ō old; ô fork; oi oil; ou out; u up; ū use; ü rule; u̇ pull; ûr turn; hw white; ng song; th thin; <u>th</u> this; zh measure; ə about, taken, pencil, lemon, circus

renewable resource (ri nü′ə bəl rē′sôrs′) A resource that can be replaced or used over and over again. (p. 296)

reproduction (rē′prə duk′shən) The way organisms make new living things just like themselves. (p. 5)

respond (ri spond′) The way a living thing reacts to changes in its environment. (p. 6)

reuse (v., rē ūz′) To use something again. (p. 314)

revolve (ri volv′) To move in a circle around an object. (p. 198)

rotate (rō′tāt) To turn around. (p. 196)

S

saliva (sə lī′və) A liquid in your mouth that helps soften and break down food. (p. 423)

satellite (sat′ə līt′) An object that orbits another, larger object in space. (p. 206)

screw (skrü) An inclined plane wrapped into a spiral. (p. 120)

simple machine (sim′pəl mə shēn′) A machine with few or no moving parts. (p. 109)

small intestine (smôl in tes′tin) A tube-like part of your body where most digestion takes place. (p. 425)

solar eclipse (sō′lər i klips′) When the Moon's shadow blocks the Sun. (p. 218)

solar system (sō′lər sis′təm) The Sun and all the objects that orbit the Sun. (p. 236)

solid (sol′id) Matter that has a definite shape and volume. (p. 142)

GLOSSARY

solution (sə lü'shən) A type of mixture that has one or more types of matter spread evenly through another. (p. 148)

speed (spēd) How fast an object moves. (p. 71)

star (stär) A hot sphere of gases that gives off energy. (p. 228)

stomach (stum'ək) Part of your body that has walls made of strong muscles that squeeze and mash food. (p. 424)

sunspot (sun'spot') A dark area on the Sun's surface. (p. 229)

switch (swich) Opens or closes an electric circuit. (p. 185)

system (sis'təm) A group of parts that work together. (p. 46)

T

taste buds (tāst budz) Thousands of cells on your tongue that send the signals for sweet, sour, bitter, and salty to your brain. (p. 423)

telescope (tel'ə skōp') A tool that gathers light to make faraway objects appear closer. (p. 240)

temperature (tem'pər ə chər) A measure of how hot or cold something is. (p. 166)

tissue (tish'ü) A group of cells that are alike. (p. 58)

V

vaccine (vak'sēn) A medicine that causes the body to form antibodies against a certain disease. (p. 404)

valley (val'ē) An area of land lying between hills. (p. 264)

PRONUNCIATION KEY

a at; ā ape; ä far; âr care; e end; ē me; i it; ī ice; îr pierce; o hot; ō old; ô fork; oi oil; ou out; u up; ū use; ü rule; u̇ pull; ûr turn; hw white; ng song; th thin; th this; zh measure; ə about, taken, pencil, lemon, circus

virus (vī'rəs) A tiny particle that can reproduce only inside a living cell. (p. 399)

vitamin (vīt'ə mən) A substance used by the body for growth. (p. 414)

volcano (vol kā'nō) An opening in the surface of Earth. Melted rock, gases, rock pieces, and dust are forced out of this opening. (p. 283)

volume (vol'ūm) How much space matter takes up. (p. 132)

W

weathering (we<u>th</u>'ər ing) The process that causes rocks to crumble, crack, and break. (p. 270)

wedge (wej) Two inclined planes placed back to back. (p. 119)

weight (wāt) The pull of gravity on an object. (p. 81)

wheel and axle (hwēl and ak'səl) A wheel that turns on a post. (p. 111)

white blood cells (hwīt blud selz) Cells in the blood that fight bacteria and viruses. (p. 400)

work (würk) When a force changes the motion of an object. (p. 100)

INDEX

* Indicates an activity related to this topic.

INDEX

CREDITS

Design & Production: Kirchoff/Wohlberg, Inc.

Maps: Geosystems.

Transvision: Ken Karp (photography); Michael Maydak (illustration).

Illustrations: Ken Batelman p.428; Ka Botzis: pp. 271, 274, 293, 325, 368, 376; Elizabeth Callen: 360; Barbara Cousins: pp. 85, 423, 424, 425; Steve Cowden pp. 350–351; Marie Dauenheimer: pp. 388–389, 390–391, 399, 400–401; Michael DiGiorgio: pp. 328, 335, 339, 364; Jeff Fagan: pp. 12, 58, 88, 89, 91, 101, 102; Lee Glynn: pp. 15, 71, 72, 82, 83, 136, 159, 230, 256, 313, 352, 357, 384, 398, 416, 432; Kristen Goeters: p. 137; Colin Hayes: p. 173 Handbook pp. R7, R11, R13, R20–R23; Nathan Jarvis: pp. 68, 69, 70; Matt Kania: pp. 264, 283; Virge Kask: pp. 14, 26–27; Fiona King: 222, 223. Tom Leonard: pp. 16, 57, 81, 90, 196, 197, 200, 208, 236–237; Olivia: Handbook pp. R2–R4, R9, R10, R13, R16–R19, R21, R23–R25; Sharron O'Neil: pp. 4, 34, 35, 36, 40, 60, 64, 288, 303, 317, 320; Pat Rasch: pp. 79, 80, 118, 119, 120, 121, 128; Rob Schuster: pp. 115, 185, 186, 192, 198–199, 206–207, 216, 218, 219, 244; Casey Shain: p. 304; Wendy Smith: pp. 338, 344, 326–327; Matt Straub: pp. 42, 61, 96, 125, 162, 166, 189, 224, 228, 253, 317, 352, 381, 408, 429; Ted Williams: pp. 154, 156, 167, 178, 182, 184; Jonathan Wright: pp. 110, 111, 113.

Photography Credits:

Contents: iii: Bob & Clara Calhoun/Bruce Coleman, Inc. iv: inset, Bob Winsett/Corbis; FPG. v: Richard Megna/Fundamental Photographs. vi: ESA/Science Photo Library. vii: Roger Werth/Woodfin Camp & Associates, Inc. viii: Gregory Ochocki/Photo Researchers, Inc. ix: Walter Bibikow/FPG.

National Geographic Invitation to Science: S2: Emory Kristof; inset, Harriet Ballard. S3: t. Woods Hole Oceanographic Institution; b. Jonathan Blair.

Be a Scientist: S5: David Mager. S6: NASA. S7: t. Corbis; b, Francois Gohier/Photo Researchers, Inc. S8: l, Jonathan Blair/Woodfin Camp & Associates; r, Wards SCI/Science Source/Photo Researchers, Inc. S11: NASA. S12: John Sanford/Science Photo Library/Photo Researchers, Inc. S13: t, b, NASA. S14: Michael Marten/Science Photo Library/Photo Researchers, Inc. S15: Peter Beck/The Stock Market. S16: l, K. Preuss/The Image Works; r, Richard A. Cooke III/Tony Stone Images. S17: Jean Miele/The Stock Market.

Unit 1: 1: Dieter & Mary Plage/Bruce Coleman, Inc.; Randy Morse/Animals Animals, inset b.r. 2: Richard Nowitz/FPG. 3: Ken Karp. 5: Ken Karp, t.r.; R. Calentine/Visuals Unlimited, b. 6: Barry L. Runk/Grant Heilman, b.l.; Runk/Schoenberger/Grant Heilman, b.r. 7: Ken Karp. 8: Sullivan & Rogers/Bruce Coleman, Inc., t.r.; Tom J. Ulrich/Visuals Unlimited, b.c. 9: Cart Roessler/Animals Animals. 10: Ronald H. Cohn. H. S. Terrence 11: Animals Animals. 13: Ken Karp. 15: Ken Karp, t.r.; C. Bradley Simmons/Bruce Coleman, Inc., t.r.; Jerry Cooke/Animals Animals. 18: Jim Zipp/Photo Researchers, Inc., c.; Kim Taylor/Bruce Coleman, Inc., r.; Lefever/Grushow/Grant Heilman, l. 19: Arthur Tilley/FPG. 20: Ken Lucas/Visuals Unlimited, l. 20–21: Skip Moody/Dembinsky Photo Assoc. 21: The Blake School, t. 22: Tim Davis/Zipp/Photo Researchers, Inc. 23: Ken Karp. 24: Dwight R. Kuhn, t.l.; Glenn M. Oliver/Visuals Unlimited, t.c.; Pat Lynch/Zipp/Photo Researchers, Inc., t.r.; Robert P. Carr/Bruce Coleman, Inc., b.l. 25: John Mielcarek/Dembinsky Photo Assoc., b.l.; Nuridsany et Perennou/Zipp/Photo Researchers, Inc. t.l.; Robert L. Dunne/Bruce Coleman, Inc., t.r.; Sharon Cummings/Dembinsky Photo Assoc., b.r.. 26: Henry Ausloos/Animals Animals. 28: Debra P. Hershkowitz/Bruce Coleman, Inc., t.l.; Ken Karp, b.r. 29: Rhoda Sidney/PhotoEdit. 30: Bill Banaszewski/Visuals Unlimited, bkgrd. 30–31: J.C. Carton/Bruce Coleman, Inc., bkgrd. 32: Toyohiro Yamada/FPG. 33: Ken Karp. 34: Inga Spence/Visuals Unlimited, t.c.; Patti Murray/Animals Animals, l. 36: George F. Mobley, l. 37: Bill Bachman/Photo Researchers, Inc. 38: D. Cavagnaro/Visuals Unlimited, t.l.; Dwight R. Kuhn, b.r.; Dwight R. Kuhn, b.l.; John Lemker/Animals Animals, b.c.. 39: Larry Lefever/Grant Heilman. 40–41: Randy Green/FPG, bkgrd.; Stan Osolinski/Dembinsky Photo Assoc. inset t.;. Larry West/FPG., inset b. 41: John M. Roberts/The Stock Market, inset t.; J. H. Robinson/Photo Researchers, Inc., inset b. 43: Superstock; Peter Cade/Tony Stone Images, inset b.r.

44: PhotoDisc., all. 45: Ken Karp. 46: Rob Gage/FPG. 47: Joe McDonald/Animals Animals, b.r.; John Shaw/Bruce Coleman, Inc., t.r.. 48: Leonard Rue III/Visuals Unlimited, b.; Robert P. Carr/Bruce Coleman, Inc., t.l. 49: F.C. Millington-TCL/Masterfile, b.r.; Tom McHugh/Photo Researchers, Inc., t.r. 51: Bonnie Kamin/PhotoEdit. 52: Joyce Photographics/Photo Researchers, Inc., t.; Sonya Jacobs/The Stock Market, l. 53: John D. Cunningham/Visuals Unlimited, r.; John Sohlden/Visuals Unlimited, b.l.; Michael T. Stubben/Visuals Unlimited, t.c.; R.J. Erwin/Photo Researchers, Inc., t.l. 54: Ken Karp. 55: Margaret Oechsli/Fundamental Photographs. 56: Dwight R. Kuhn, t.l.; Ken Karp, b.r. 59: Dennis MacDonald/PhotoEdit. 60: Phillip Hayson/Photo Researchers, Inc.

Unit 2: 65: ZEFA Stock Imagery, Inc. 66: Anderson Monkmeyer, b.l.; Dollarhide/Monkmeyer, b.r. 67: Ken Karp, b.r.; Will Hart/PhotoEdit, t.r.. 69: Ken Karp. 70: Barbara Leslie/FPG, b.r.; K.H. Switak/Photo Researchers, Inc., b.l. 71: K. & K. Amman/Bruce Coleman, Inc./PNI. 73: Jacob Taposchaner/FPG. 74: Dan McCoy/Rainbow/PNI. 75: David Young-Wolff/PhotoEdit. 76: Ken Karp. 77: Ken Karp. 78: Ken Karp. 80: RubberBall Productions. 84: Ken Karp. 86: Ken Karp. 87: Ken Karp. 90: NASA. 91: Ken Karp. 92: Ken Karp. 93: Jade Albert/FPG. 94–95: Stephen J. Shaluta, Jr./Dembinsky Photo Assoc. 95: Ken Karp. 97: Chris Salvo/FPG. 98: Camelot/Photonica, b.r.; Jacob Taposchaner/FPG, b.l.; Will & Deni McIntyre/Photo Researchers, Inc., t.c. 99: Ken Karp. 100: Camelot/Photonica, b.l.; Ken Karp, t.l. & m.l. 101: Ken Karp. 103: R. Hutchings/PhotoEdit. 104–105: Ed Degginger/Bruce Coleman, Inc., bkgrd. 105: Jeff Foott/Bruce Coleman, Inc. b. inset; Jonathan Nourok/PhotoEdit, t. inset. 106: Ken Karp. 107: Ken Karp. 109: Ken Karp. 110: Ken Karp, t. & b. 112: Ken Karp. 114–115: The Granger Collection New York. 116: Carl Purcell/Photo Researchers, Inc. 117: Ken Karp. 118: Dollarhide/Monkmeyer. 119: W. Metzen/Bruce Coleman, Inc. 123: Ken Karp. 124: David Mager.

Unit 3: 129: Bkgrd: MMSD Joe Sohm/ChromoSohm. 130: Ken Karp. 131: Ken Karp. inset 132: PhotoDisc. 133: MMSD, m.r.; PhotoDisc, m.c., b.l. & b.r.; Sylvain Grandadam/Photo Researchers, Inc., t.r. 134: Stockbyte. 135: PhotoDisc, b.l.; Ken Karp, t.r. 138: Robert Rathe/NIST; inset, Joe Sohm/Stock, Boston/PNI. 140: Gerry Ellis/ENP Images. 141: Ken Karp. 142: PhotoDisc. 143: PhotoDisc, b.c. & b.r.; Ken Karp, b.l. 144: Lawrence Migdale, l. & b.m.; Margerin Studio/FPG, t.r. 145: Ken Karp. 146: Peter Scoones-TCL/Masterfile. 147: PhotoDisc. 148: Ken Karp. 149: Arthur Tilley/FPG. 150: McGraw Hill School Division. 150–151: Ken Karp, insets. 152: Ken Karp. 153: Ken Karp. 154: Leonard Lessin/Peter Arnold, Inc. 155: PhotoDisc, t.r.; Ken Karp, b.r. 156: Telegraph Colour Library/FPG. 157: Ken Karp. 158: PhotoDisc. 160: Stan Osolinski/Dembinsky Photo Assoc. Charles D. Winters/Photo Researchers, Inc.161: t. Mehau Kulyk/Photo Researchers, Inc. b. William Waterfall/The Stock Market. 163: Eric Meola/The Image Bank; Tom Bean, inset b.r. 164: Ken Karp. 165: Ken Karp. 168: Ben Simmons/The Stock Market, l.; Eric Gay/AP/World Wide Photos, b.r. 169: Ken Karp. 170: Nakita Ovsyanikov/Masterfile, b.r.; Robert P. Carr/Bruce Coleman, Inc., l. 171: Ken Karp. 172: Culver Pictures, Inc. 172–173: Gary Buss FPG, bkgrd. 174: Ken Karp. 175: Ken Karp. 176: Ron Thomas/FPG. 177: Gary Withey/Bruce Coleman, Inc., b.r.; Jerome Wexler/Photo Researchers, Inc., t.r.; Ken Karp, b.l.; Telegraph Colour Library/FPG, b.c. 179: Tim Davis/Photo Researchers, Inc., b.l. 180: Frank Krahmer/Bruce Coleman, Inc., b.l. 181: Telegraph Colour Library/FPG, bkgrd.; Ken Karp, inset. 183: Ken Karp. 188: PhotoDisc bkgrd.; Ken Karp, insets.

Unit 4: 193: NASA/FPG; inset, GSO Images/The Image Bank. 194: George D. Lepp/Photo Researchers, Inc. 195: Ken Karp. 197: Jim Cummins. FPG. 200: Ken Karp. 201: Andy Levin/Photo Researchers, Inc. 202: Michael R. Whelan, inset; Jim Ballard/AllStock/PNI, t. 204–205: Edward R. Degginger/Bruce Coleman, Inc. 205: Ken Karp. 206–207: John Sanford/Science Photo Researchers, Inc. 208–209: NASA. 210: NASA, b.l.; Michael P. Gadomski/Photo Researchers, Inc., t.l. 211: Richard T. Nowitz/Corbis. 212: Chris Dube. 212–213: t. Photo Disc. 213: The Granger Collection New York. 214: Matt Bradley/Bruce Coleman, Inc. 215: Ken Karp. 217: Archive Photos/PNI, b.r.; Ken Karp, b.l. 218: Frank Rossotto/The Stock Market. 219: Rev. Ronald Royer/Photo Researchers, Inc. 220–221: Pekka/Photo Researchers, Inc. 222-223: Visuals Unlimited. 225: Science Photo Library/Photo Researchers, Inc. 226: Mike Yamashita/Woodfin Camp & Associates. 227: Ken Karp. 228: Jerry Schad/Photo Researchers, Inc. 229: Francois Gohier/Photo Researchers, Inc., b.; Jerry Lodriguss/Photo Researchers, Inc., t. 231: Detlev Van/Photo Researchers, Inc., t.; Ken Karp, b. 232: Jim Cummins/FPG. 233: t. NASA/Photo Researchers, Inc. b. Telegraph

Colour Library/FPG 234: Palomar Observatory/Caltech. 235: Ken Karp. 238: NASA/Mark Marten/Photo Researchers, Inc., b.; US Geological/Photo Researchers, Inc., t. 239: NASA/Science Source/Photo Researchers, Inc., b.; US Geological Survey/Photo Researchers, Inc., t. 240: Ken Karp. 241: Mugshots/The Stock Market. 242: A. Ramey Stock Boston, l. NASA/JPL/Corbis; 242–243: USGS/Photo Researchers, Inc., bkgrd. 243: NASA/Corbis, b.r. Photo Researchers, Inc., bkgrd. 245: Ken Karp. 246: Science Photo Library/Photo Researchers, Inc. 247: Ken Karp. 248: NASA, t.; NASA/Mark Marten/Photo Researchers, Inc., b. 249: NASA Science Photo Library/Photo Researchers, Inc., b.; Space Telescope/Photo Researchers, Inc., t. 250–251: Jerry Lodriguss/Photo Researchers, Inc. 251: Nieto/Jerrican/Photo Researchers, Inc. 252: Sam Zarembar/The Image Bank, bkgrd.; The Granger Collection, inset.

Unit 5: 257: ZEFA/Stock Imagery, Inc. 258: PhotoDisc, b.l.; Ann Purcell/Photo Researchers, Inc., b.r.; Jeffrey Myers/FPG., t.r. 259: Ken Karp. 260: Joyce Photographics/Photo Researchers, Inc., b.c.; Ken Karp, t.l., m.l., b.l., b.r. 261: Ken Karp. 262: PhotoDisc, bkgrd; Ken Karp, insets. 263: l. col. from top, Stephen Ogilvy, Ken Karp, Stephen Ogilvy, E.R. Degginger/Photo Researchers, Inc.; r. col. from top, Stephen Ogilvy, Ken Karp, Ken Karp, Charles R. Belinky/Photo Researchers, Inc. 264: Diane Rawson; Photo Researchers, Inc., b.l.; Josef Beck/FPG, m.l.; Tim Davis/Photo Researchers, Inc, b.r. 265: Yann Arthus-Bertrand/Corbis. 266: Art Wolfe/AllStock/PNI, t.; Robert Harding Picture Library, inset; 267: Fergus O'Brien/FPG International, t.; D. E. Cox/Tony Stone Images, m. 268: Francois Gohier/Photo Researchers, Inc. 269: Ken Karp. 270: Keith Kent/Science/Photo Researchers, Inc., bkgrd.; Susan Rayfield/Photo Researchers, Inc., inset l & r. 271: Ken Karp. 272: Farrell Grehan/Photo Researchers, Inc., t.; Ken M. Johns/Photo Researchers, Inc., b. 273: Ken Karp. 274: Dan Guravich/Photo Researchers, Inc. 275: Ralph N. Barrett/Bruce Coleman, Inc. 276: Adam Jones/Photo Researchers, Inc., t.r.; John Sohlden/Visuals Unlimited, b.r.; W. E. Ruth/Bruce Coleman, Inc., b.l. 276–277: PhotoDisc., bkgrd. 277: The National Archives/Corbis, t.r.; Pat Armstrong/Visuals Unlimited, b.l.; Sylvan H. Wittaver/Visuals Unlimited, t.l. 278: Warren Faidley/International Stock. 279: Ken Karp. 280: NASA/GSFC/Photo Researchers, Inc. 281: PhotoDisc. 282: Paul Sakuma/AP/Wide World Photos, b.; Will & Deni McIntyre/Photo Researchers, Inc., t. 283: PhotoDisc. 284: Arthur Rothstein/AP Photo, b.; Sergio Dorantes, t. 285: The Weather Channel. 286: Jeffrey Howe/Visuals Unlimited. 286–287: Telegraph Colour Library/FPG, bkgrd. 287: Frank Rossotto/The Stock Market, t.r.; NOAA/Science Photo Library/Photo Researchers, Inc., m.r.; Dr. Denise M. Stephenson-Hawk, b.r. 289: PhotoDisc, bkgrd.; Stock Imagery, Inc., inset. 290: PhotoDisc, b.r.; Michael P. Gadomski/Photo Researchers, Inc., b.l.; Peter Skinner/Photo Researchers, Inc., t.r. 291: Ken Karp. 292: Craig K. Lorenz/Photo Researchers, Inc. 294: Ken Karp. 295: Ken Karp. 296: Jim Foster/The Stock Market, b.; M. E. Warren/Photo Researchers, Inc., t. 297: Debra P. Hershkowitz/Bruce Coleman, Inc. 298: The National Archives/Corbis, inset. 298–299: John Elk III/Bruce Coleman, Inc., bkgrd. 299: G. Buttner/Okapia/Photo Researchers, Inc., b.r.; Roy Morsch/The Stock Market, t.r. 300: Liaison Agency, b.r.; Owen Franken/Corbis., b.l. 301: Ken Karp. 302: Phillip Hayson/Photo Researchers, Inc., t.; Richard Hamilton Smith/Corbis., b. 303: Ray Ellis/Photo Researchers, Inc. 304: Will McIntyre/Photo Researchers, Inc. 305: Ken Karp. 306: Bruce Byers/FPG, b.c.; Ken Karp., t.b.l. 306–307: Jeffrey Sylvester/FPG. 307: Norman Owen Tomalin/Bruce Coleman, Inc., r. & b.;Steve Kline/Bruce Coleman, Inc., inset. 308: Lawson Wood/Corbis. 309: Ken Karp. 310: PhotoDisc. 311: Ken Karp. 312: PhotoDisc. b.l. Stuart Cahill/AFP/BETTMAN. 315: PhotoDisc. 316: David Sucsy/FPG bkgrd.; Barbara Comnes, inset.

Unit 6: 321: Craig K. Lorenz/Photo Researchers, Inc., bkgrd; Richard Price/FPG, inset. 322: Renee Lynn/Photo Researchers, Inc. 323: Ken Karp. 324: Gary Randall/FPG, b.; Lee Foster/Bruce Coleman, Inc., t. 329: Jon Feingersh/The Stock Market. 330: George F. Mobley, t.; 1998 Comstock, Inc., inset. 331: Emory Kristof. 332: Tim Davis/Photo Researchers, Inc. 333: Ken Karp. 334: Gary Meszaros/Visuals Unlimited. 336: Farrell Grehan/Photo Researchers, Inc., r. ; Rod Planck/Photo Researchers, Inc., l. 337: Ken Karp. 340–341: clockwise

from top: Charles Gold/The Stock Market; Denise Cupen/Bruce Coleman, Inc.; Roy Morsch/The Stock Market. Don Mason/The Stock Market; Ed Bock/The Stock Market; Elaine Twichell/Dembinsky Photo Assoc.; J. Barry O'Rourke/The Stock Market; J Sapinsky/The Stock Market; Rex A. Butcher/Bruce Coleman, Inc. 340–341: Telegraph Colour/FPG. 342: Ken Karp. 343: Ken Karp. 345: Dennie Cody/FPG, l; DiMaggio/Kalish/The Stock Market, r. 346: Paul A. Zahl, l; William E. Townsend/Photo Researchers, Inc., r. 347: Arthur Norris/Visuals Unlimited, l.; Biophoto Associates/Photo Researchers, Inc., r. 348: Ken Karp, b.; Zig Leszcynski/Animals Animals, t. 349: Lynwood Chase/Photo Researchers, Inc. 353: Gil Lopez-Espina/Visuals Unlimited, inset; K & K Ammann/Bruce Coleman, Inc., bkgrd. 354: Michael Gadomski/Photo Researchers, Inc. 355: Ken Karp. 356: Joe McDonald/Bruce Coleman, Inc., t.; John Shaw/Bruce Coleman, Inc., b. 358: Ken Karp. 359: Kenneth W. Fink/Bruce Coleman, Inc. 361: Ken Lucas/Visuals Unlimited. 362: Richard Kolar/Animals Animals, l.; Richard & Susan Day/Animals Animals, b. 363: Ken Karp. 365: Barbara Gerlach/Visuals Unlimited, t.; Zefa Germany/The Stock Market, b. 366: A. Cosmos Blank/Photo Researchers, Inc., b.l.; Breck P. Kent/Animals Animals, t.; Robert P. Carr/Bruce Coleman, Inc., b.r. 367: Ken Karp. 369: Emily Stong/Visuals Unlimited. 370: Art Wolfe/Tony Stone Images t.c.; Tom Brakefield/The Stock Market, b. 371: Gerald & Buff Corsi/Visuals Unlimited, t.l.; Stephen Dalton/Photo Researchers, Inc., t.r.; Dan Suzio/Photo Researchers, Inc., b. 372: David Weintraub/Photo Researchers, Inc. 373: Ken Karp. 374: Keith Gunnar/Bruce Coleman, Inc., l.; Phil Degginger/Bruce Coleman, Inc., r. 375: Pat & Tom Leeson/Photo Researchers, Inc. 376: Joe McDonald/Visuals Unlimited. 377: Joe & Carol McDonald/Visuals Unlimited. 378: Ken Karp., b.; Omikron/Photo Researchers, Inc., t. 379: Pat & Tom Leeson/Photo Researchers, Inc. 380: Photo Disc t.; Janis Burger/Bruce Coleman, Inc., t.r.; Jen and Des Bartlett/Bruce Coleman, Inc., b.l.; Tom Van Sant/The Stock Market, bkgrd.

Unit 7: 385: George Schiavone/The Stock Market. 386: Gary Landsman/The Stock Market. 387: Ken Karp. 388: Yoav Levy/Phototake. 389: Barbara Peacock/FPG. 392: Ken Karp. 393: Ken Karp. 394: Michael Townsend/Tony Stone Images, t.; Randy Taylor/Liaison Agency, inset; 395: Bob Daemmrich/The Image Works. 396: David Waldorf/FPG. 397: Ken Karp. 399: David M. Phillips/Visuals Unlimited. 401: Manfred Kage/Peter Arnold, Inc. 402: Ken Karp. 403: Mary Kate Denny/ PhotoEdit. 404: CORBIS/BETTMANN–UPI. 405: Sandy Fox/MMSD. 406: Howard Sochurek/The Stock Market, inset; Deborah Gilbert/The Image Bank, b. 407: Telegraph Colour Library/FPG, bkgrd. r. McGraw Hill School Division. 409: Otto Rogge/The Stock Market; t. Tracy/FPG. 410: Joyce Photographics/Photo Researchers, Inc., l.; Steven Needham/Envision, r. 411: Ken Karp. 412–413: Ken Karp. 414: David Young-Wolff/PhotoEdit, t.; Ken Karp, b. 417: Michael Newman/PhotoEdit. 418: NASA/Photri, b.r. & m.r. 419: NASA/Photri, t.r., m.r. & b.r.; NASA/Corbis, inset top. 418–419: Ronald Royer/Photo Researchers, Inc. 420: David Young-Wolff/PhotoEdit. 421: Ken Karp. 422: Michael A. Keller/The Stock Market. 426: Ken Karp. 428: Bkgrd: PhotoDisc.

Handbook: Steven Ogilvy: pp. R6, R8, R12, R14, R15, R26.

PERIODIC TABLE OF THE ELEMENTS

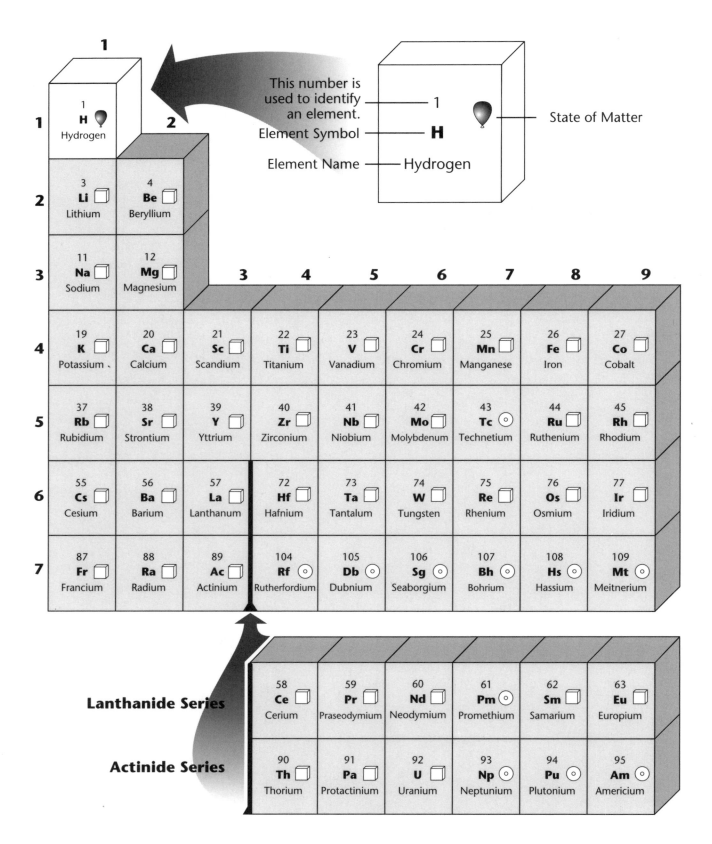